TATTOO MAGIC

La magia del tatuaje Magia da tatuagem La magia del tatuaggio

promopress

TATTOO MAGIC

La magia del tatuaje Magia da tatuagem La magia del tatuaggio

Aymara Arreaza

Tattoo Magic
La magia del tatuaje Magia da tatuagem La magia del tatuaggio

Editorial coordination: Cristian Campos
Editor: Aymara Arreaza
Texts: Laura Higes Castillo
Translation: Cillero & de Motta
Art direction: Emma Termes Parera
Layout assistant: Leticia Mazaira

PROMOPRESS is a brand of:
PROMOTORA DE PRENSA INTERNACIONAL, S. A.
Ausiàs March, 124
08013 Barcelona, Spain
Tel.: +34 93 245 14 64
Fax: +34 93 265 48 83
E-mail: info@promopress.es
www.promopress.es
www.promopresseditions.com

First published in English / Spanish / Portuguese / Italian: 2012
ISBN: 978-84-92810-43-7
Printed in Spain

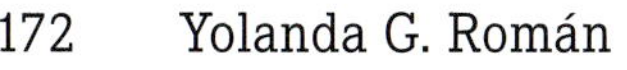

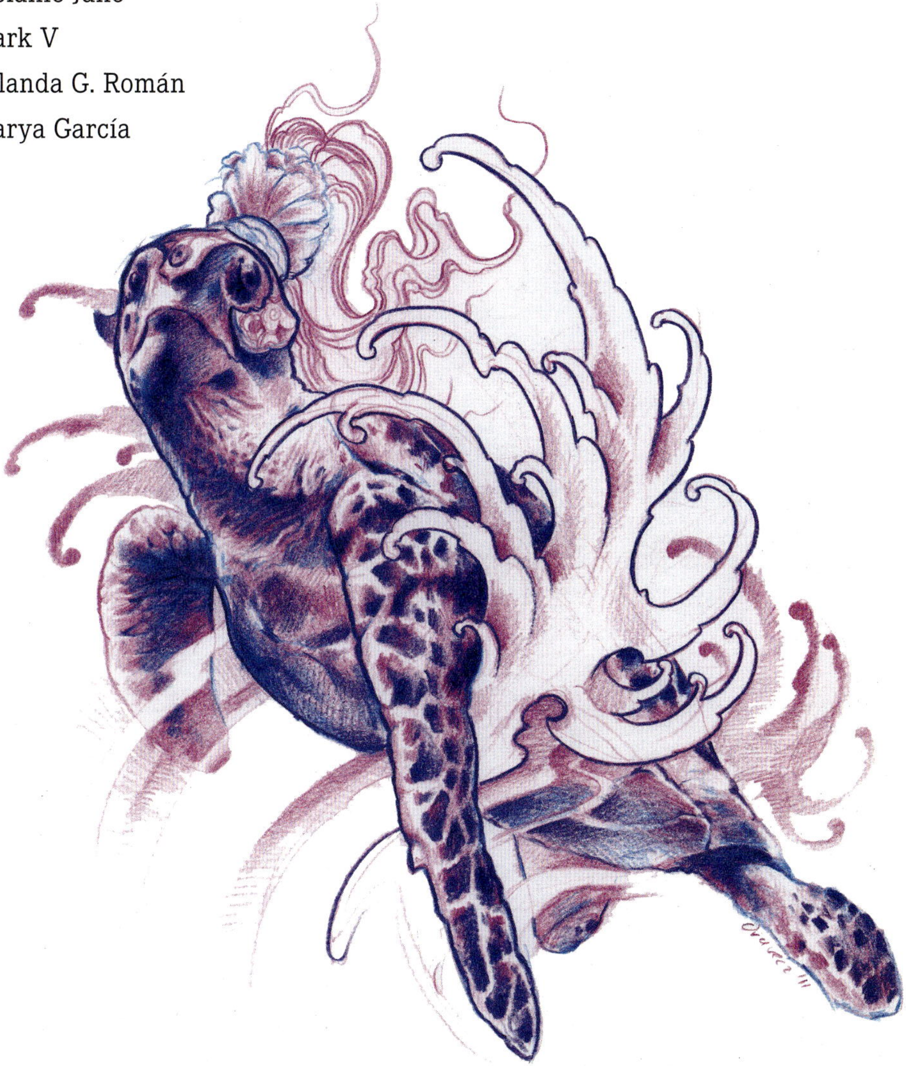

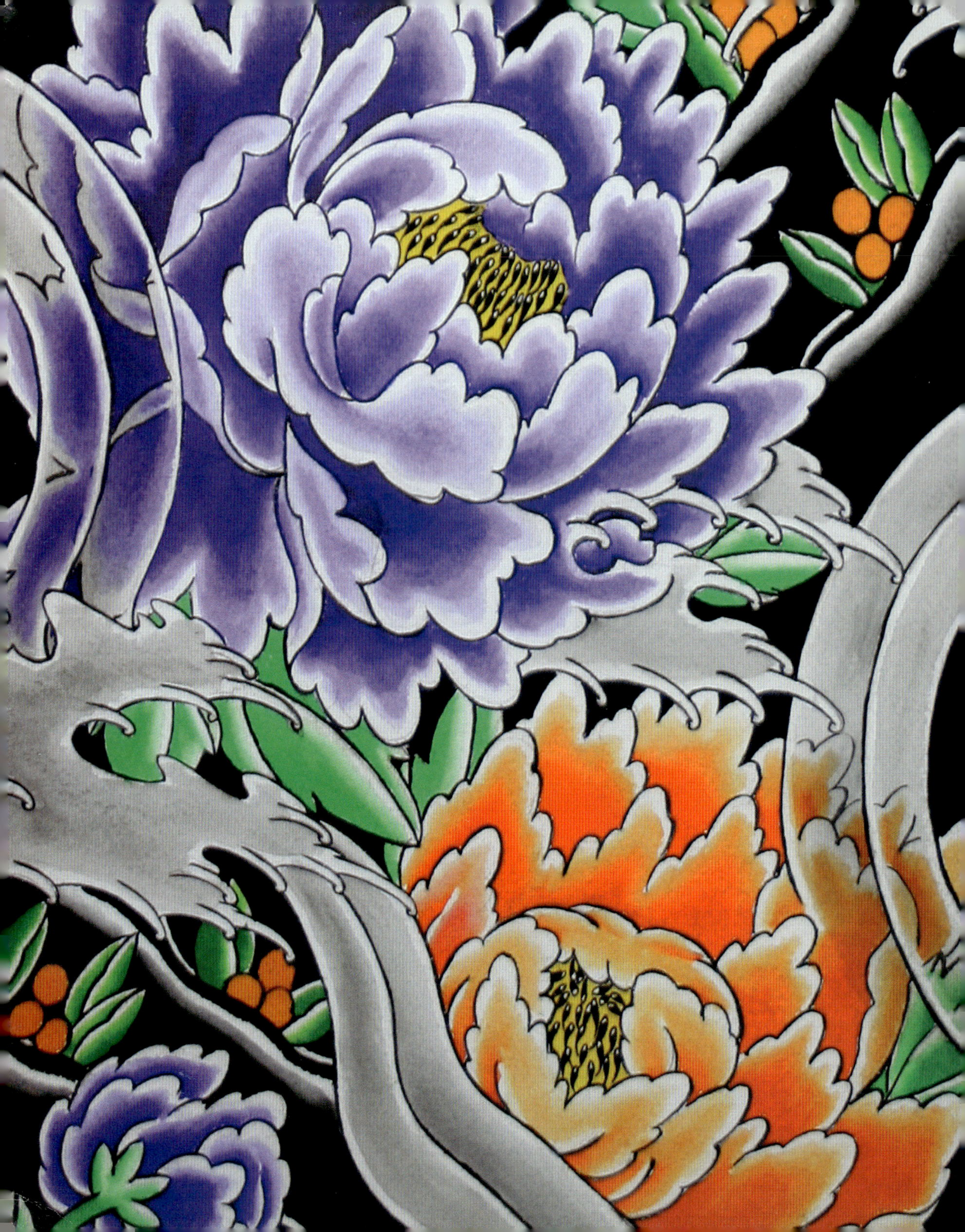

Introduction

Irezumi is the name that is given to the Japanese style tattoo in the majority of the Western world, and it is characterized broadly by presenting an oriental theme design. This style of tattooing has drawn special attention in the West since its inception and continues to fascinate both newbies and experts. But to understand this expansion, it is necessary to know its cultural evolution, since tattooing in Japan has been historically associated with crime groups such as the Yakuza and lower social classes as well as courtiers and merchants. However, its evolution has led it to be considered as one of the most beautiful and complex tattoo styles, and in Japan the same purpose of the tattoo is evolving at present among the new generations, which are increasingly getting tattoos more for aesthetic than for cultural reasons. This book includes a selection of different Japanese tattoo designs and a chapter devoted to the work of professional photographers who have portrayed the world of tattoos with their camera.

Introducción

Irezumi es el nombre con el que se conoce el tatuaje de estilo japonés en gran parte de Occidente y que se caracteriza, a grandes rasgos, por presentar un diseño de temática oriental. Este estilo de tatuaje ha llamado especialmente la atención en occidente desde sus inicios y sigue fascinando tanto a recién iniciados como expertos. Pero para entender esta expansión se hace necesario conocer su evolución cultural, ya que el tatuaje en Japón se ha asociado históricamente a organizaciones criminales cómo la *yakuza* y las clases sociales más bajas, así como a cortesanas y mercaderes. Sin embargo, su evolución lo ha llevado a ser considerado uno de los estilos de tatuaje más bellos y complejos, y la misma finalidad del tatuaje en Japón va evolucionando en la actualidad entre las nuevas generaciones, que cada vez se tatúan más por motivos estéticos que culturales. Este libro incluye una selección de diferentes diseños de tatuajes japoneses y un capítulo dedicado a la obra de fotógrafos profesionales que han retratado con su cámara el mundo del tatuaje.

Introdução

Irezumi é o nome pelo qual se conhece a tatuagem de estilo japonês em grande parte do Ocidente e que se caracteriza em grandes traços por apresentar um desenho de temática oriental. Este estilo de tatuagem chamou especialmente à atenção no ocidente desde os seus inícios e continua a fascinar tanto recém-iniciados como peritos. Mas, para entender esta expansão, torna-se necessário conhecer a sua evolução cultural, já que a tatuagem no Japão associou-se historicamente a grupos criminais como a *yakuza* e as classes sociais mais baixas, assim como a cortesãs e mercadores. No entanto, a sua evolução levou-a a ser considerada um dos estilos de tatuagem mais belos e complexos e a própria finalidade da tatuagem no Japão vai evoluindo actualmente entre as novas gerações, que cada vez se tatuam mais por motivos estéticos que culturais. Este livro inclui uma selecção de diferentes desenhos de tatuagens japonesas e um capítulo dedicado à obra de fotógrafos profissionais que retrataram com a sua câmara o mundo da tatuagem.

Introduzione

Irezumi è il nome con il quale è conosciuto il tatuaggio giapponese in gran parte dell'Occidente, caratterizzato generalmente da un un disegno con motivo orientale. Questo tipo di tatuaggio ha da subito affascinato soprattutto l'Occidente e continua ad appassionare esperti e nuovi scopritori del genere. Per comprenderne tuttavia l'espansione è necessario conoscere la sua evoluzione culturale dato che il tatuaggio in Giappone è stato storicamente associato a gruppi criminali come la Yakuza e alle classi sociali più basse, oltre che a cortigiane e mercanti. Tuttavia la sua evoluzione lo ha portato a essere considerato uno dei tipi di tatuaggio più belli e complessi e la stessa finalità del tatuaggio in Giappone si sta attualmente evolvendo tra le nuove generazioni, che si tatuano sempre più per motivi estetici che culturali. Questo libro comprende una selezione di diversi disegni di tatuaggi giapponesi, oltre a un capitolo dedicato all'opera di fotografi professionisti che hanno ritratto il mondo del tatuaggio.

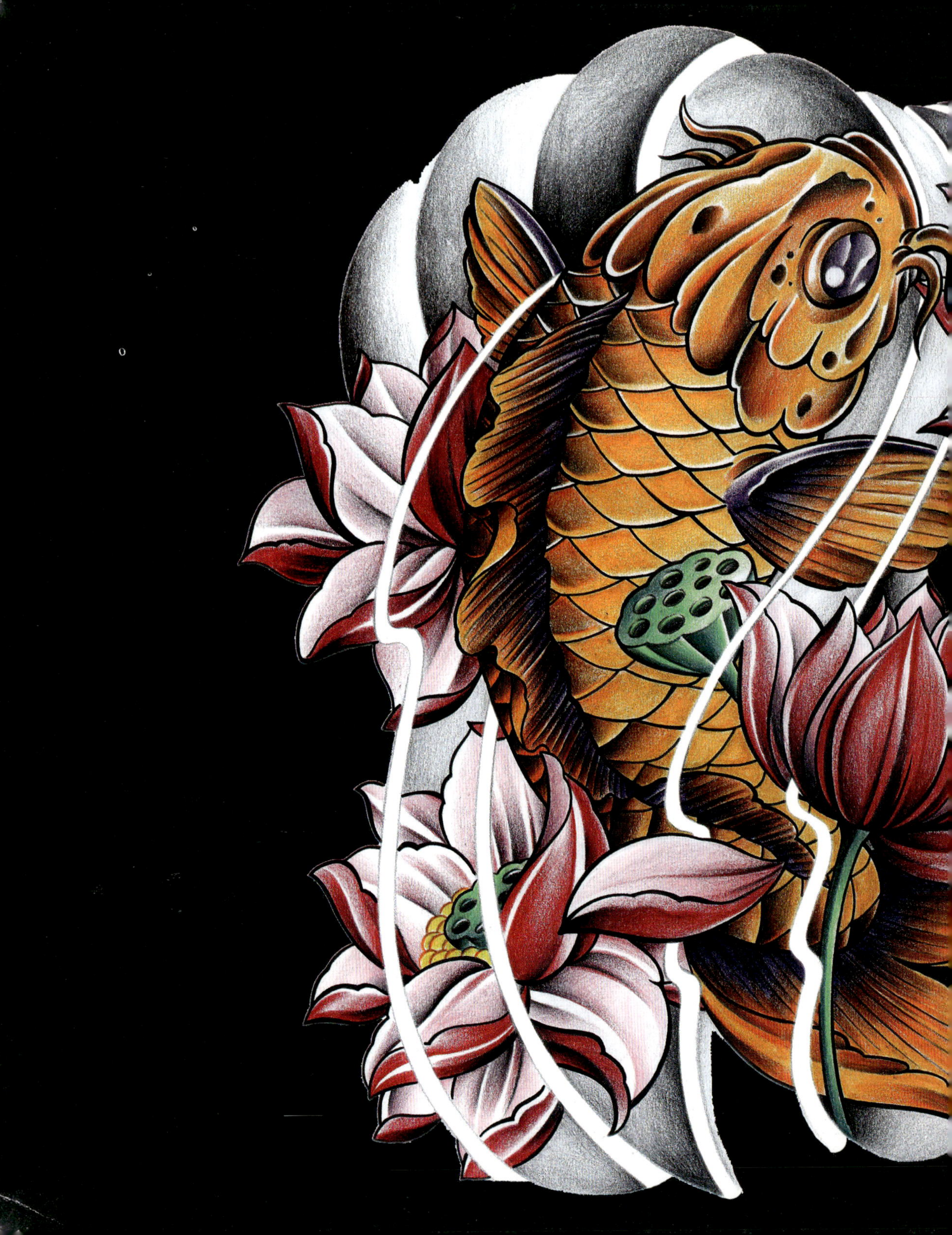

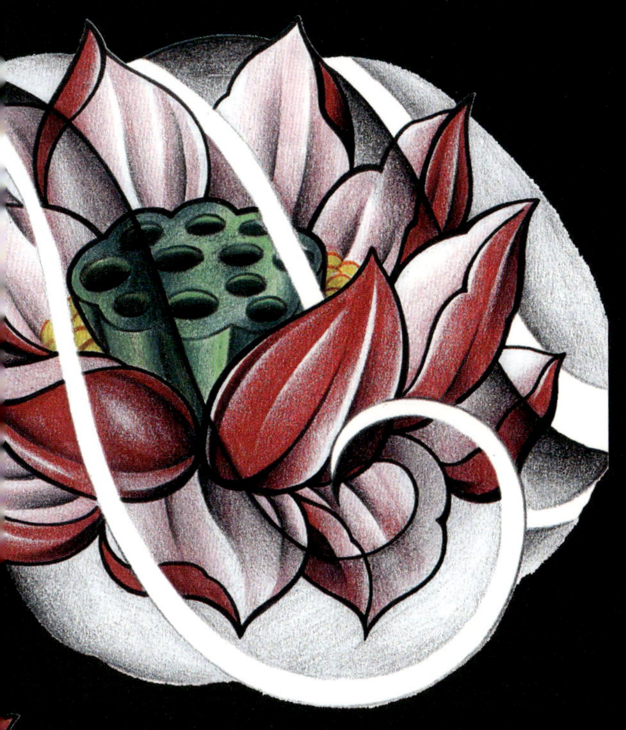

TATTOOS

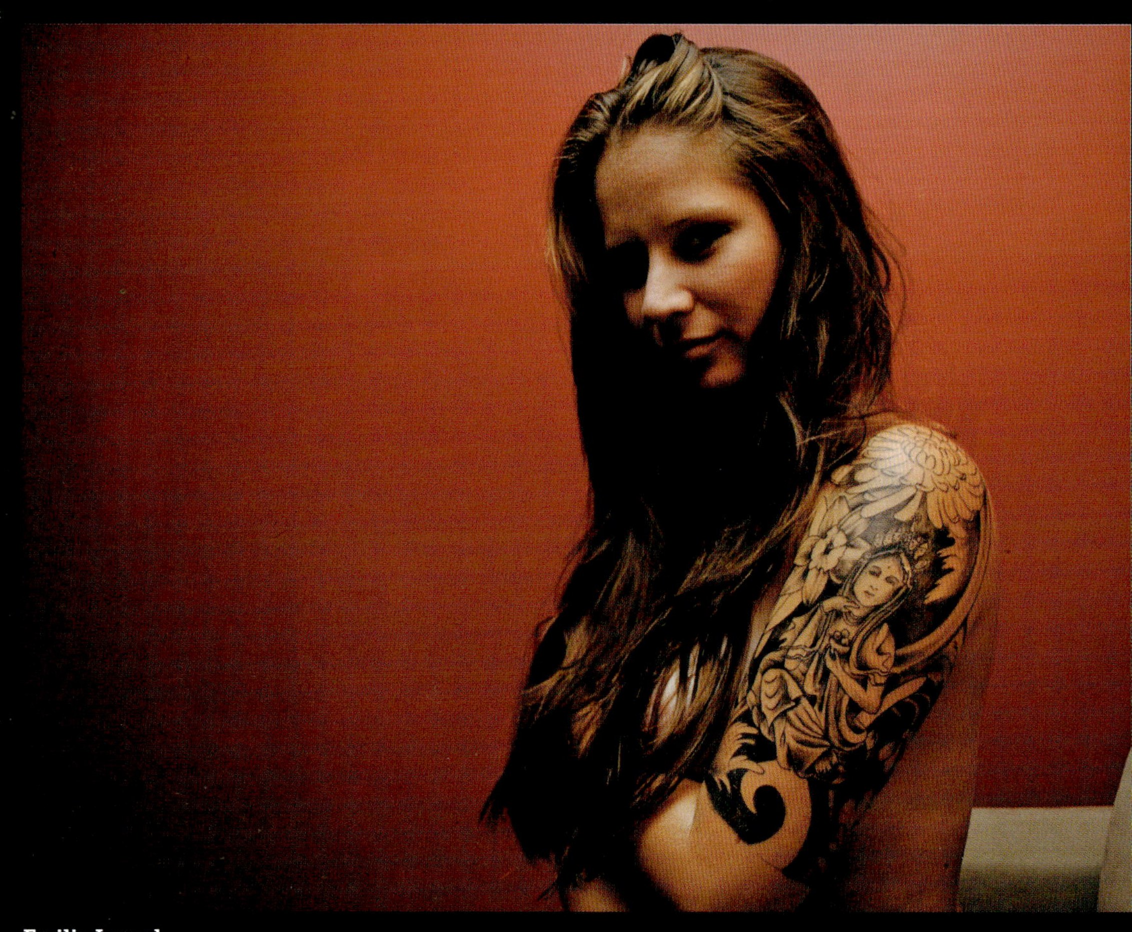

Emilia Laurel

www.emiliatattooart.com

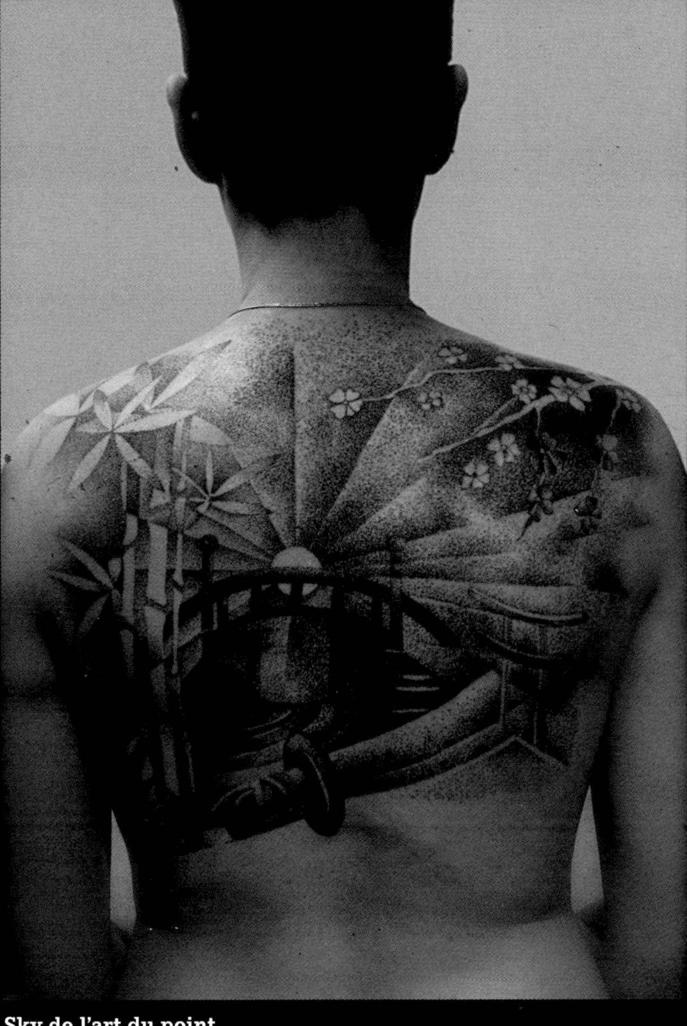

Sky de l'art du point

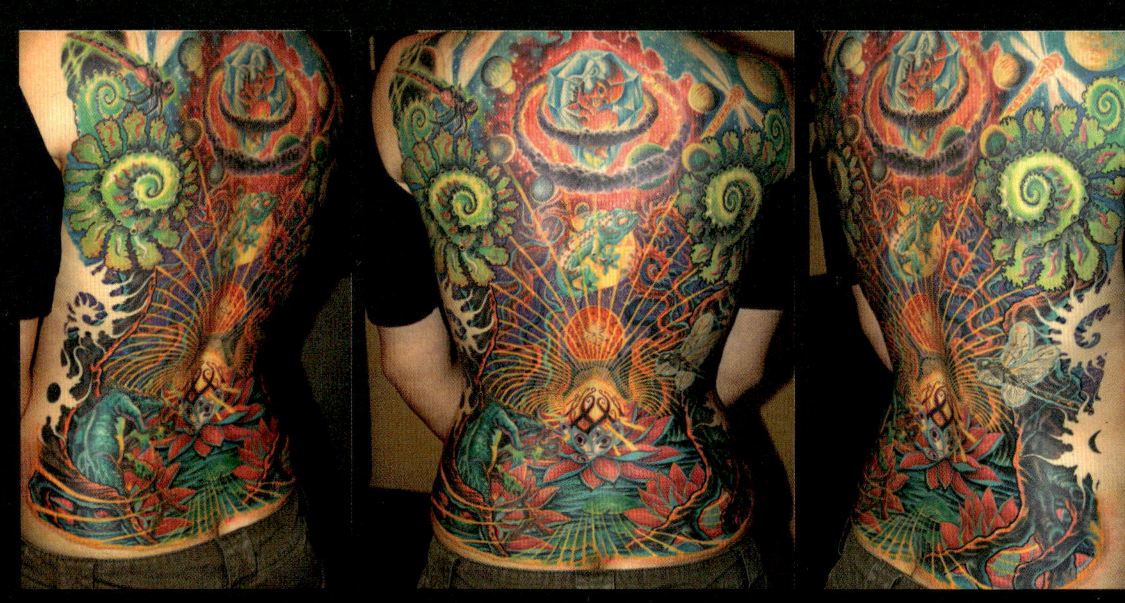

Zsolt
Dark Art Tattoo
www.darkart.hu

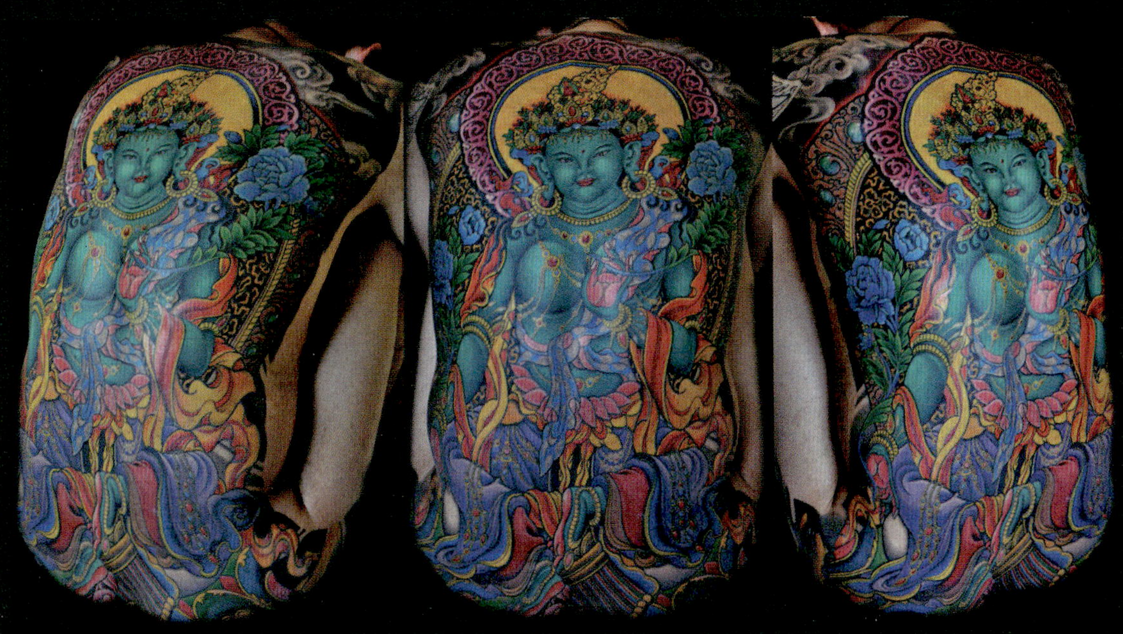

Tang Ping
Zi You Tattoo
www.myspace.com/ziyoutattoo

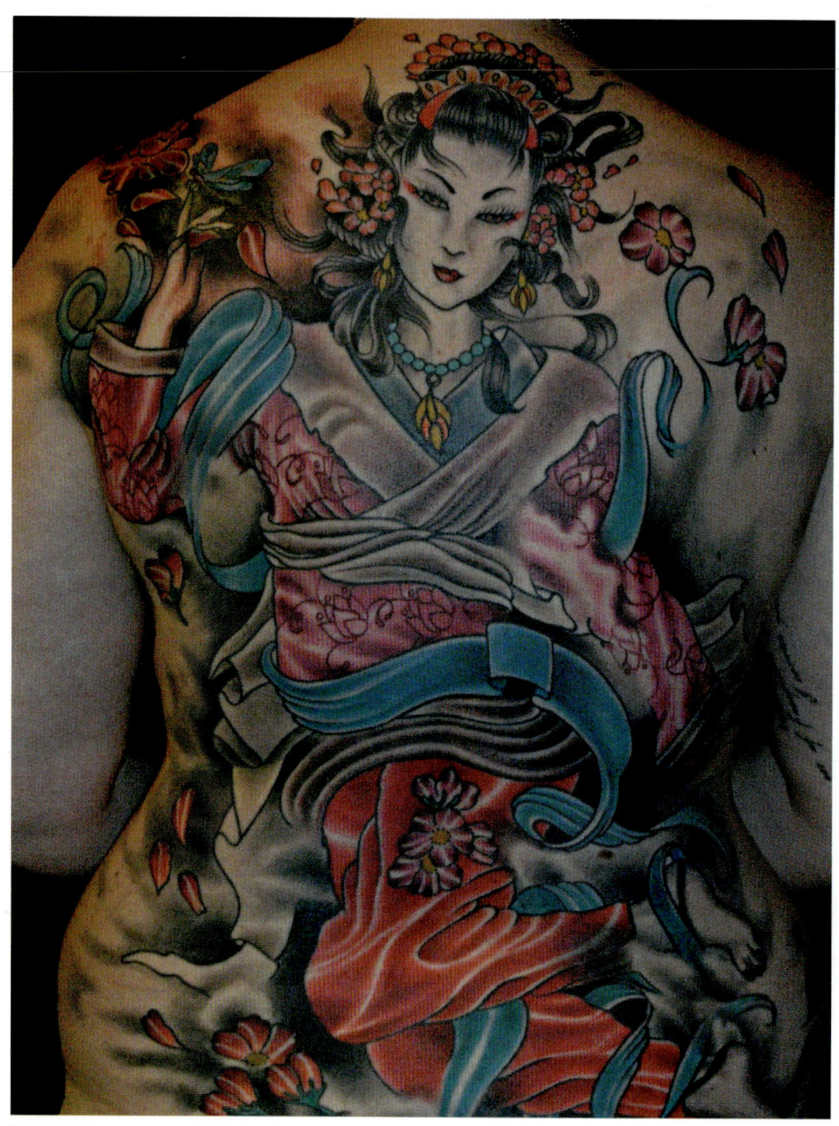

Jonny Wemmenstedt
Studio King Carlos Tattoo
www.kingcarlostattoo.com

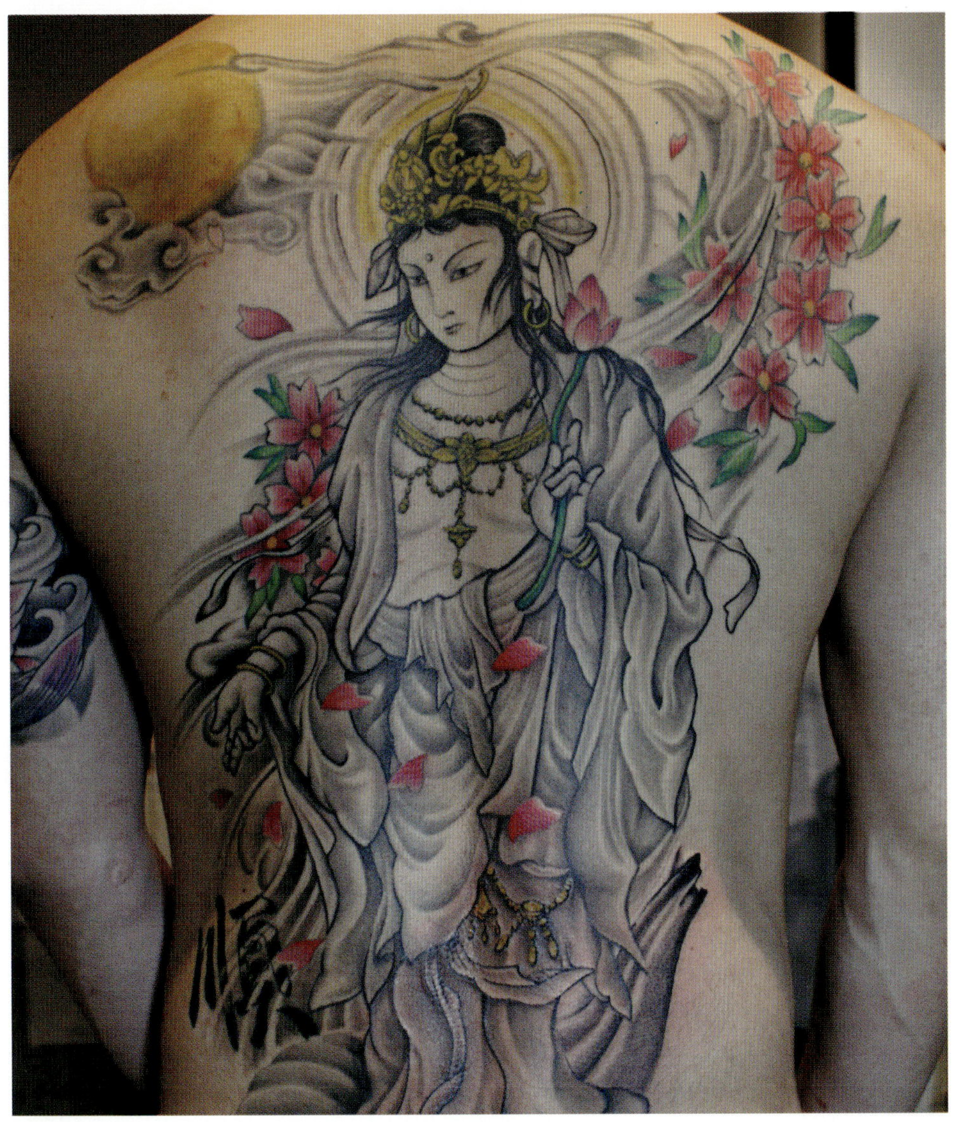

Satoshi Ohata
T3-Tattoos
www.t3-tattoos.com

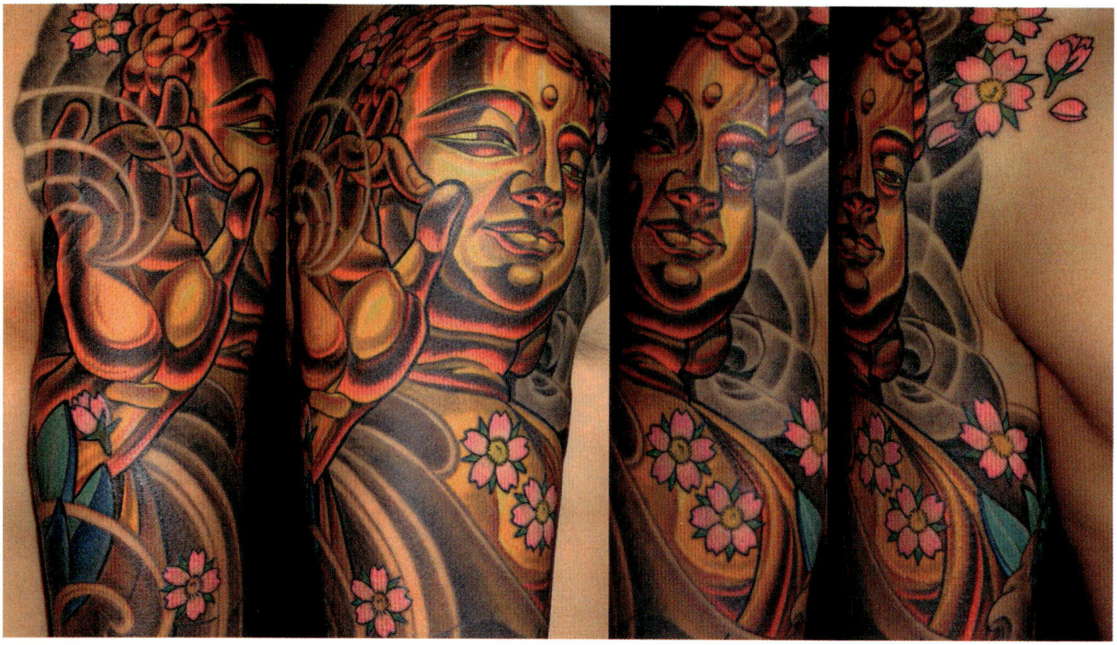

Terry Ribera
www.terryribera.com

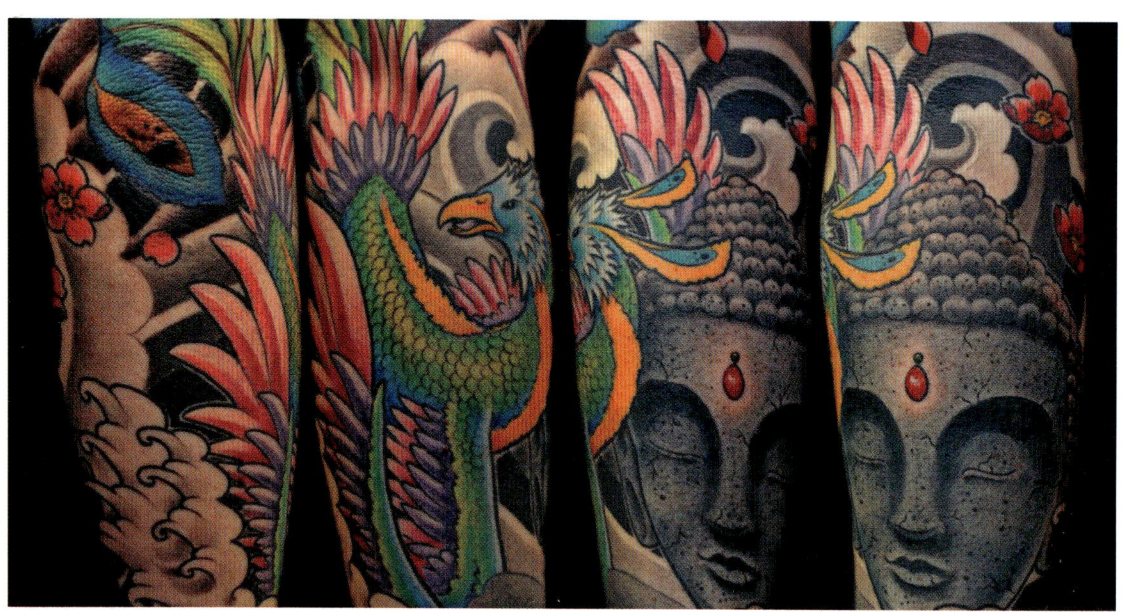

Joako
Human Fly Tattoo Studio
www.humanflytattoo.com

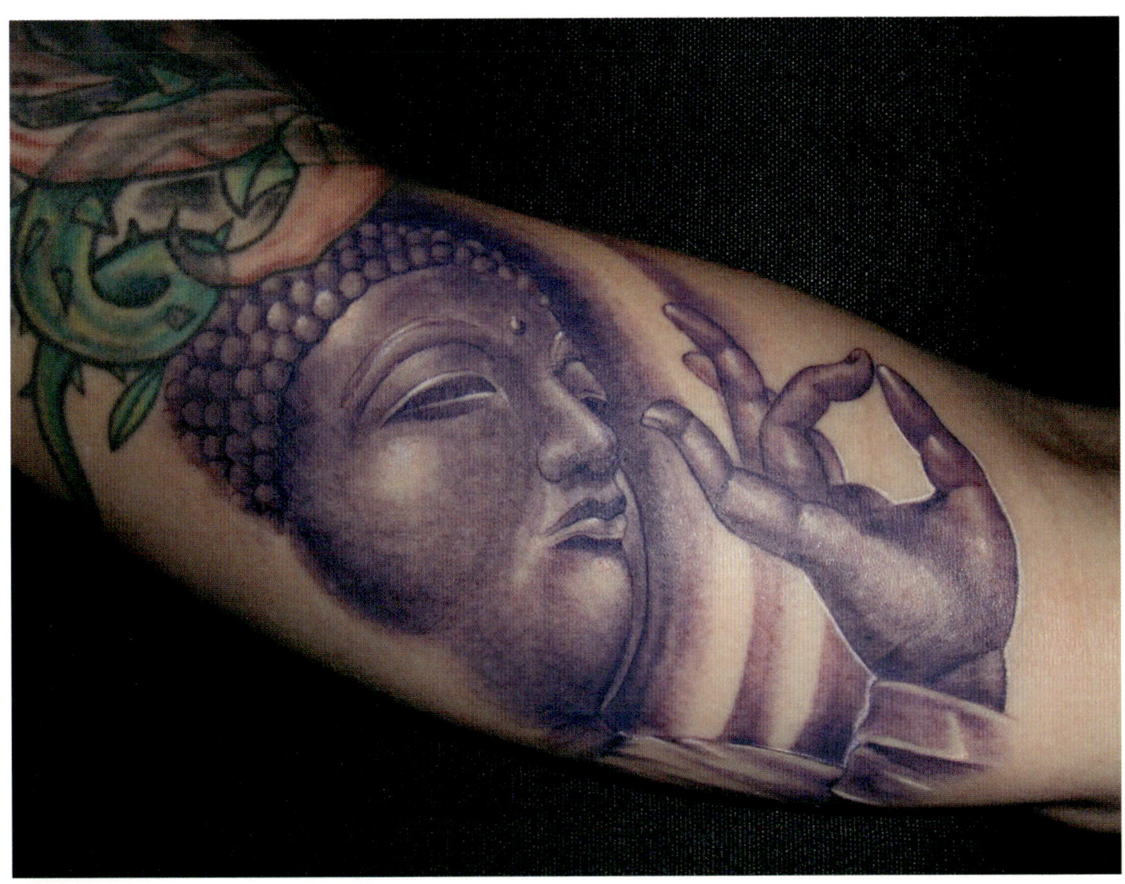

Samu Wanted
V Tattoo
www.vtattoo.es

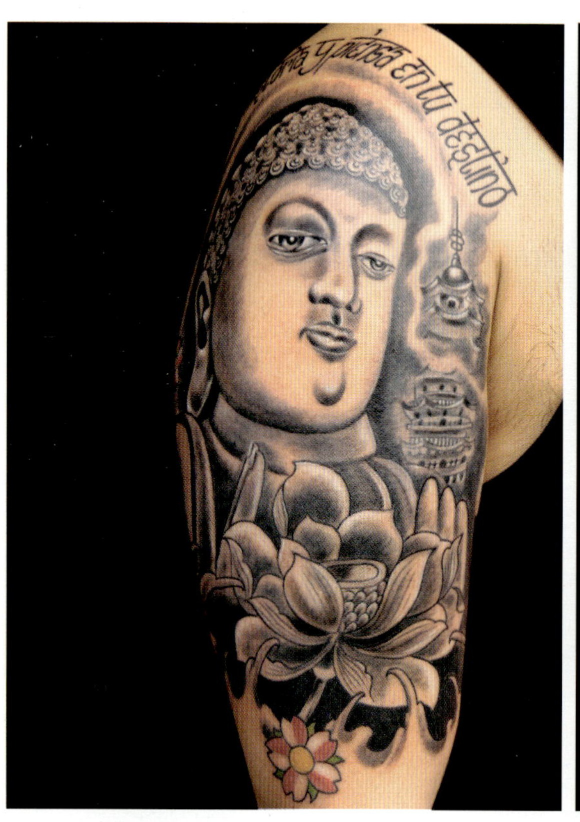

Alfonso Sánchez
Balinese Tattoo Studio
www.balinesetattoo.com

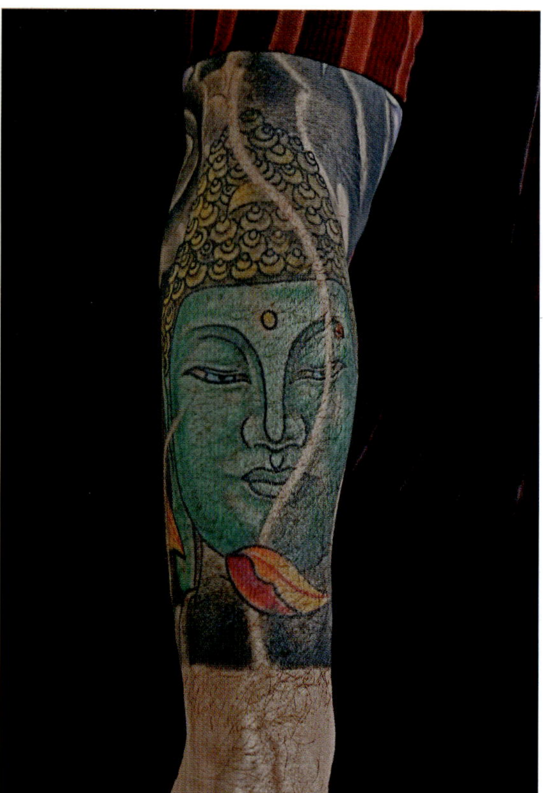

Javier Acero
Tattoo & Co. Miami
www.tattooandco.com

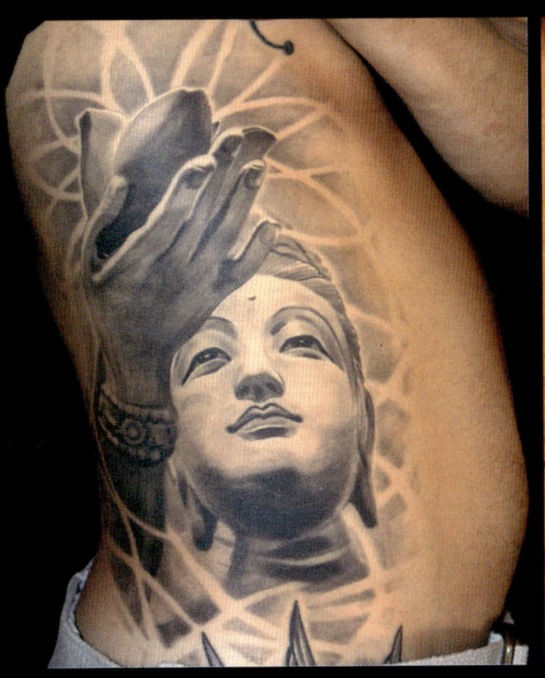

Zsolt
Dark Art Tattoo
www.darkart.hu

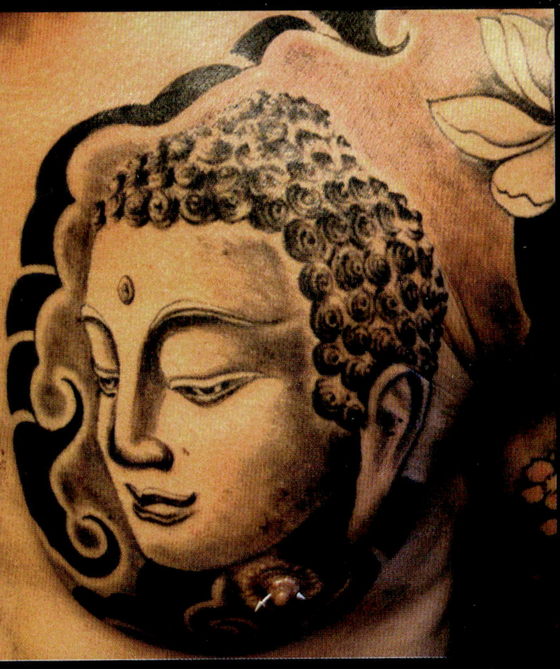

Falke
Pro-Arts Tattoo
www.pro-arts.com

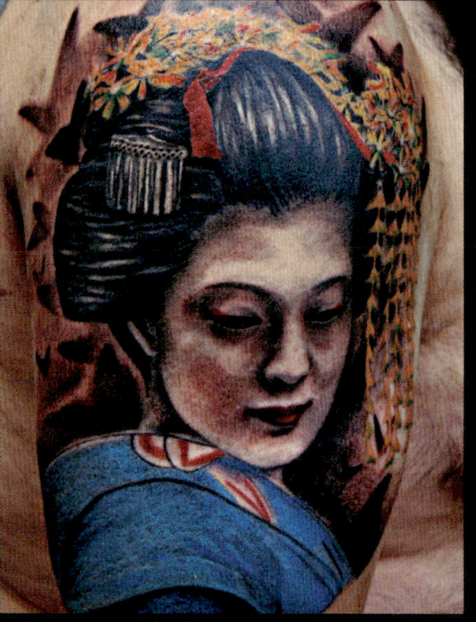

Jordi Pinzell
Brush Planet Tattoo
www.facebook/jordi.pinzell

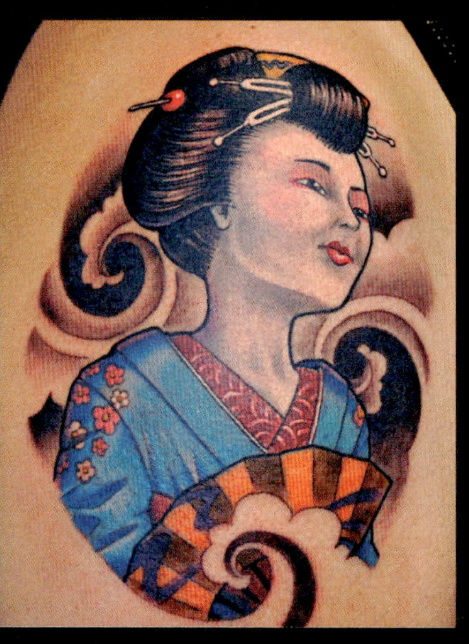

Joako
Human Fly Tattoo Studio
www.humanflytattoo.com

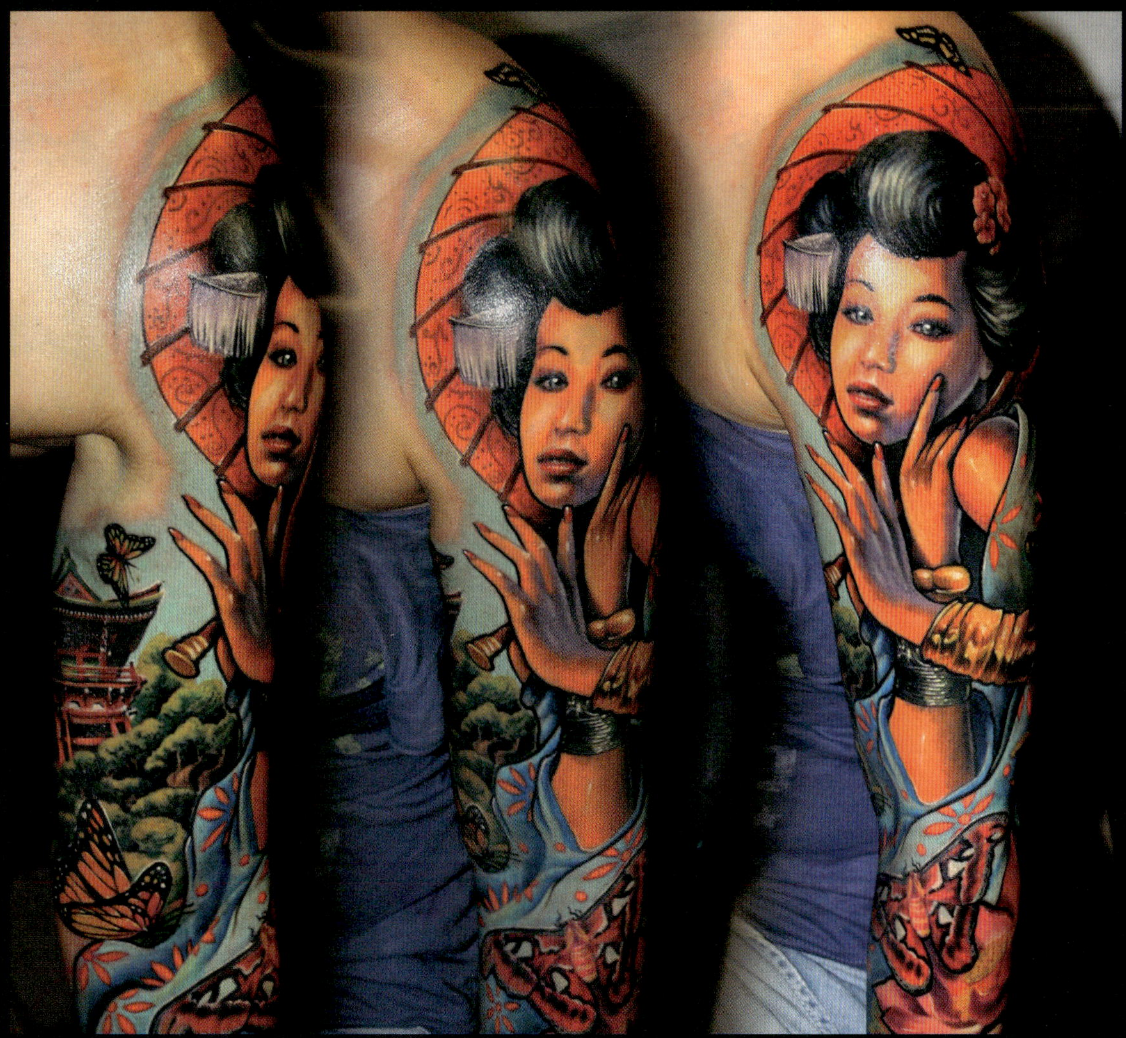

Csaba Mullner
www.csabamullnertattoos.com

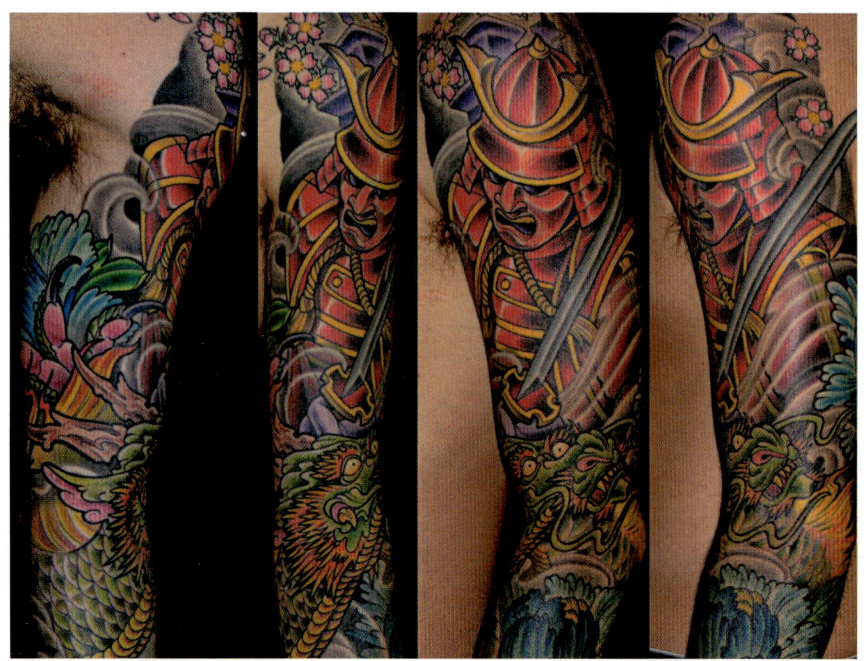

Terry Ribera
Remington Tattoo
www.terryribera.com

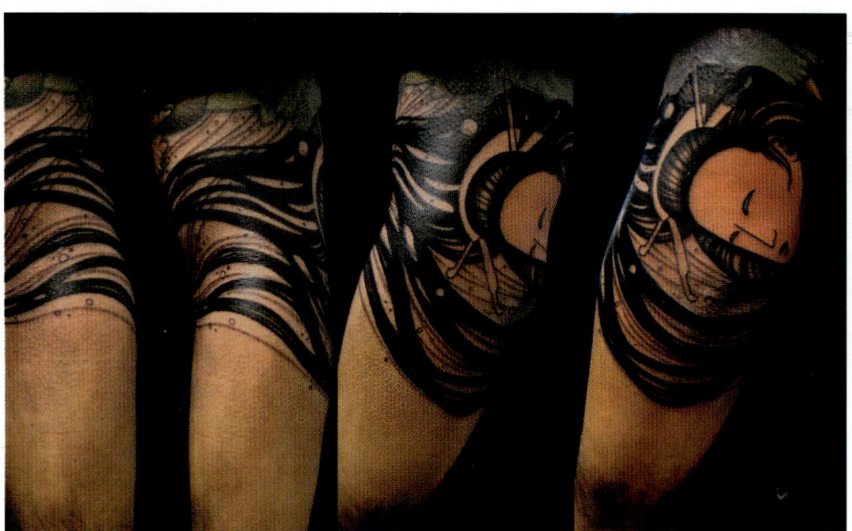

Gustavo Rizeiro
Studio invisible nyc
www.gustavorizeiro.com

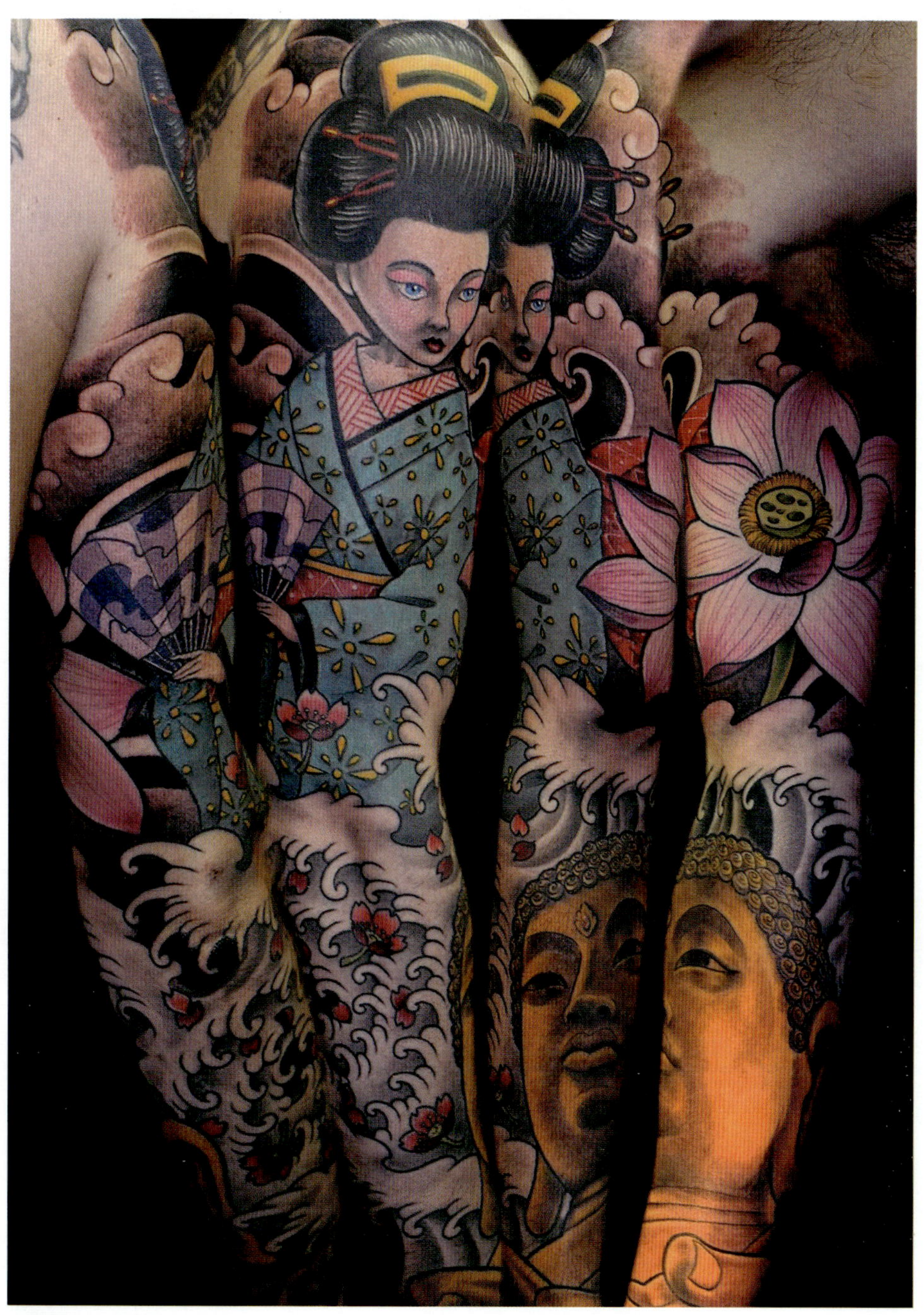

Joako
Human Fly Tattoo Studio
www.humanflytattoo.com

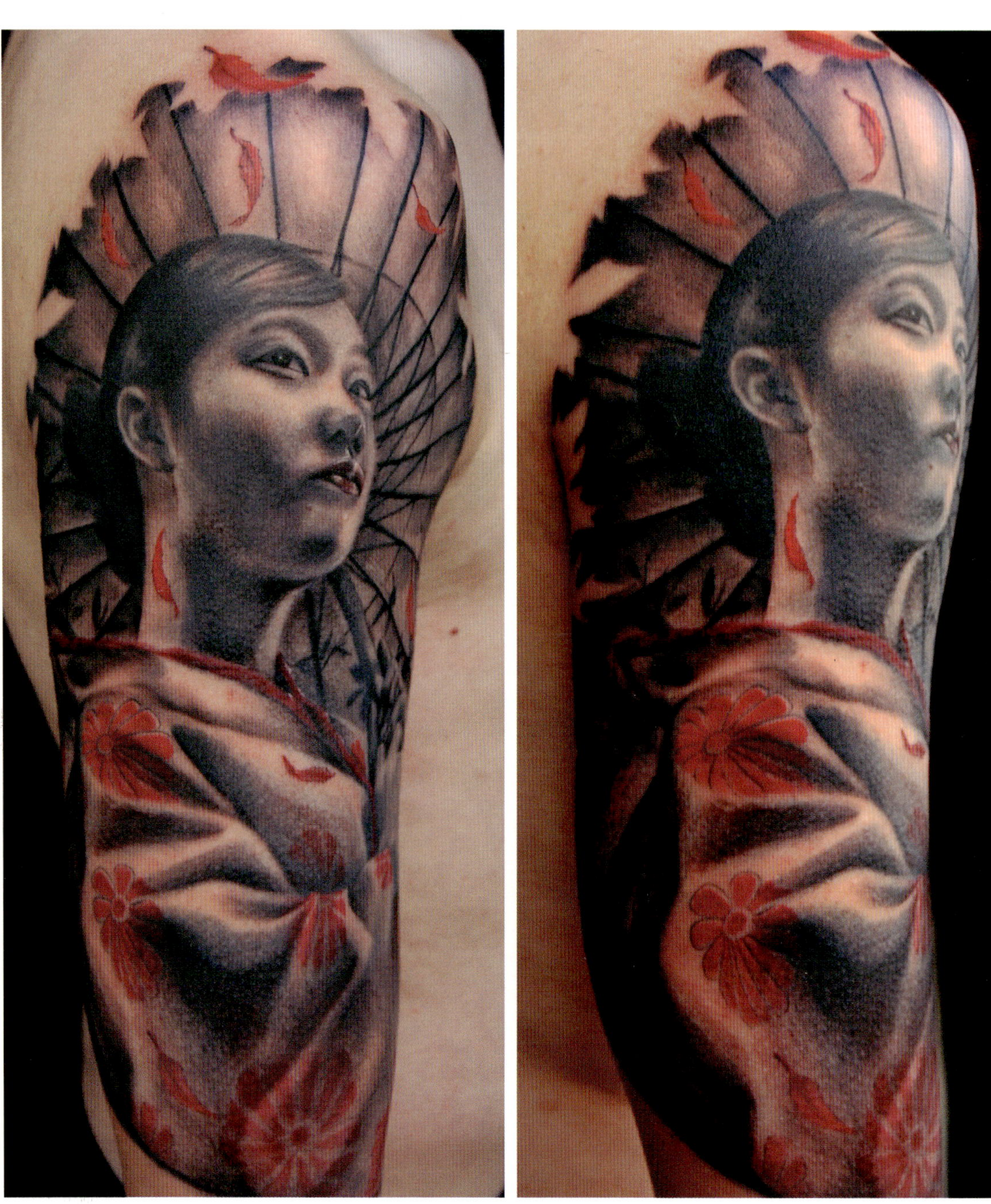

Jordi Pinzell
Brush Planet Tattoo
www.facebook/jordi.pinzell

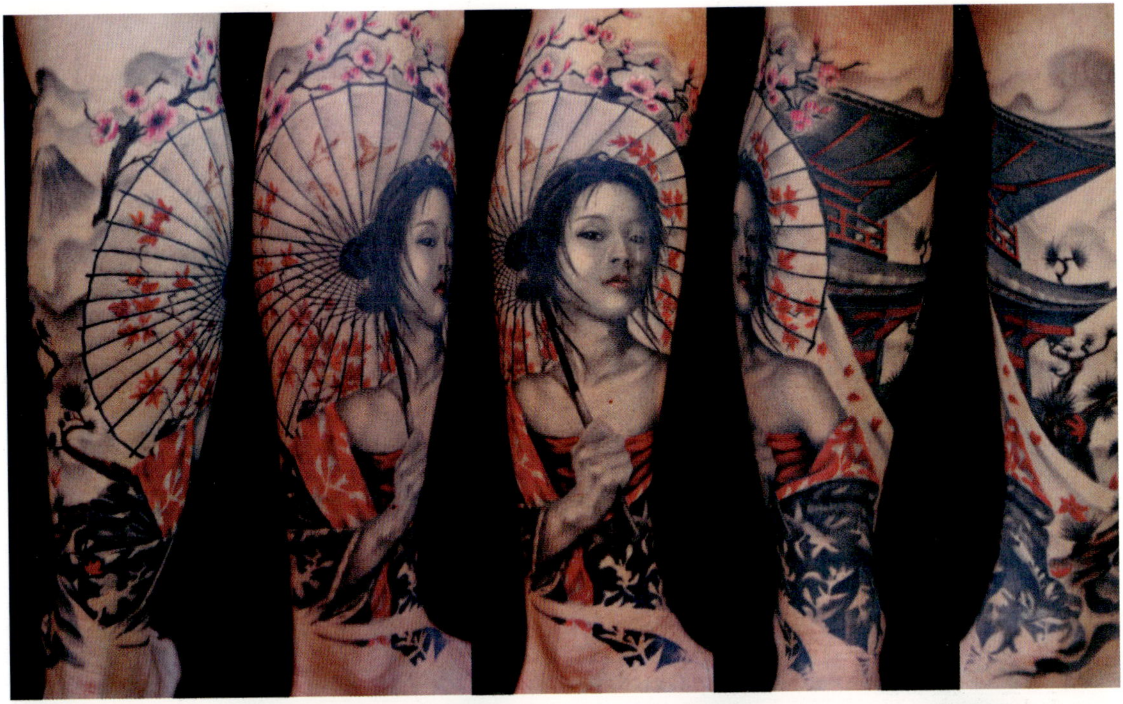

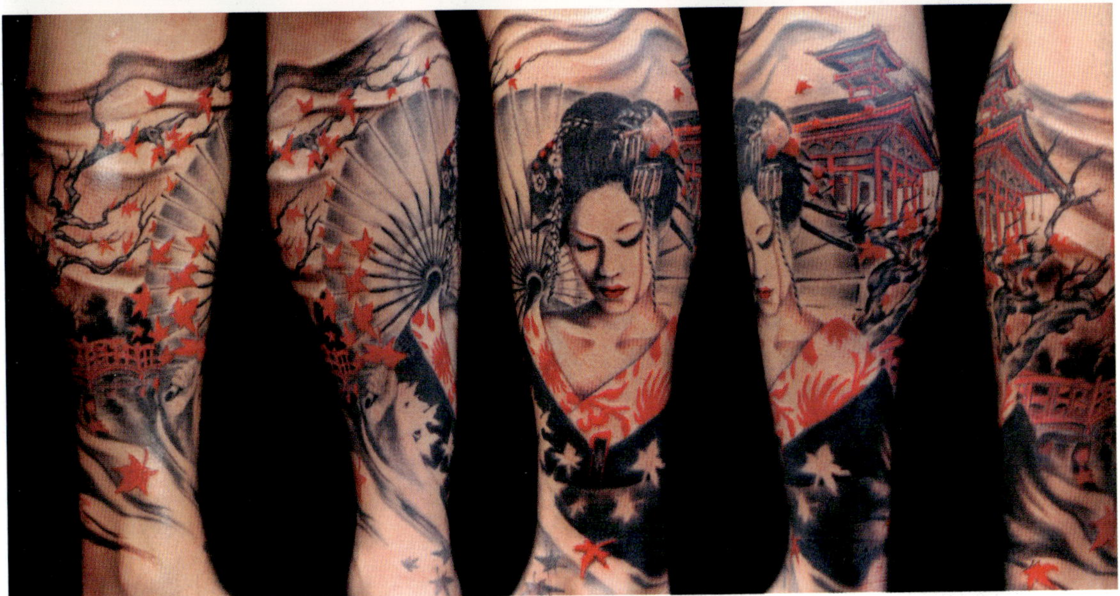

Jordi Pinzell
Brush Planet Tattoo
www.facebook/jordi.pinzell

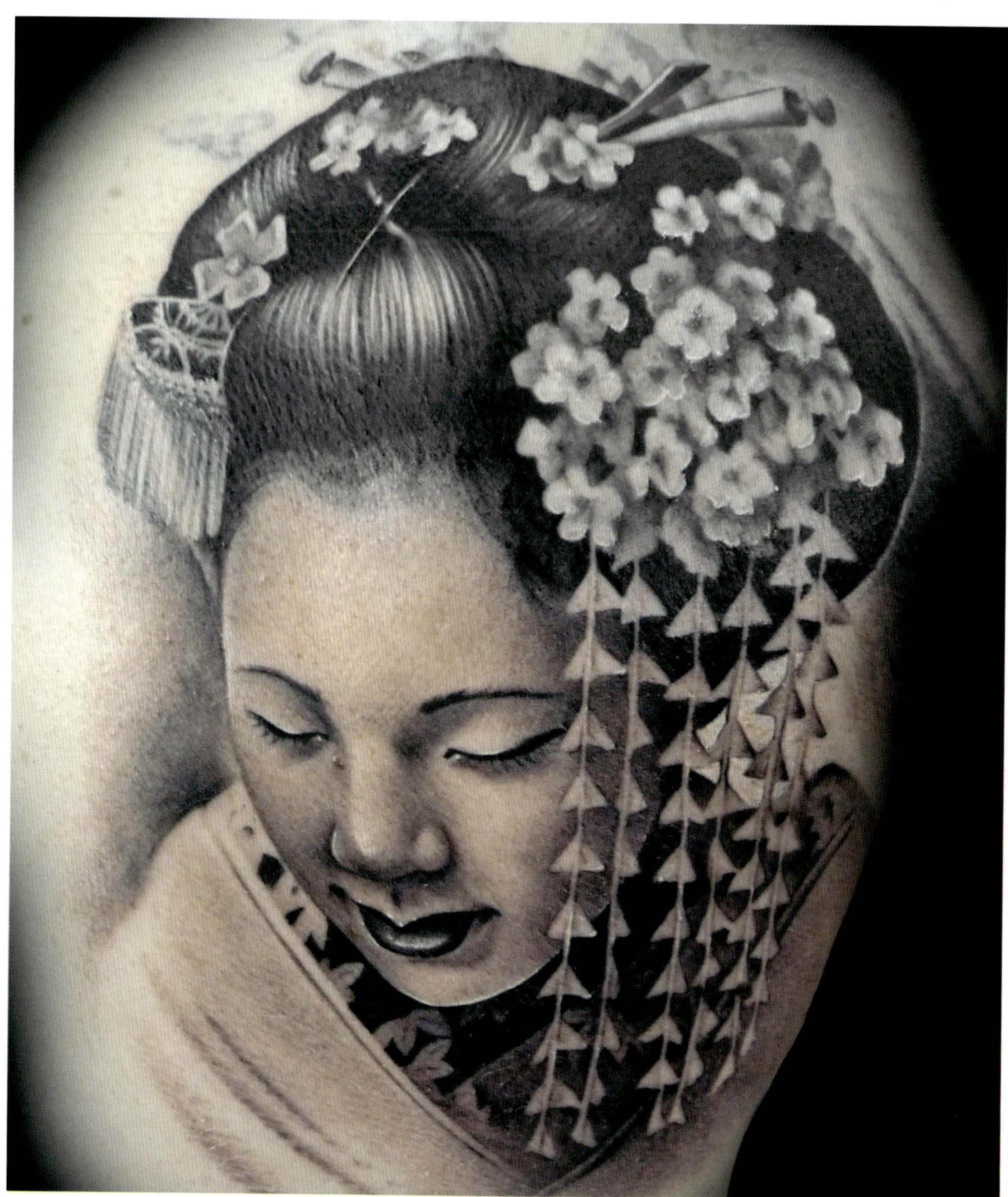

Daniel Martos
Studio Demon Tattoo
www.tatuajesdemon.com

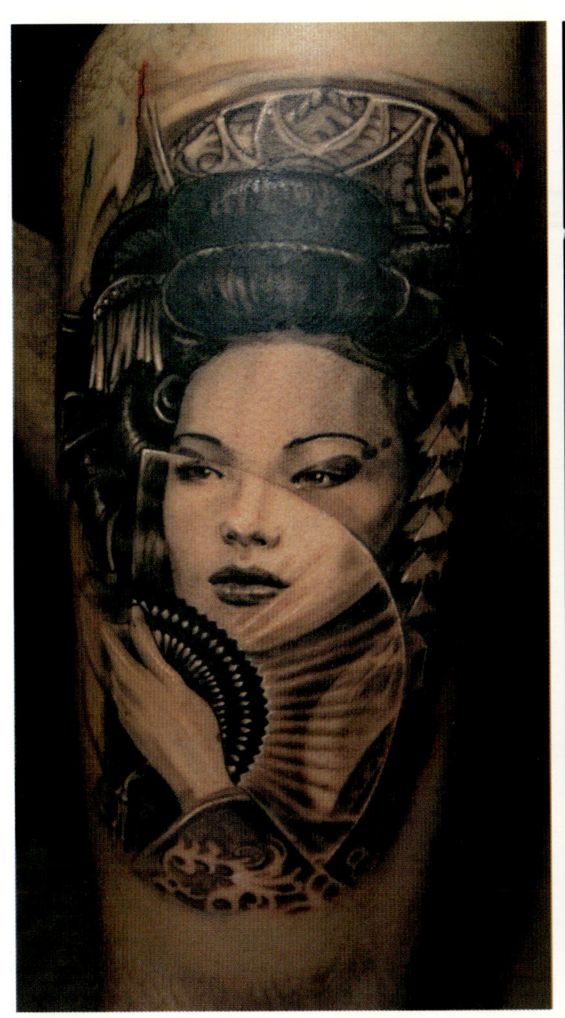

Zsolt
Dark Art Tattoo
www.darkart.hu

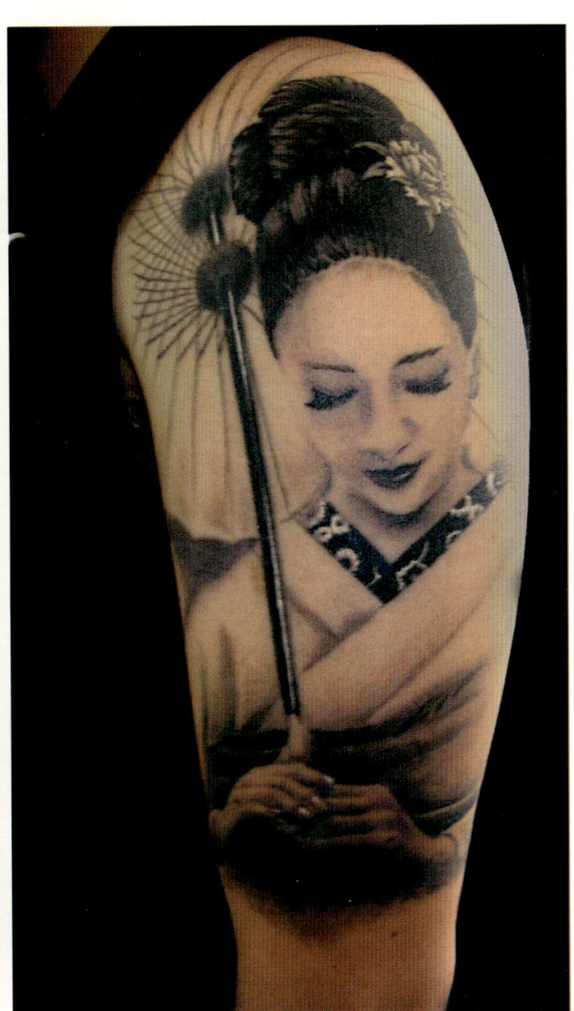

Falke
Pro-Arts Tattoo
www.pro-arts.com

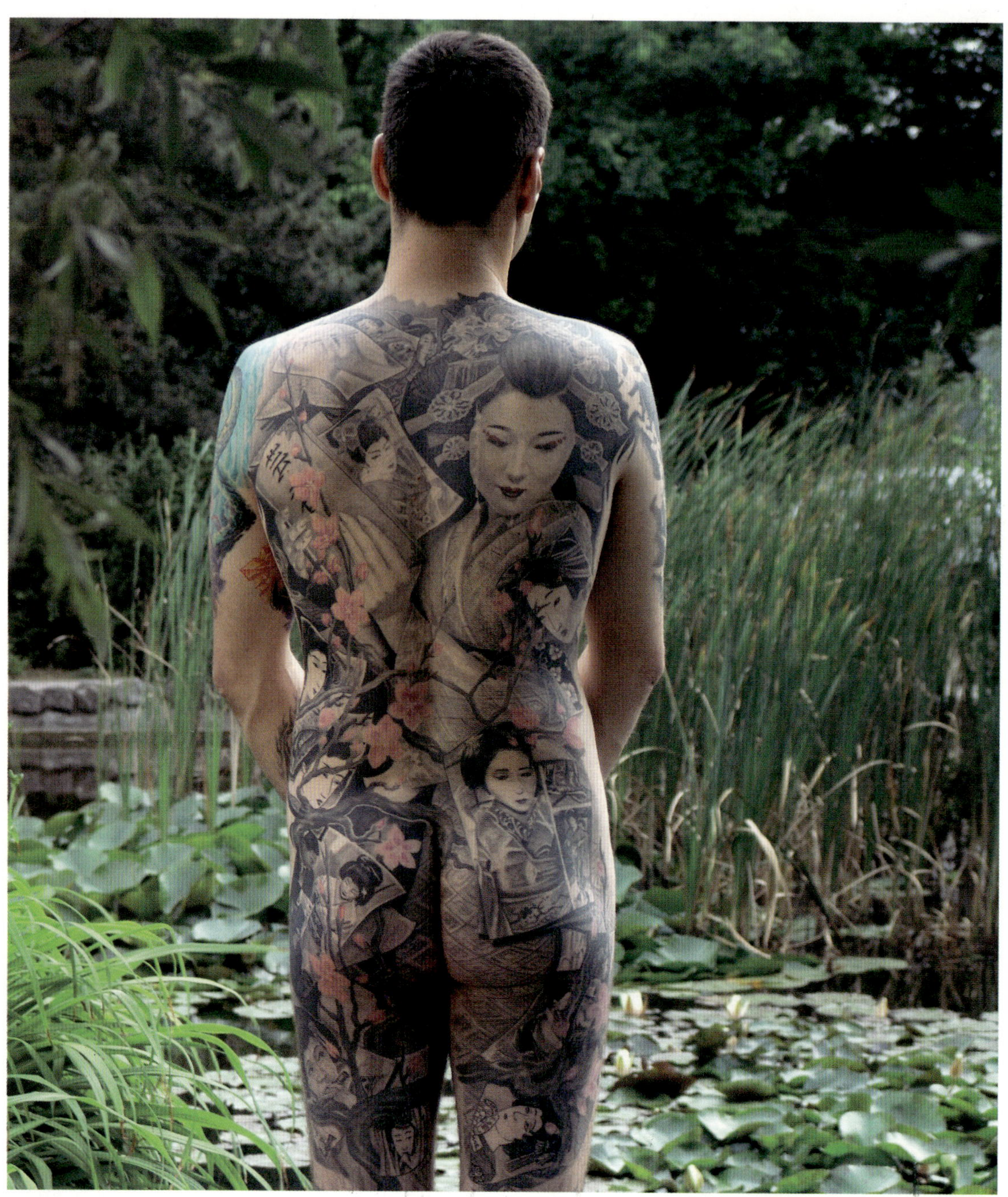

Zsolt
Dark Art Tattoo
www.darkart.hu

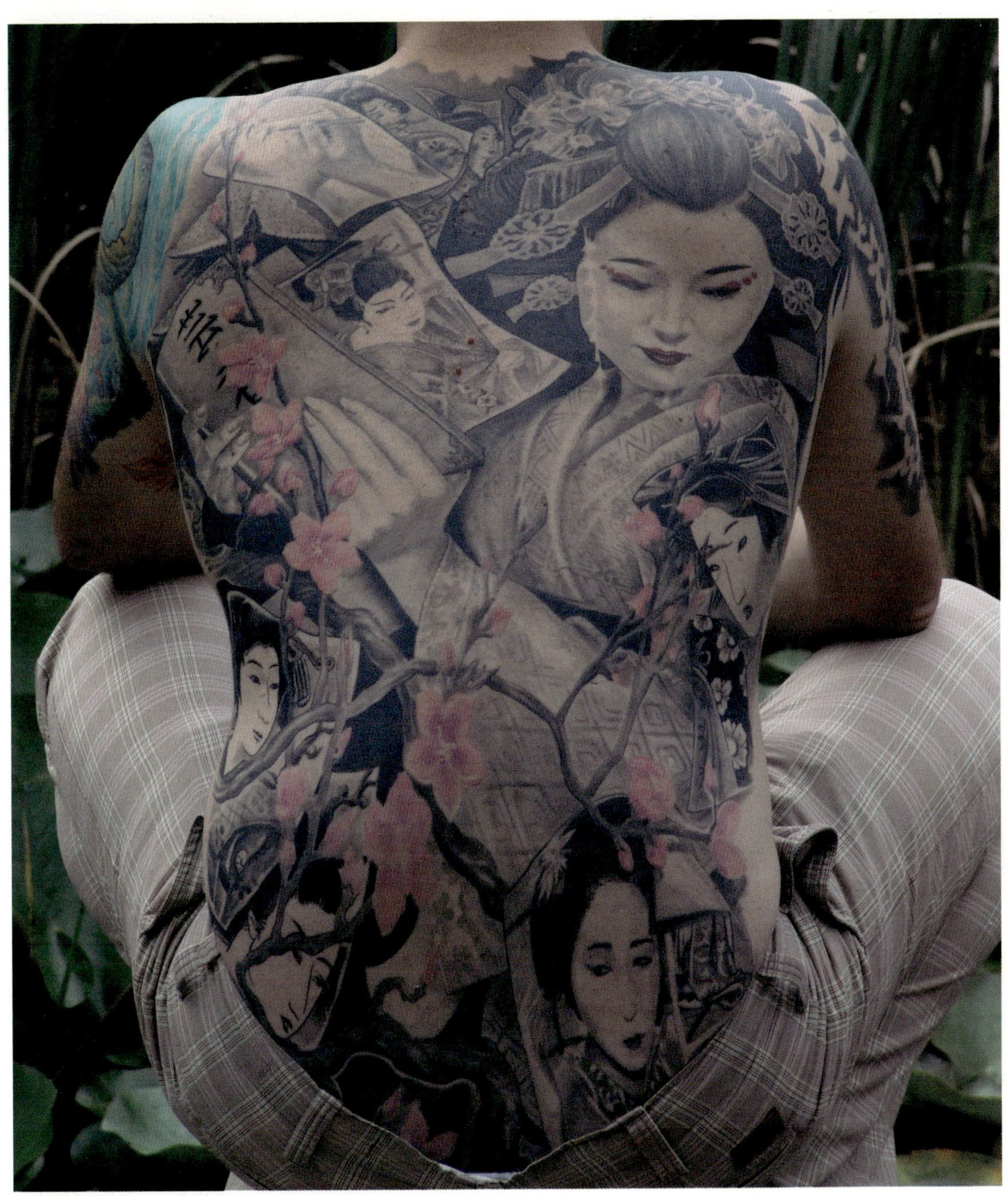

Zsolt
Dark Art Tattoo
www.darkart.hu

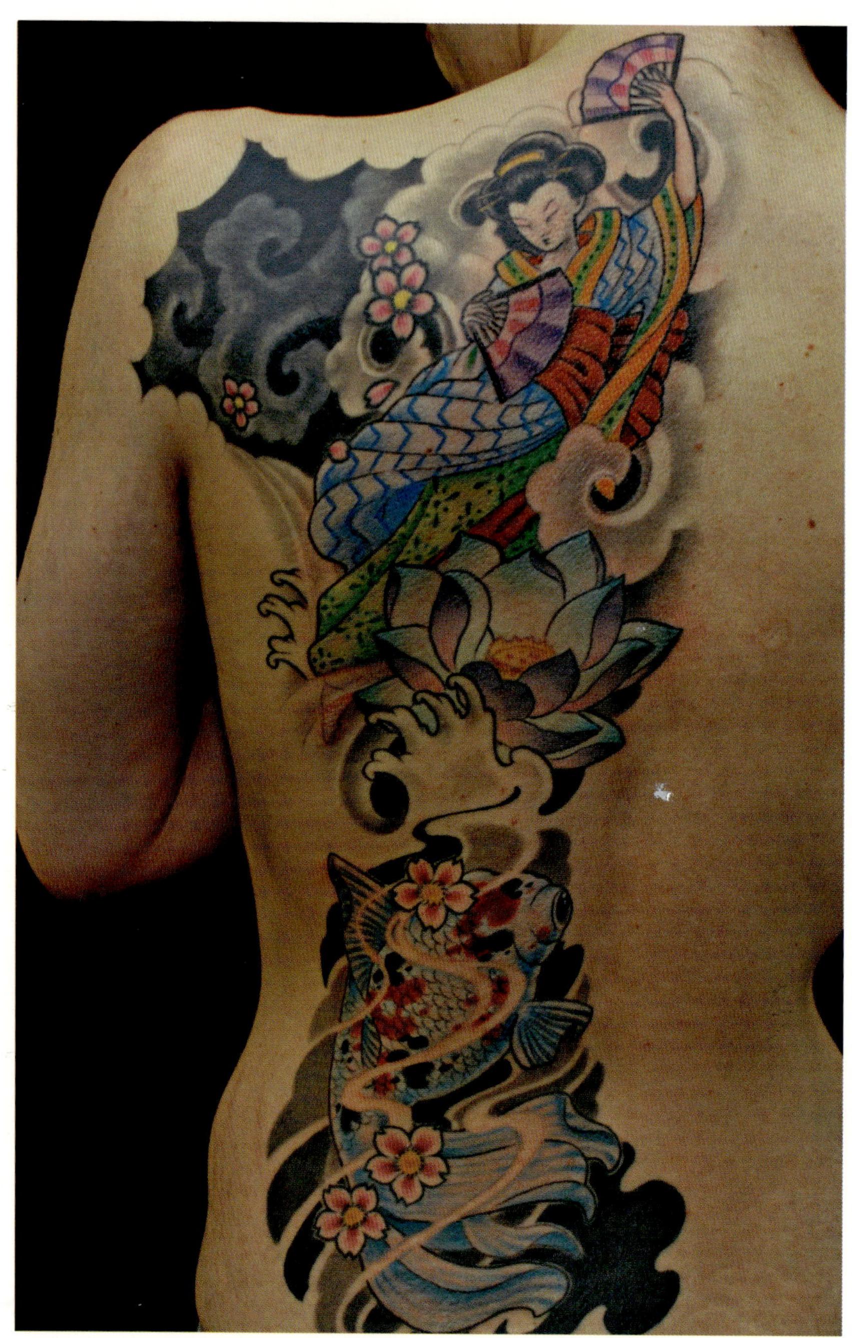

Joako
Human Fly Tattoo Studio
www.humanflytattoo.com

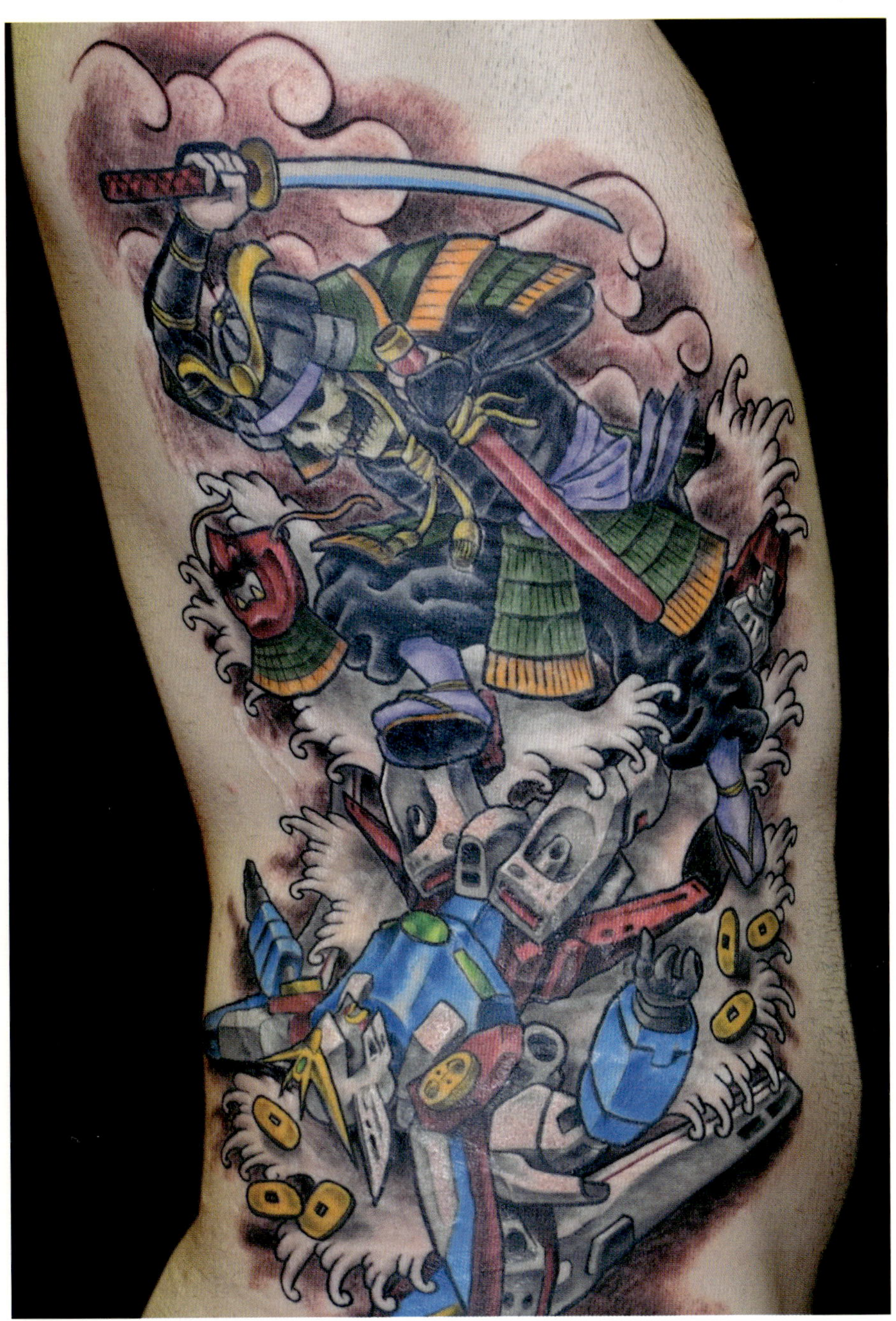

Joako
Human Fly Tattoo Studio
www.humanflytattoo.com

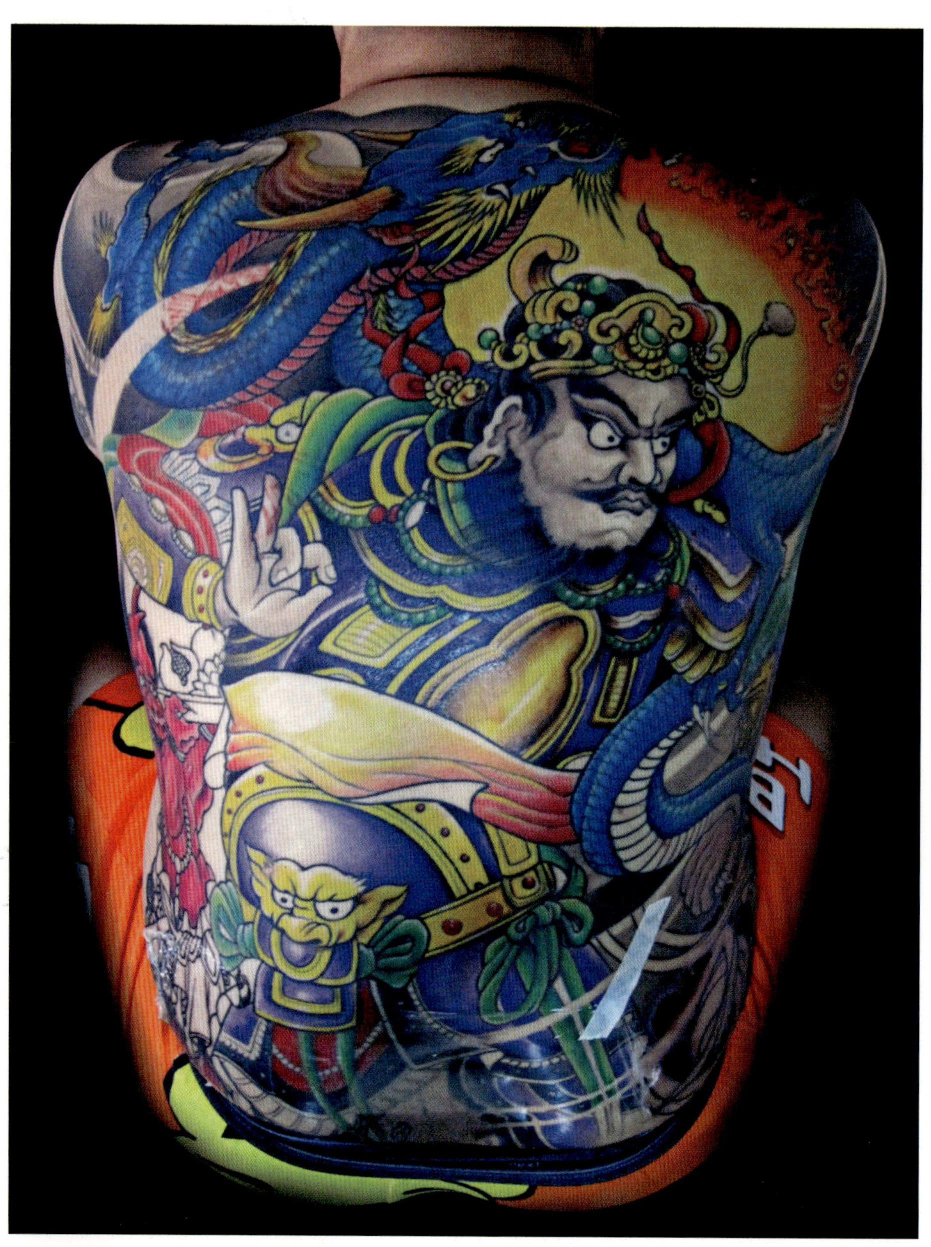

Tang Ping
Zi You Tattoo
www.myspace.com/ziyoutattoo

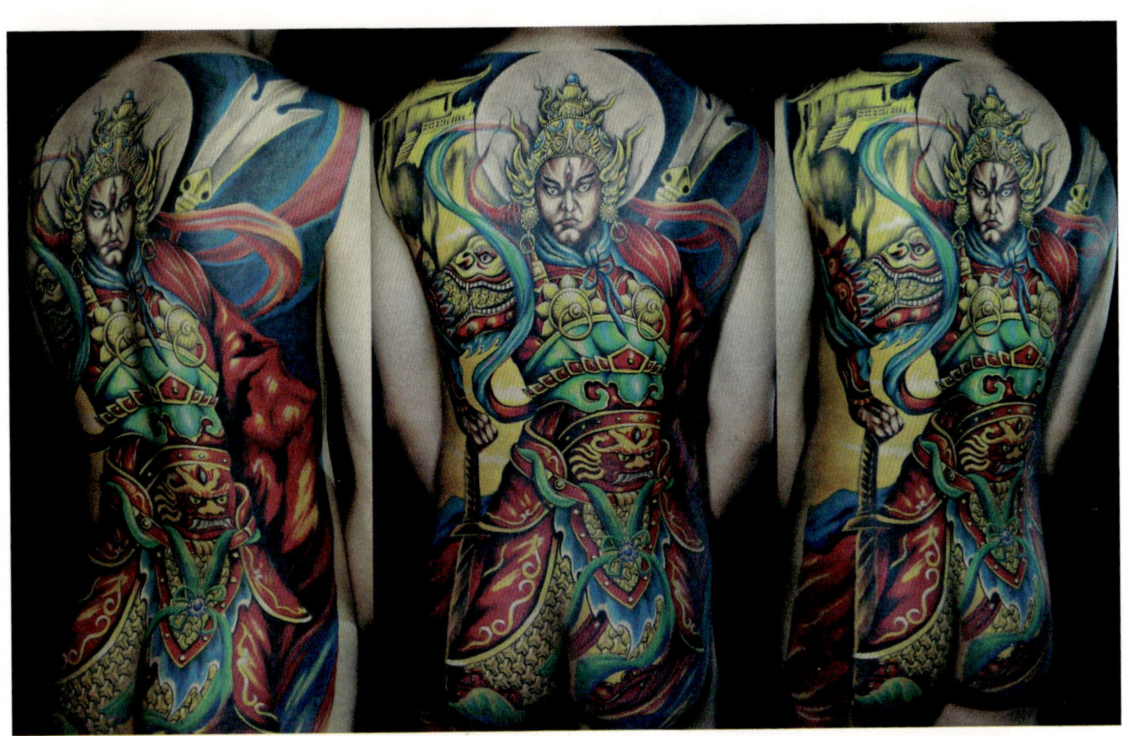

Tang Ping
Zi You Tattoo
www.myspace.com/ziyoutattoo

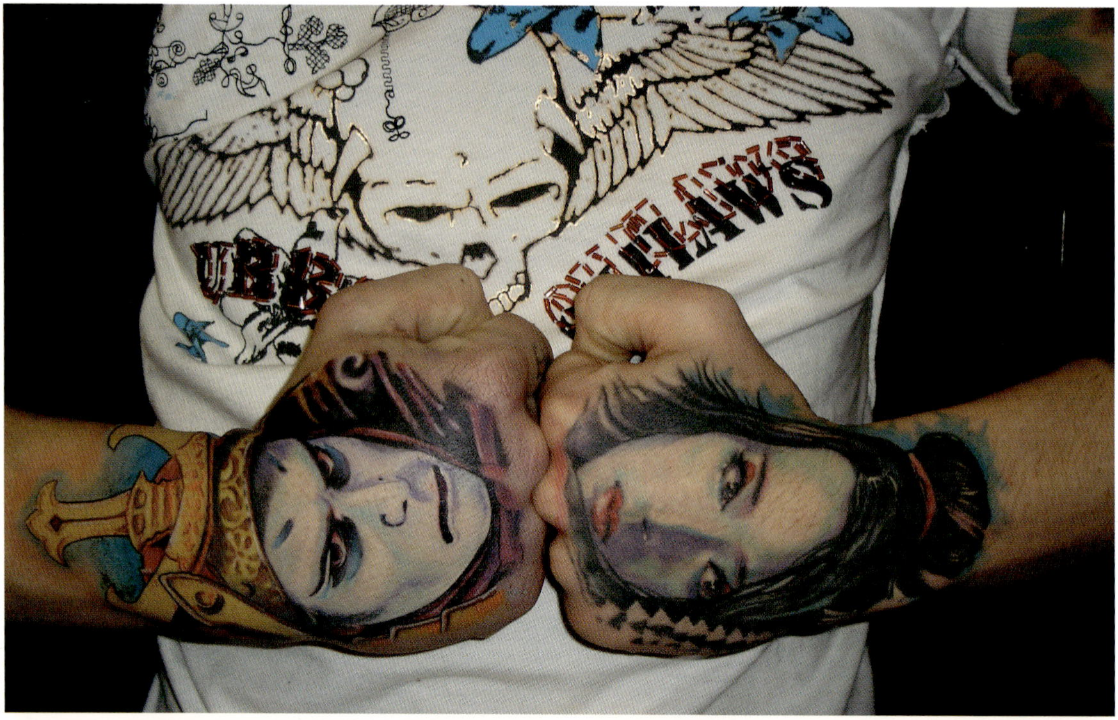

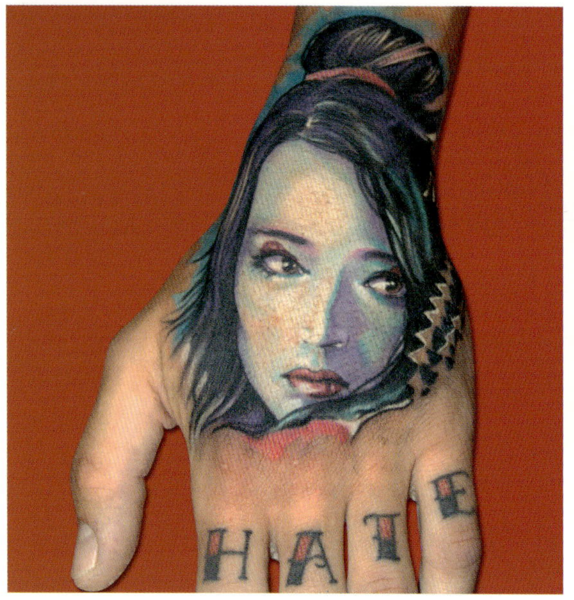

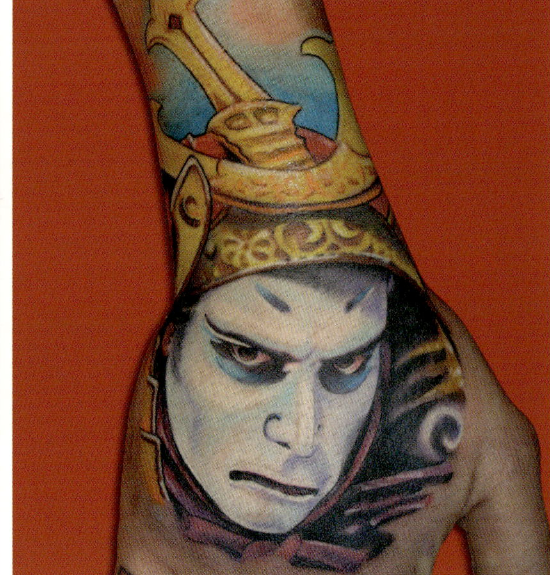

Zsolt
Dark Art Tattoo
www.darkart.hu

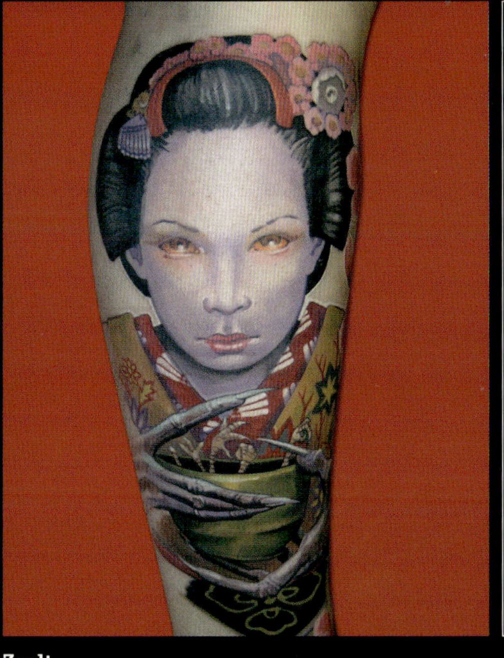

Zsolt
Dark Art Tattoo
www.darkart.hu

Mirek vel Stotker
www.stotkertattoo.com

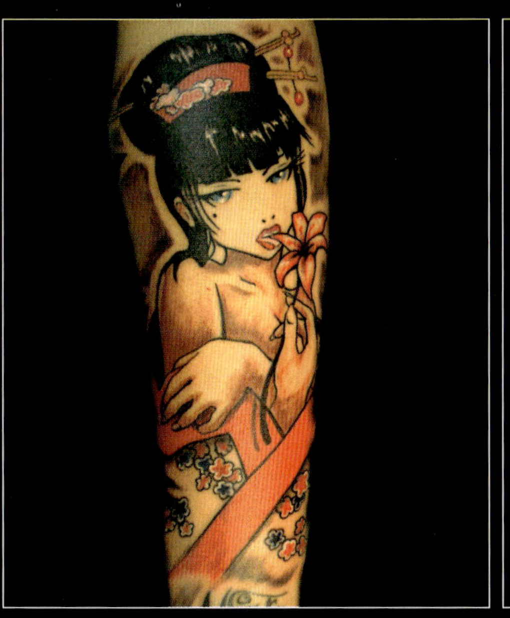

Falke

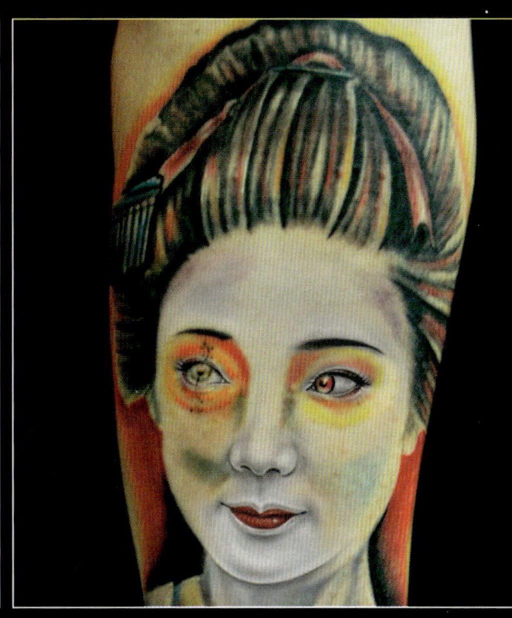

Alfonso Sánchez

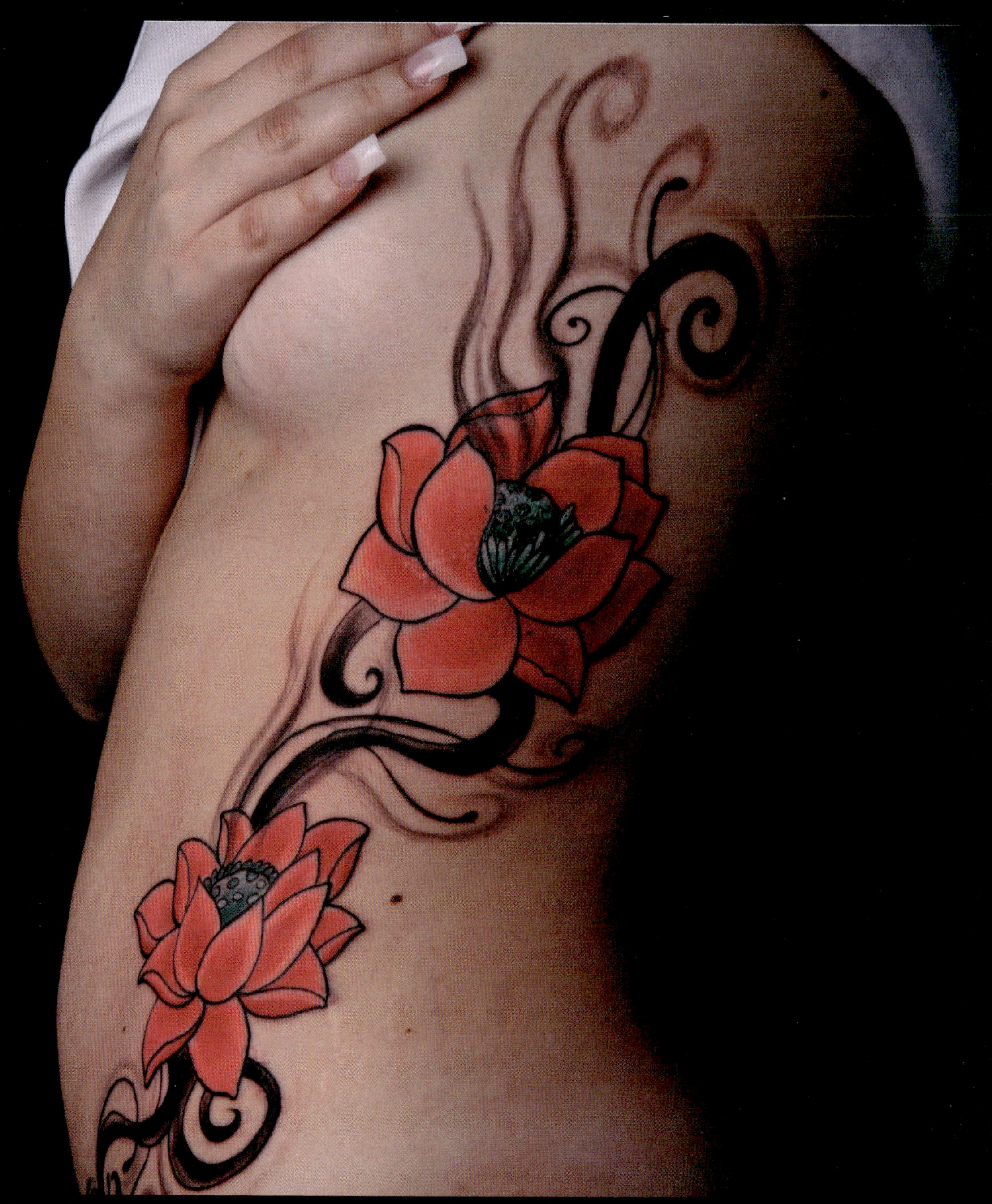

Javier Acero
Tattoo & Co. Miami
www.tattooandco.com

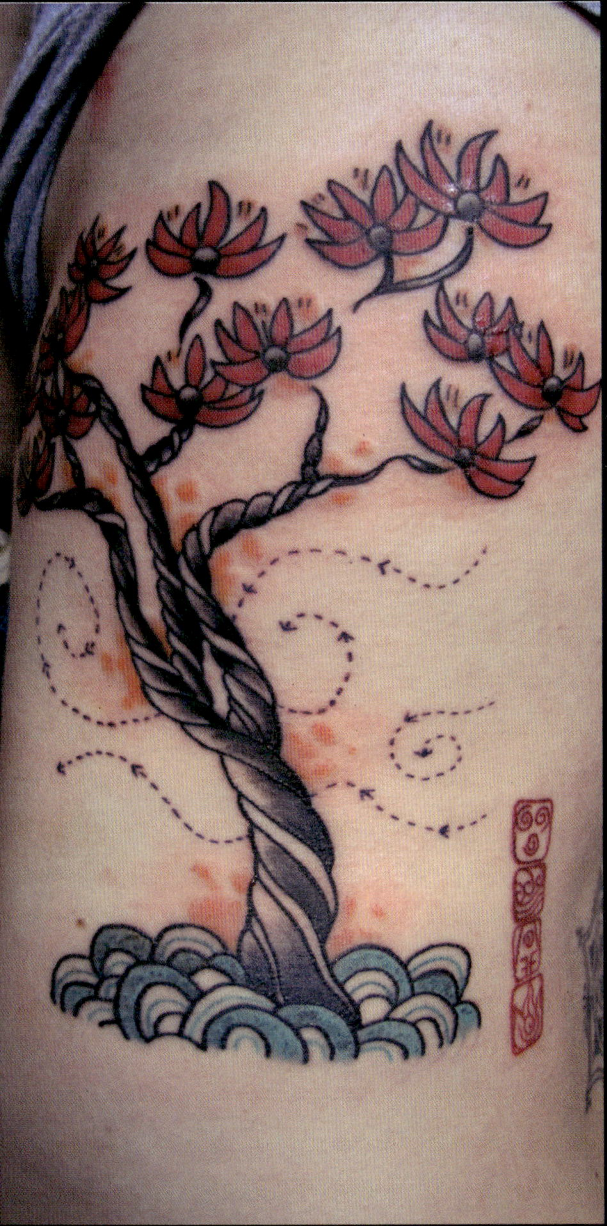

Kat Scarlet
Kat Scarlet Tattoo
www.facebook.com/katscarlettattoo

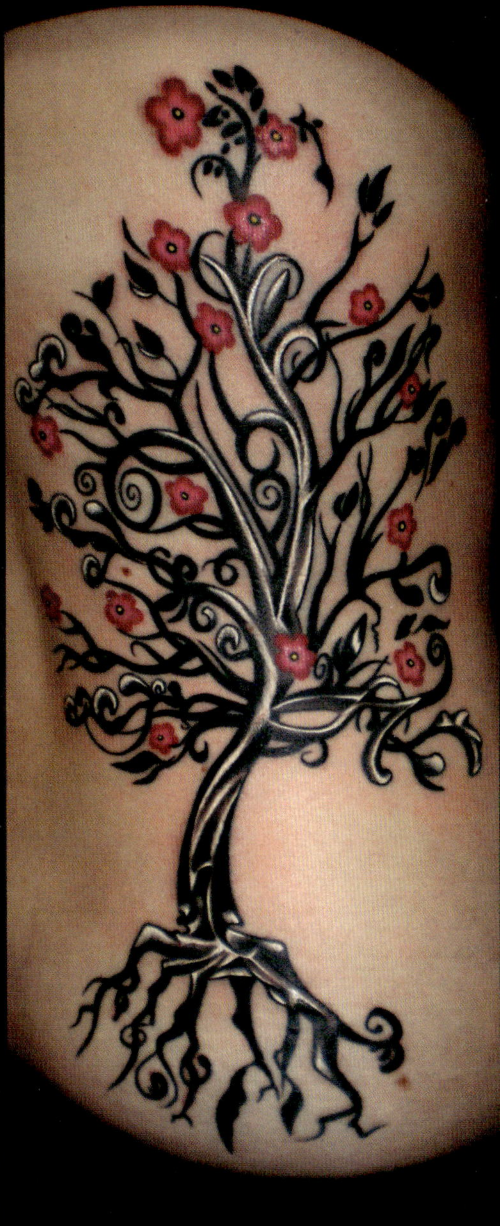

Tomás "Psycho" Dacej
Psycho Tattoo
www.facebook.com/tomas.dacej

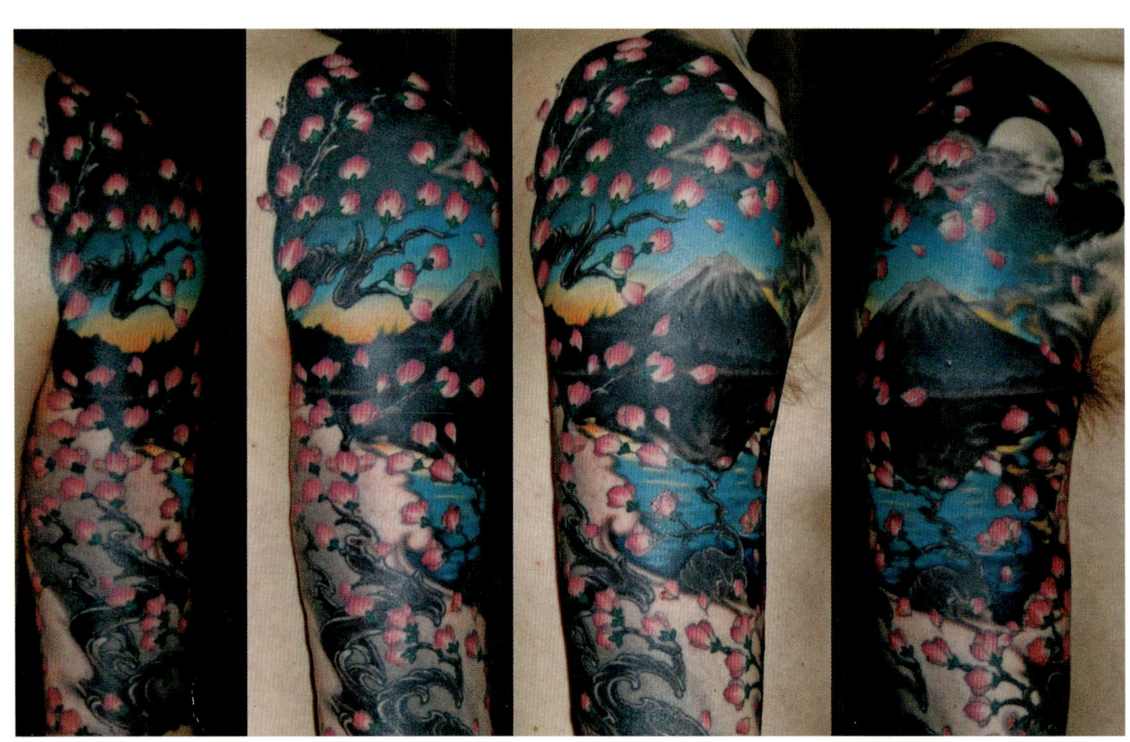

Carl Corson
Studio King Carlos Tattoo
www.kingcarlostattoo.com

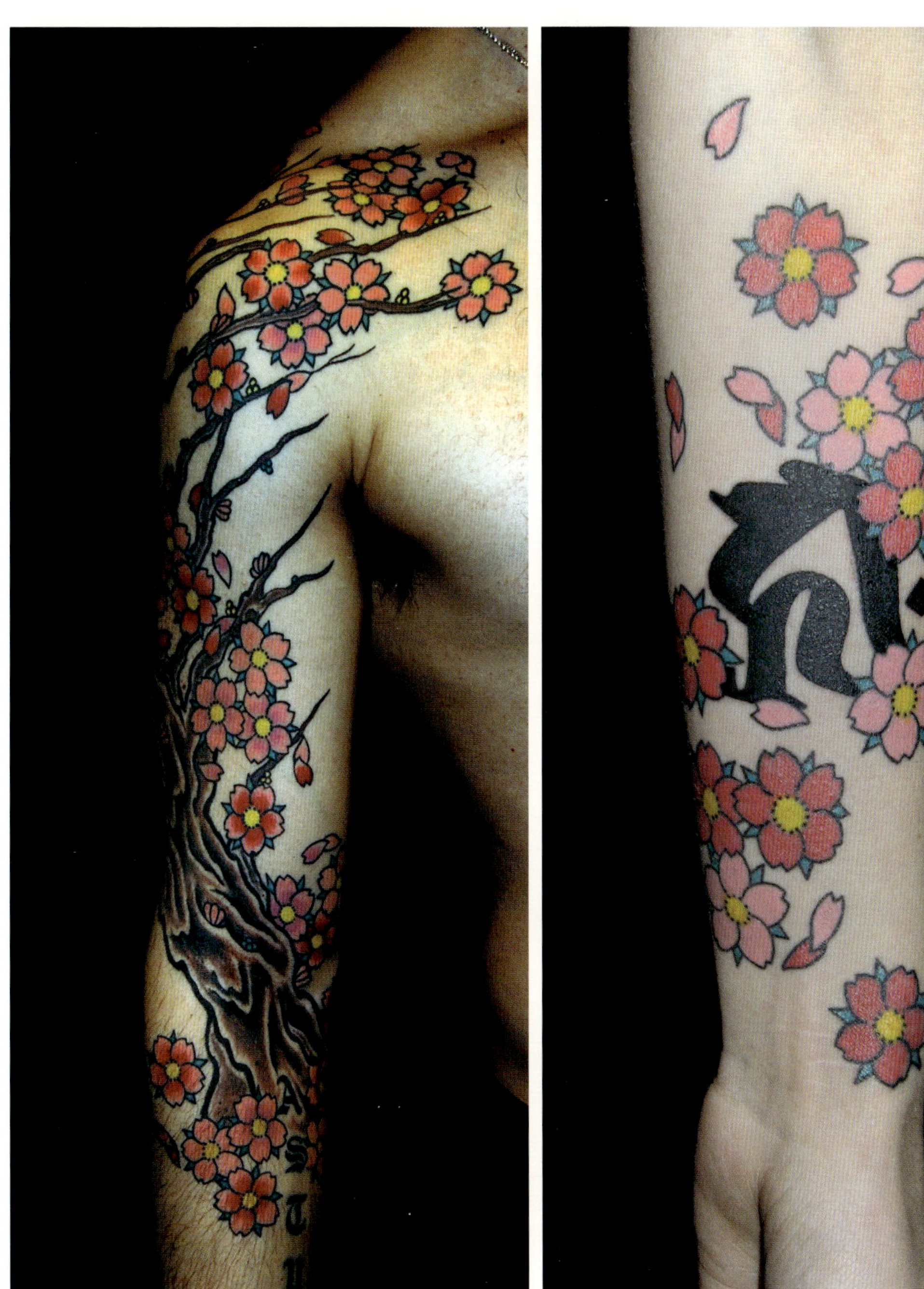

João Paulo Rodrigues
Acqua Santa Tattoo
www.jprodrigues.com

João Paulo Rodrigues
Acqua Santa Tattoo
www.jprodrigues.com

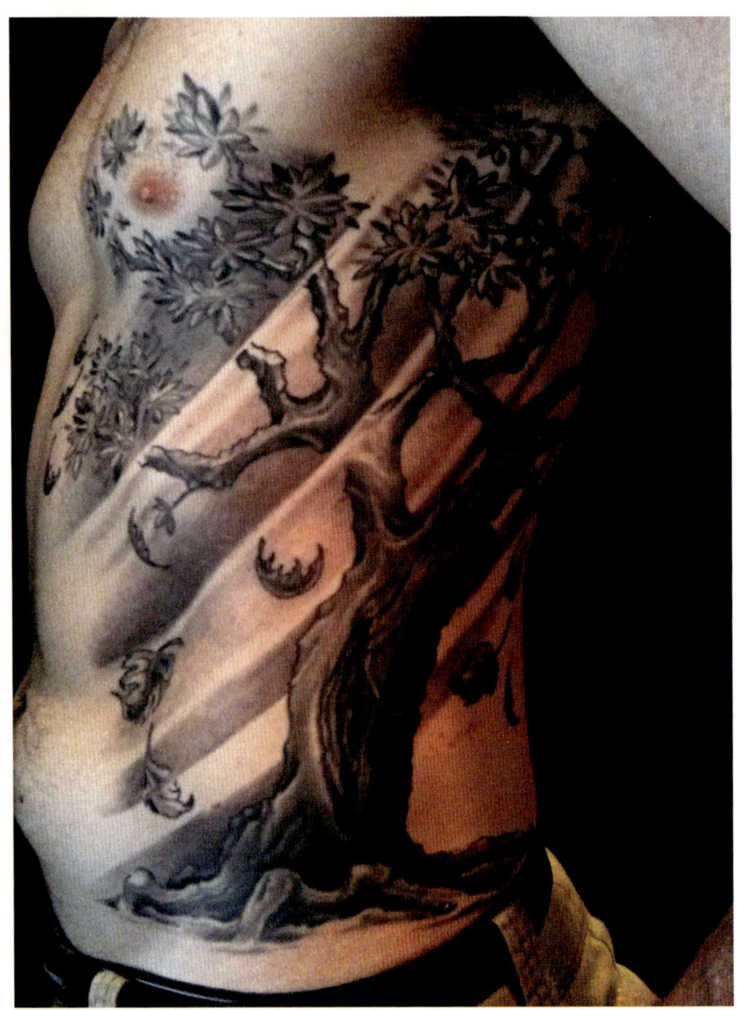

Bill Funk
Body Graphics
www.bodygraphics.com

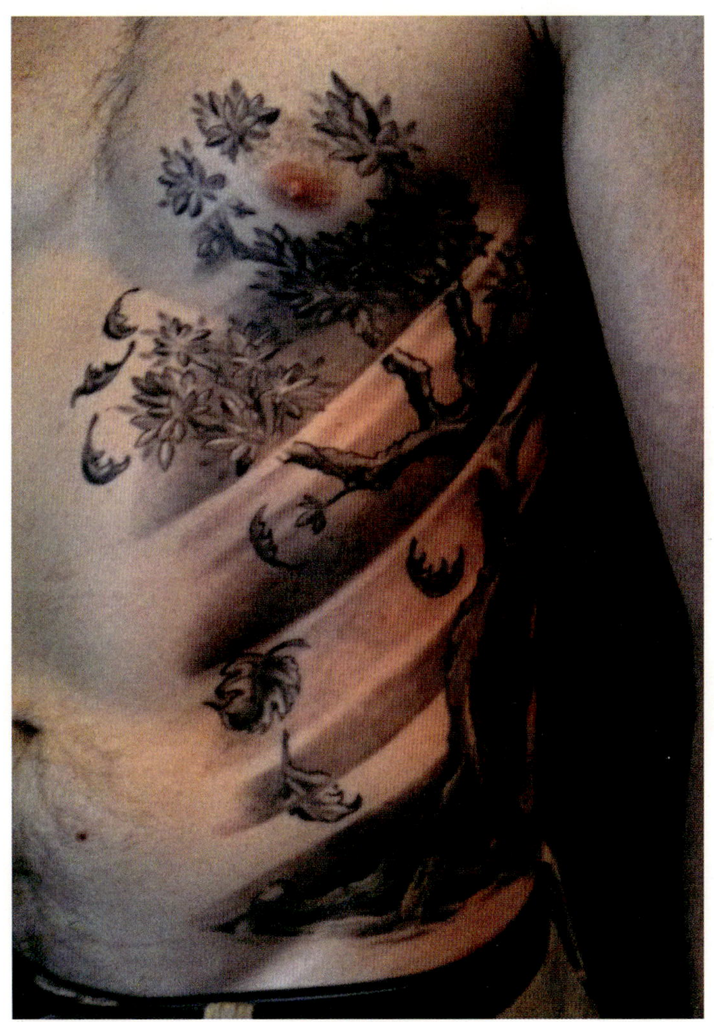

Bill Funk
Body Graphics
www.bodygraphics.com

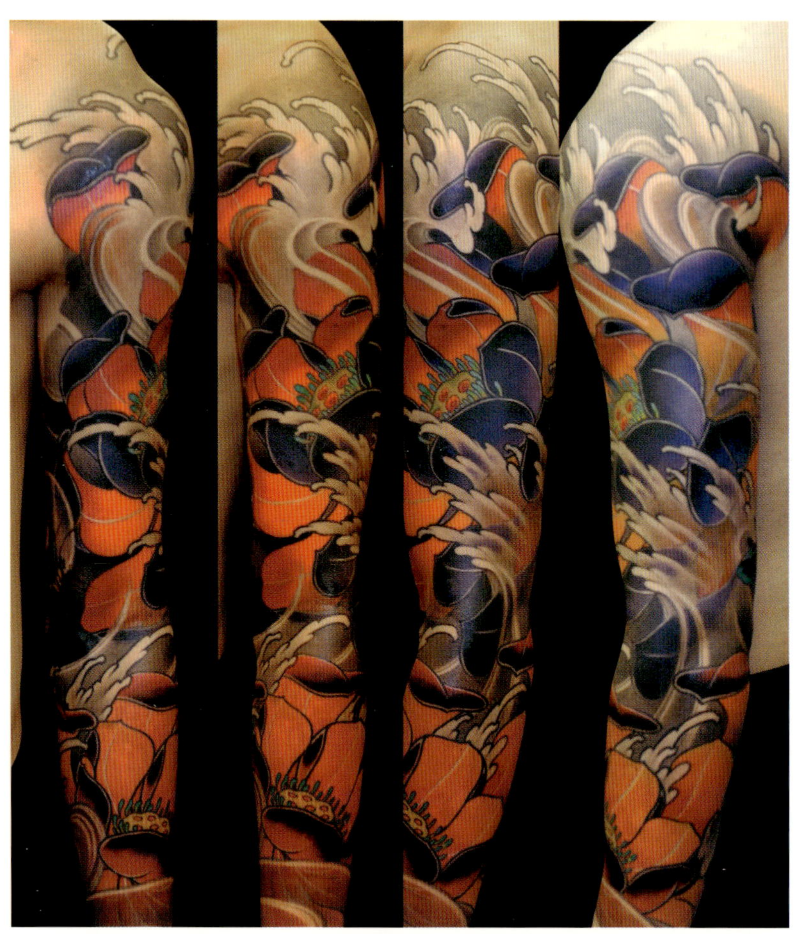

Carl Corson
Studio King Carlos Tattoo
www.kingcarlostattoo.com

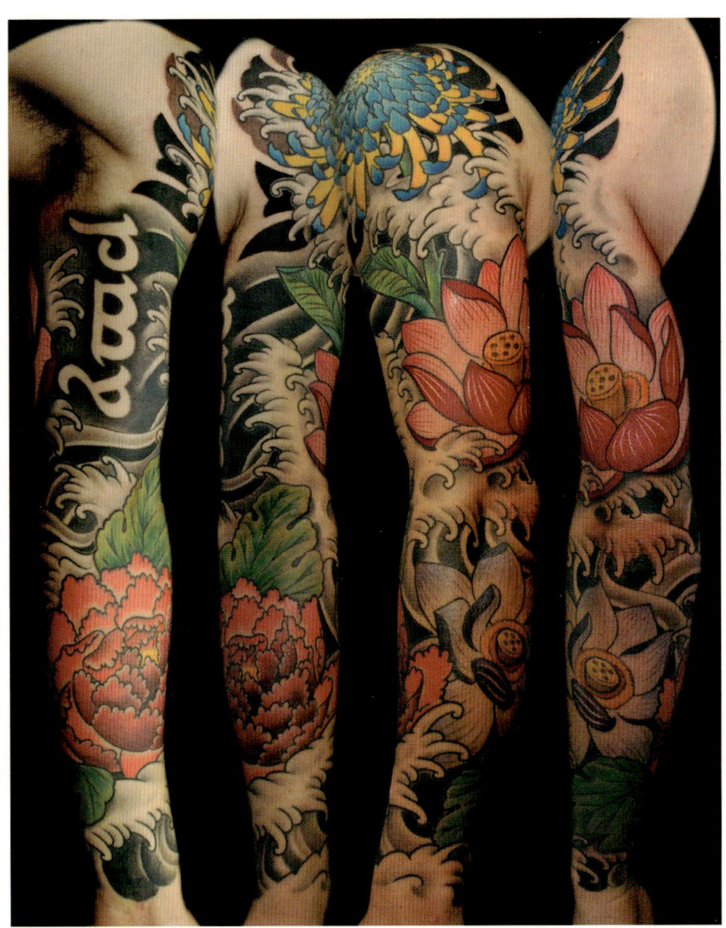

Joako
Human Fly Tattoo Studio
www.humanflytattoo.com

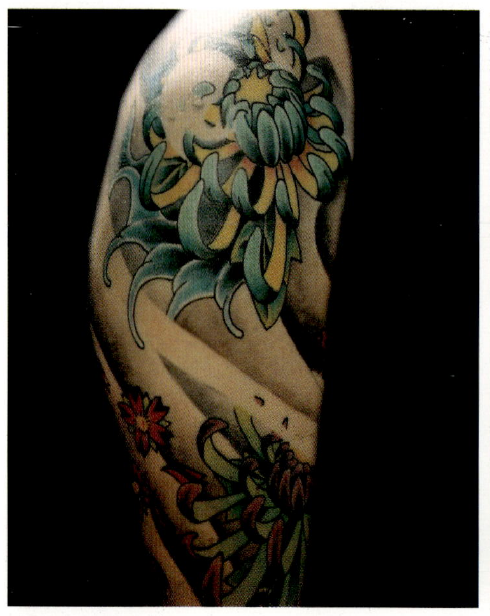

Matt Hugill
Tattoo UK – Twickenham branch
www.tattoouk.com

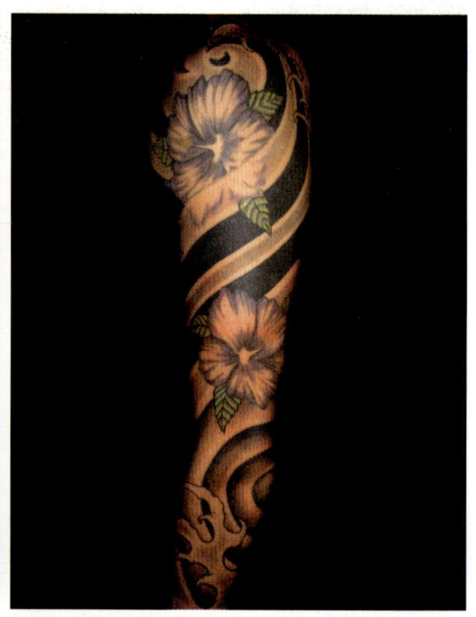

Falke
Pro-Arts Tattoo
www.pro-arts.com

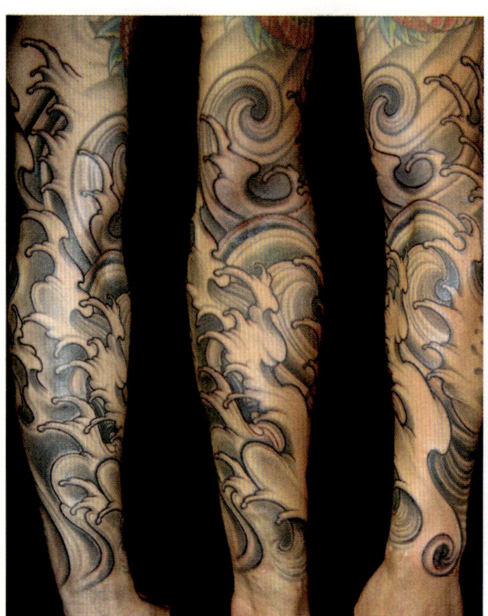

Gustavo Rizeiro
Studio invisible nyc
www.gustavorizeiro.com

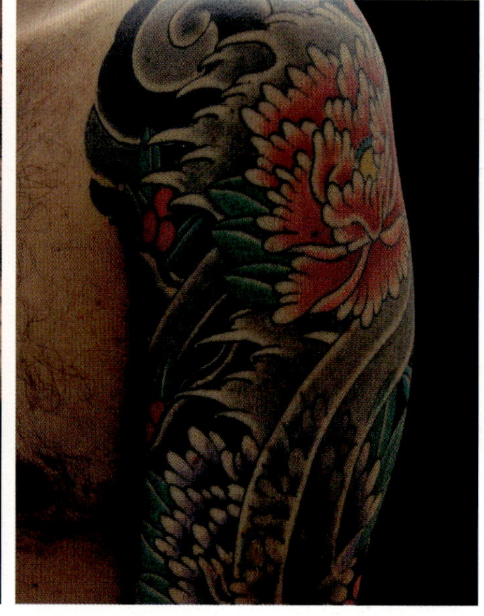

João Paulo Rodrigues
Acqua Santa Tattoo
www.jprodrigues.com

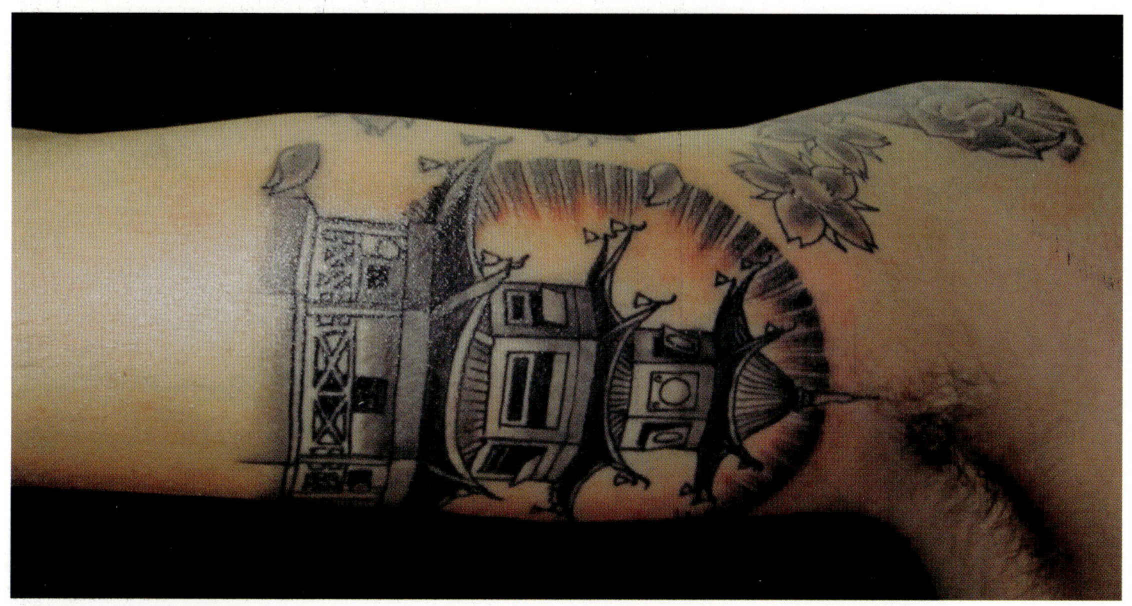

Vallekas Tattoo Zone
www.vallekastattoozone.es

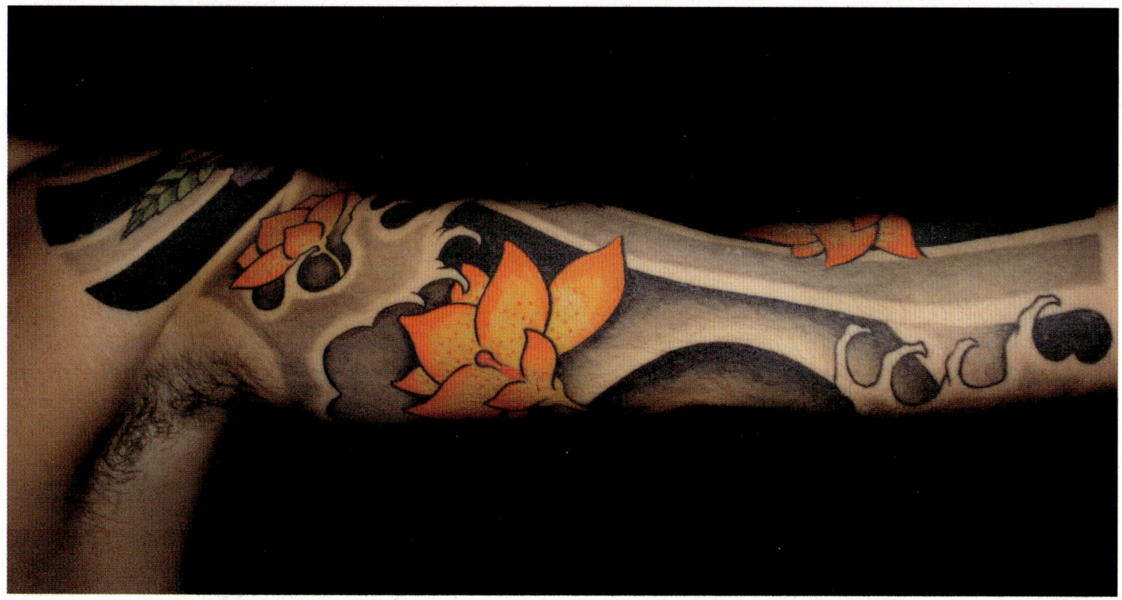

Falke
Pro-Arts Tattoo
www.pro-arts.com

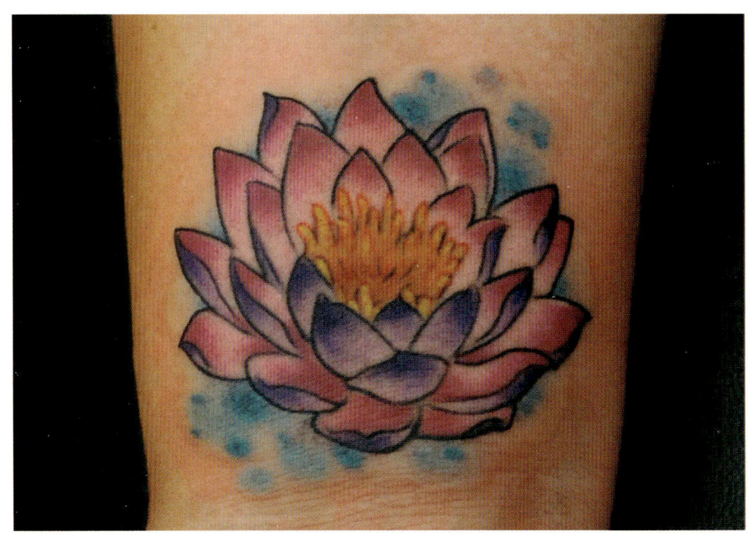

Joako
Human Fly Tattoo Studio
www.humanflytattoo.com

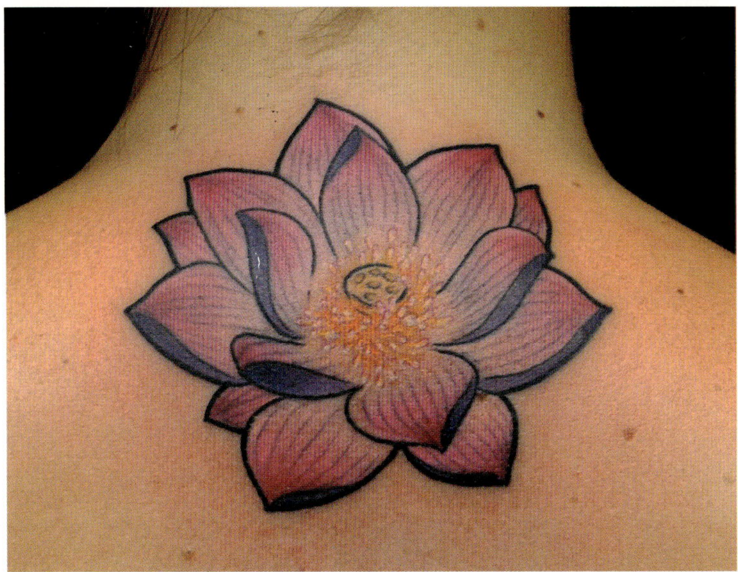

Joako
Human Fly Tattoo Studio
www.humanflytattoo.com

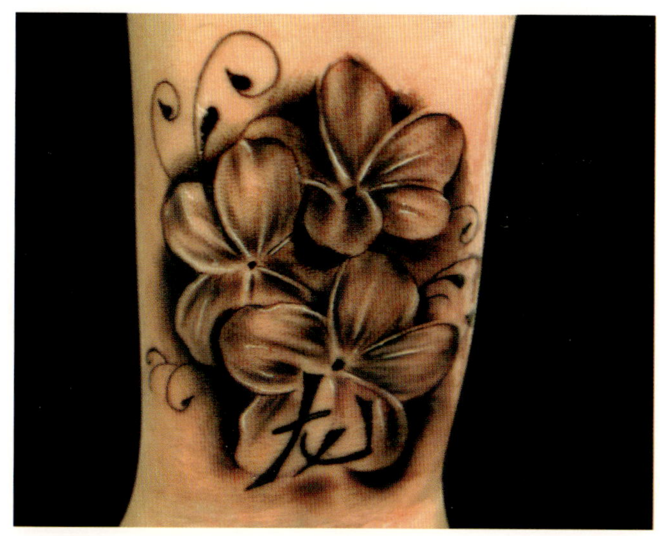

Dani Leiva
V Tattoo
www.vtattoo.es

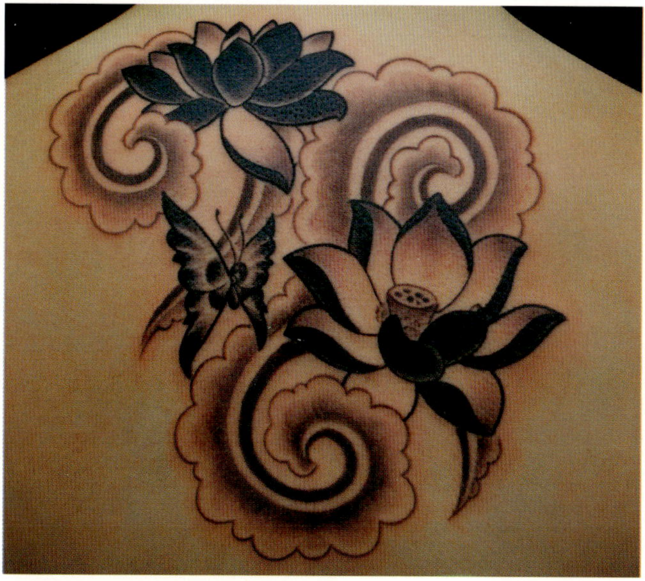

Joako
Human Fly Tattoo Studio
www.humanflytattoo.com

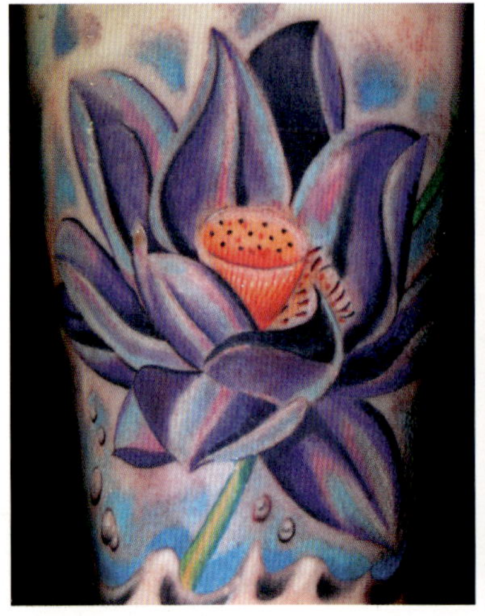

Alfonso Sánchez
Balinese Tattoo Studio
www.balinesetattoo.com

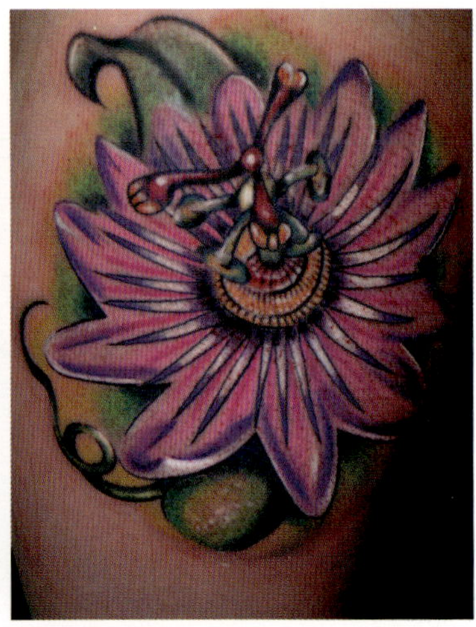

Alfonso Sánchez
Balinese Tattoo Studio
www.balinesetattoo.com

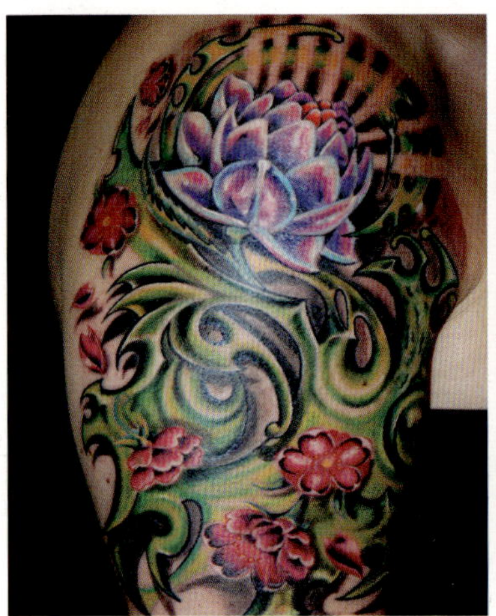

Alfonso Sánchez
Balinese Tattoo Studio
www.balinesetattoo.com

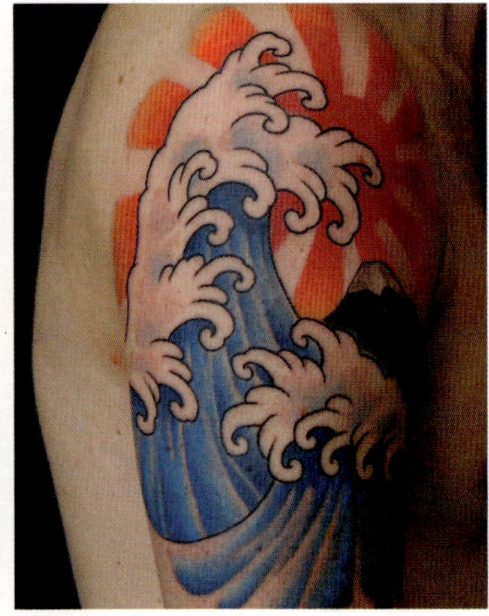

Joako
Human Fly Tattoo Studio
www.humanflytattoo.com

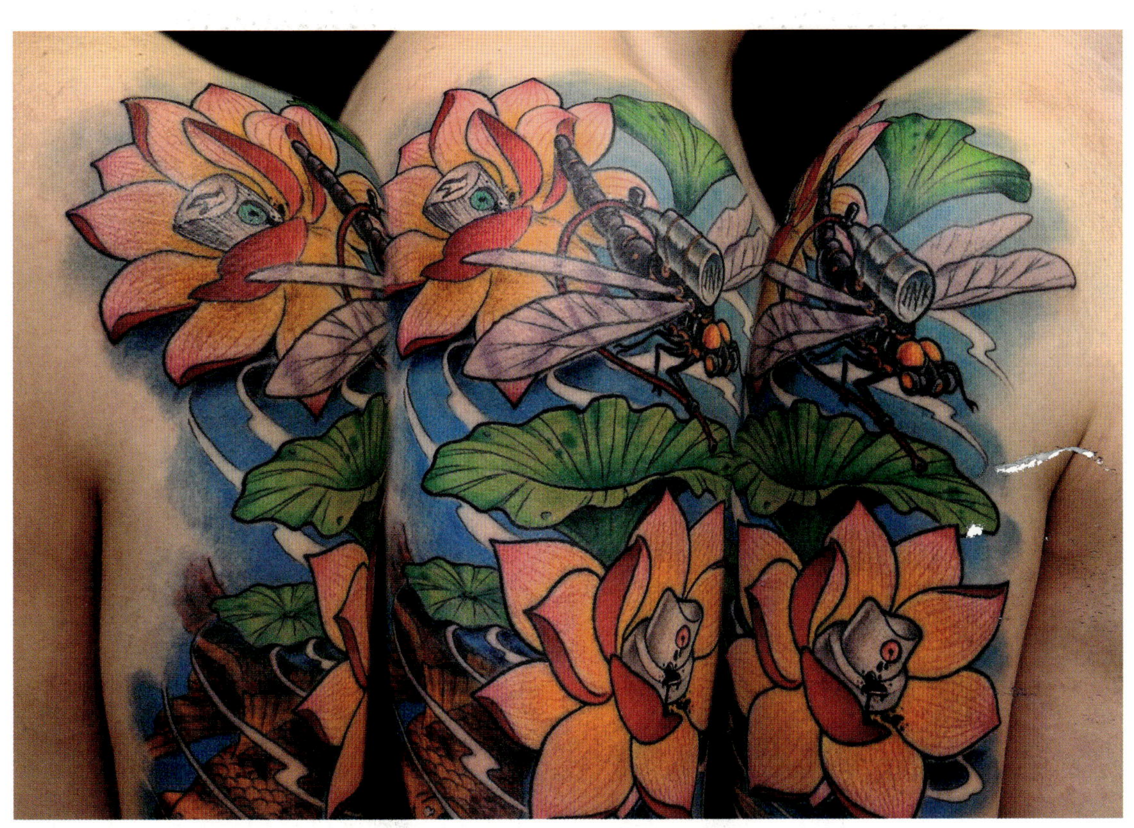

Joako
Human Fly Tattoo Studio
www.humanflytattoo.com

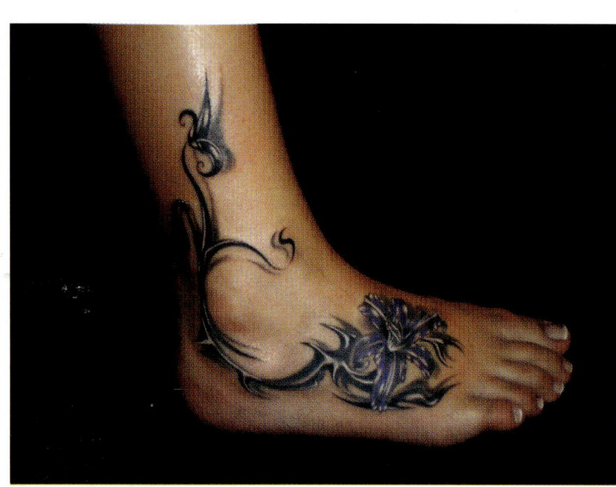

Tomás "Psycho" Dacej
Psycho Tattoo
www.facebook.com/tomas.dacej

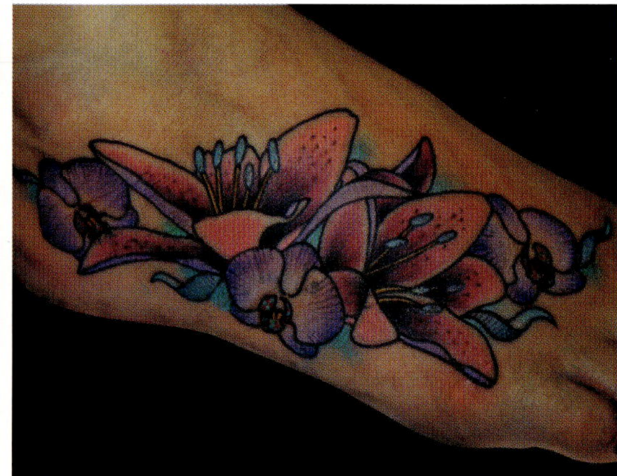

Aimée Lou
Bespoke Tattoo Company
www.facebook.com/aimeeloutattoo

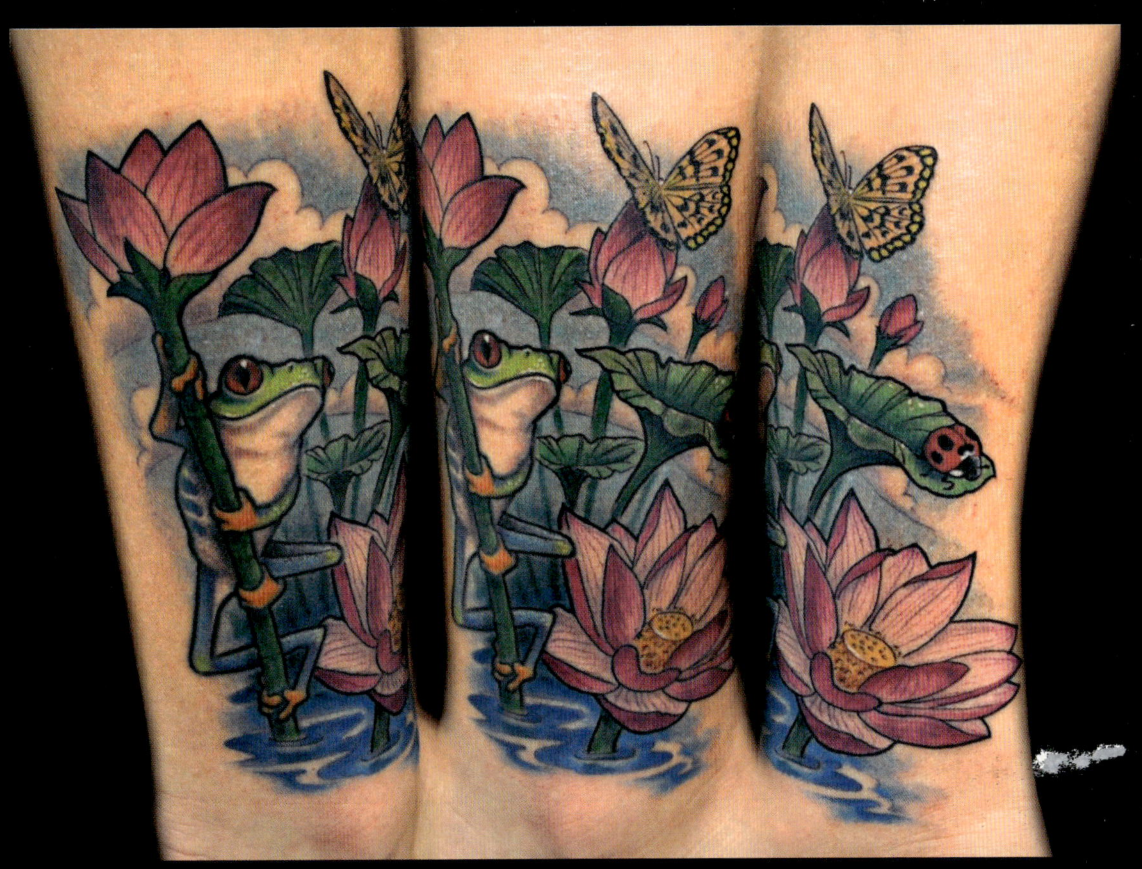

Joako
Human Fly Tattoo Studio
www.humanflytattoo.com

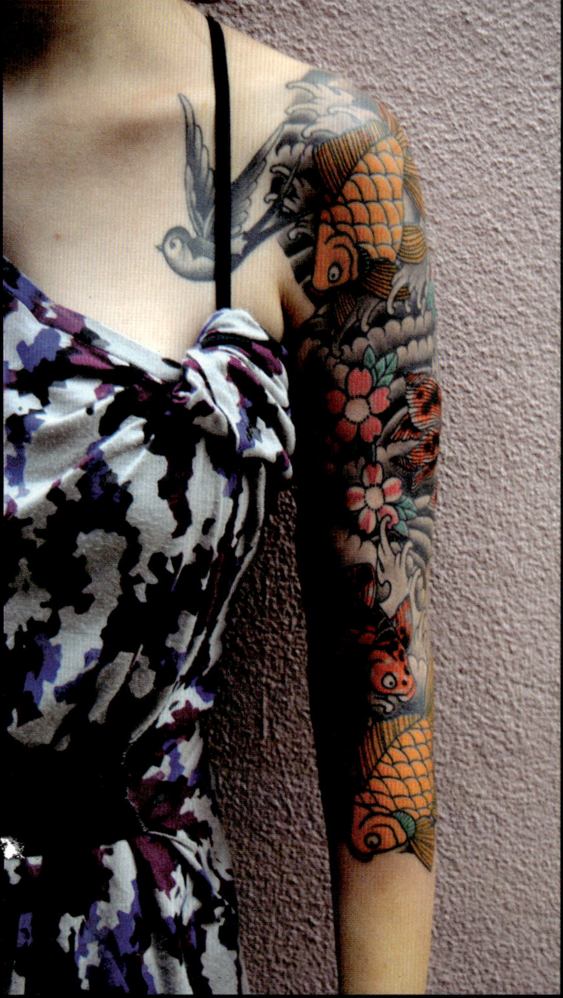

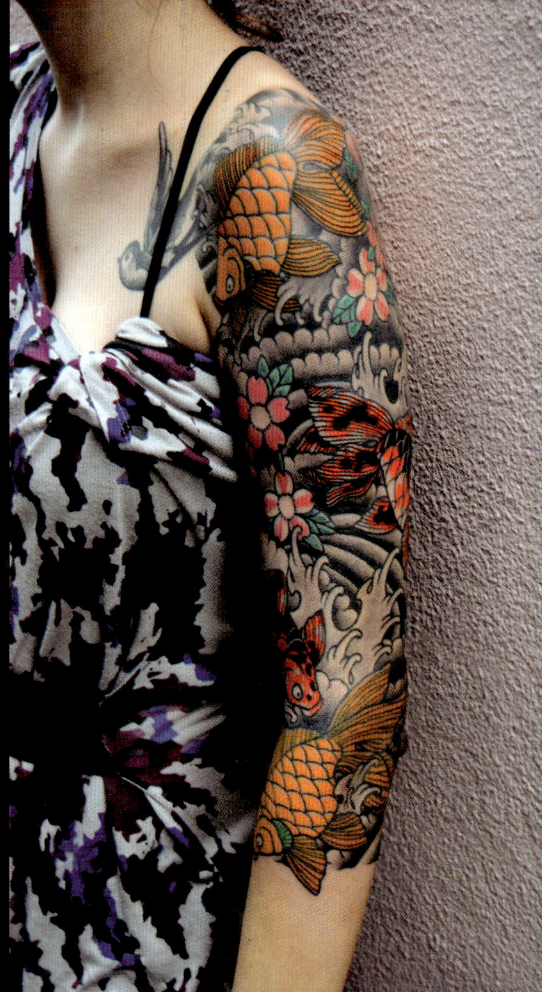

Pedro.soos
Ohana Tattoo Company
www.tattoosbypedro.org

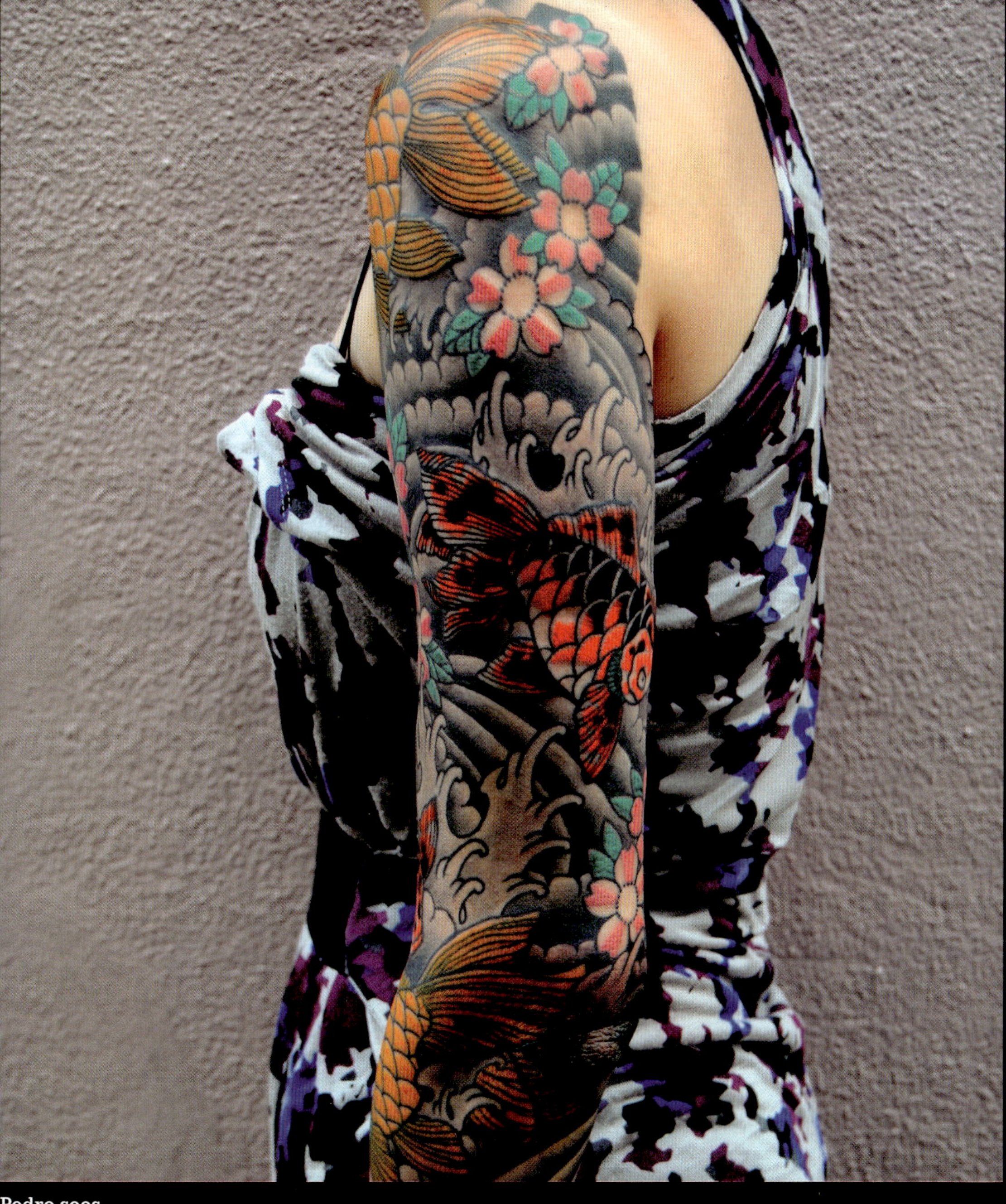

Pedro.soos

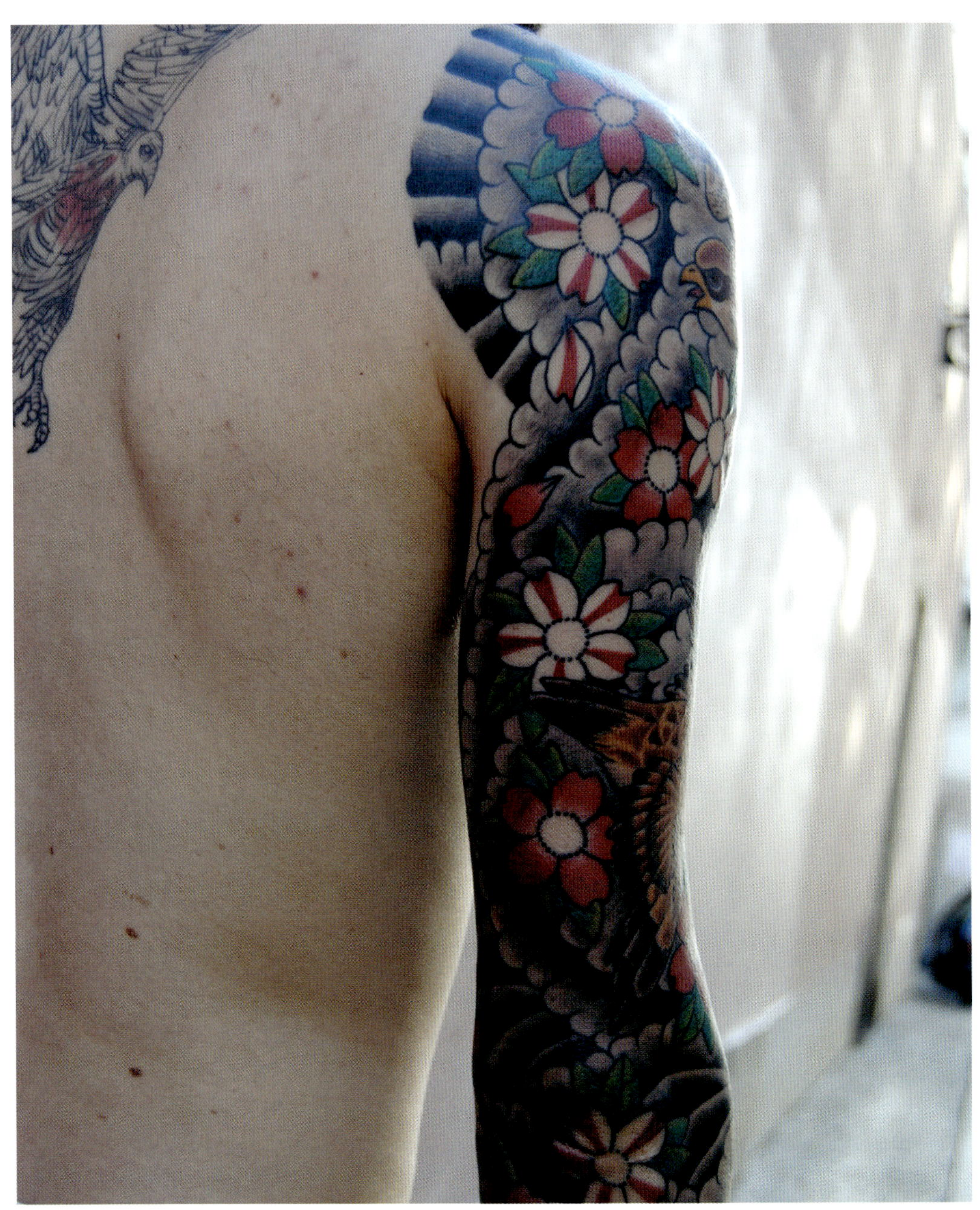

Pedro.soos
Ohana Tattoo Company
www.tattoosbypedro.org

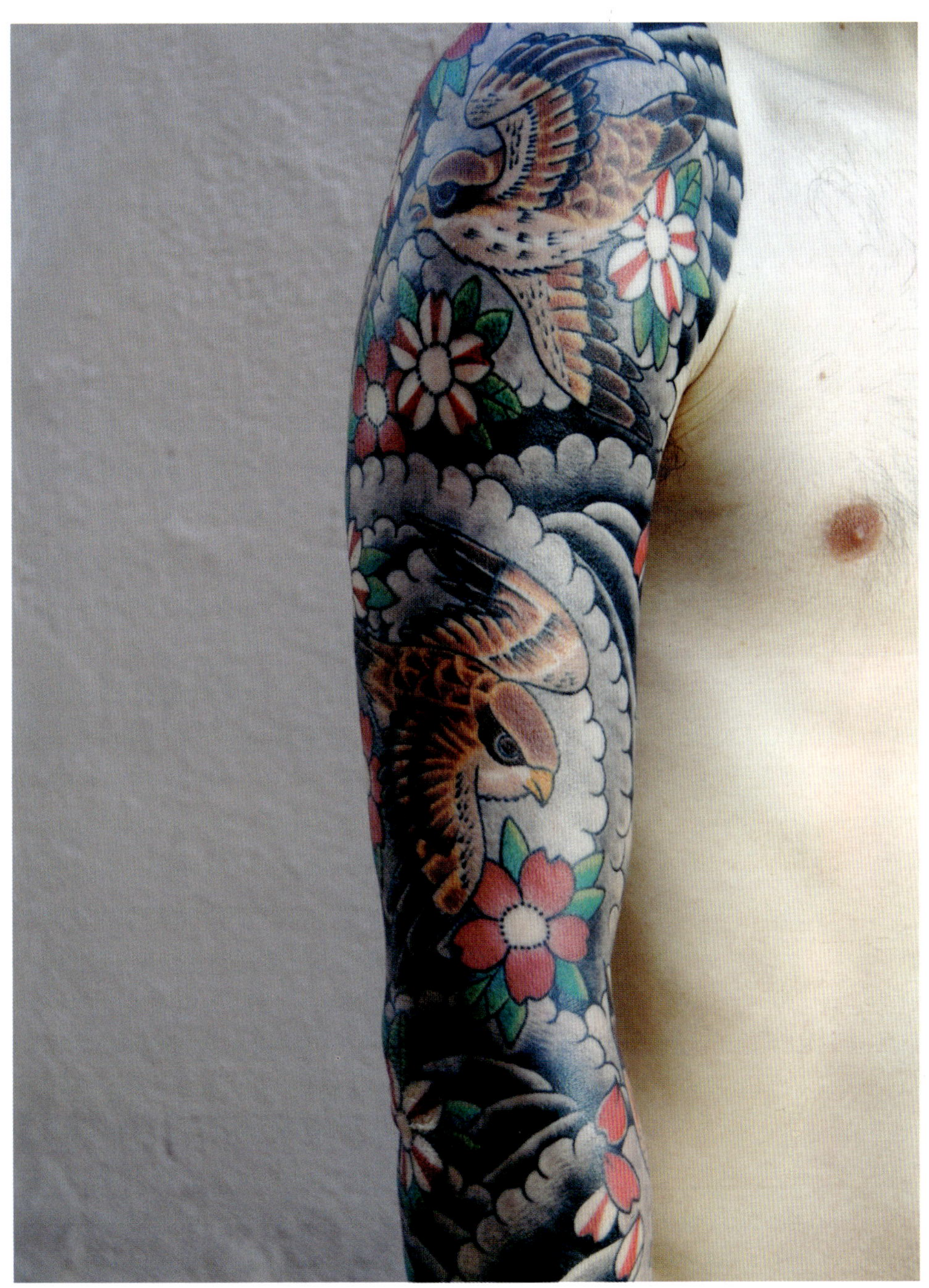

Pedro.soos
Ohana Tattoo Company
www.tattoosbypedro.org

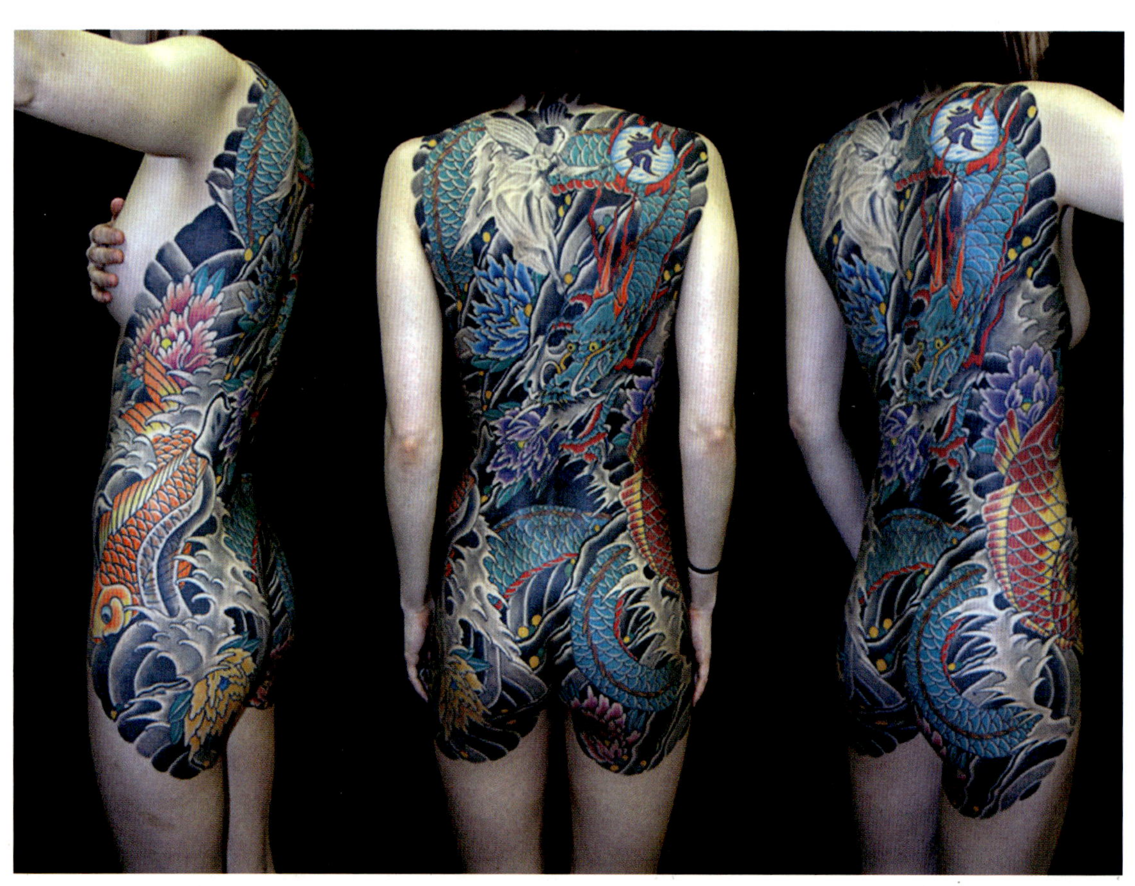

João Paulo Rodrigues
Acqua Santa Tattoo
www.jprodrigues.com

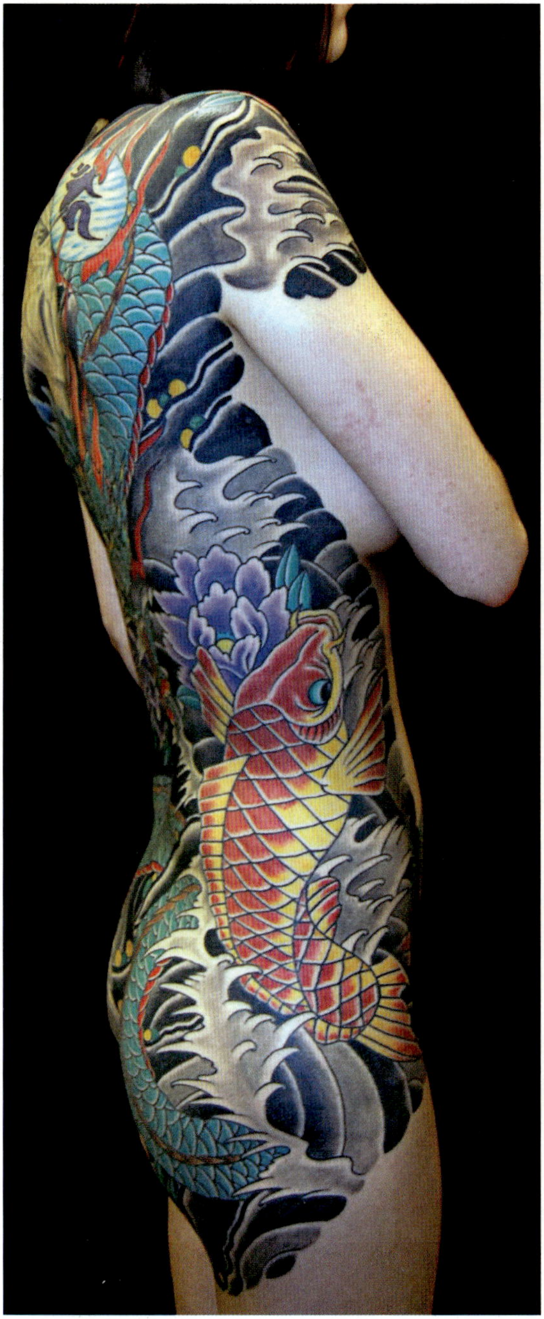

João Paulo Rodrigues
Acqua Santa Tattoo
www.jprodrigues.com

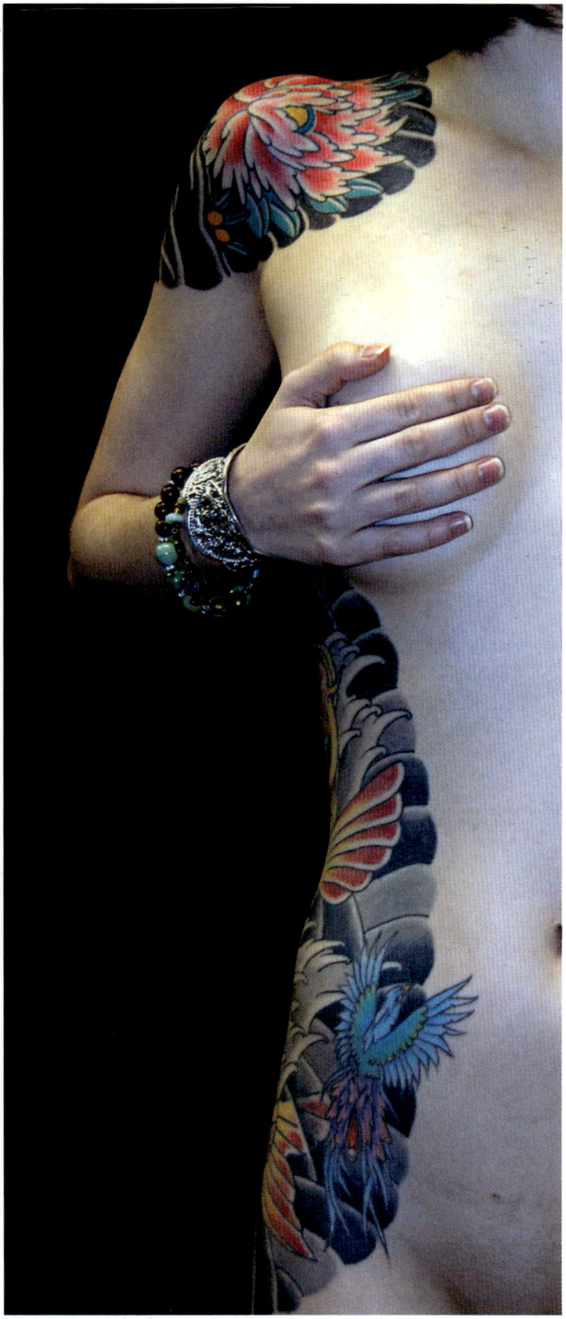

João Paulo Rodrigues
Acqua Santa Tattoo
www.jprodrigues.com

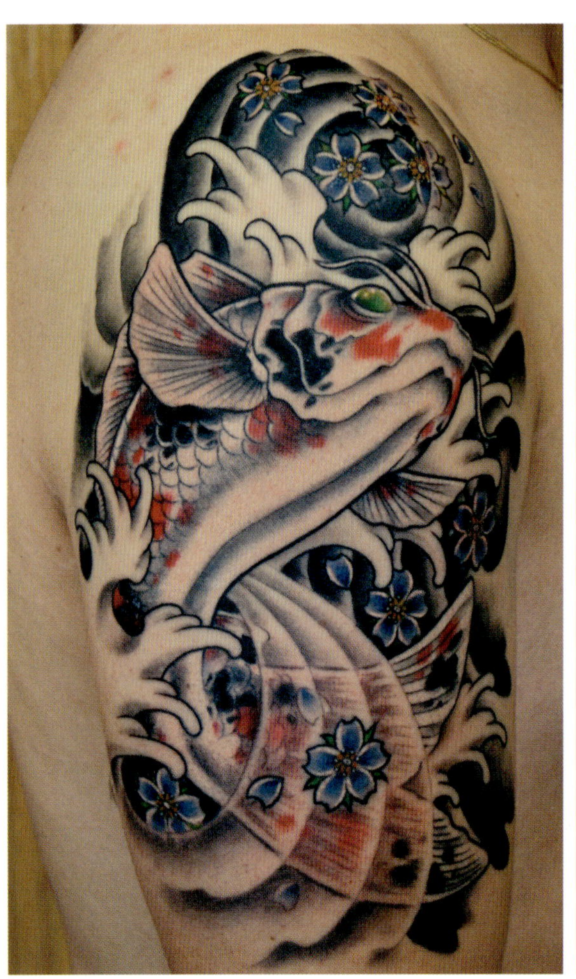

Joako
Human Fly Tattoo Studio
www.humanflytattoo.com

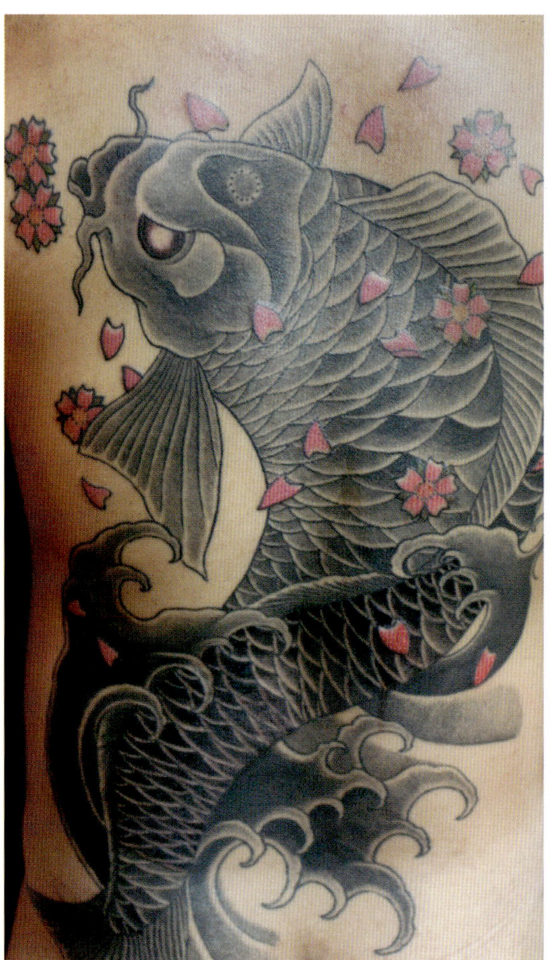

Horijin
Tatau Confort
tataucomfort@io.ocn.ne.jp

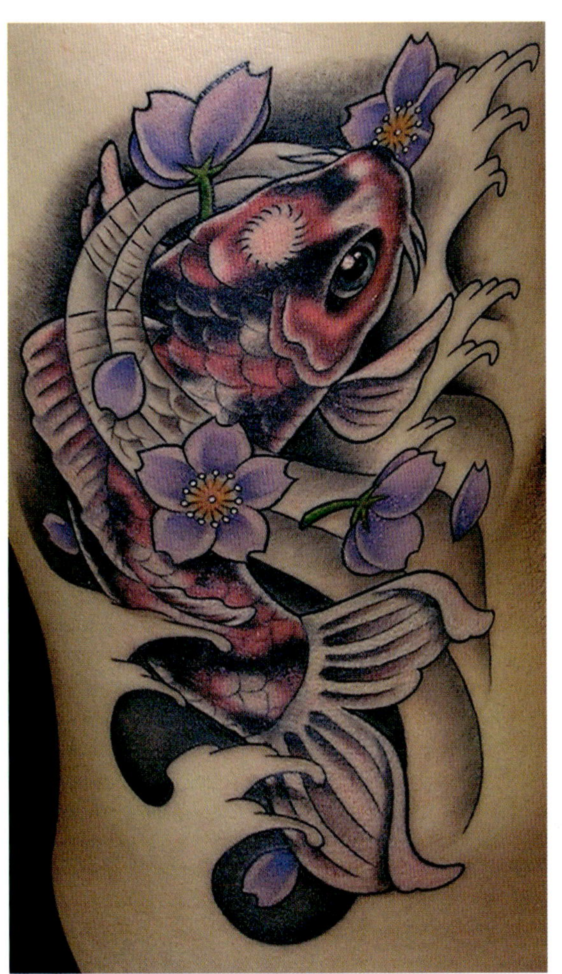

Joako
Human Fly Tattoo Studio
www.humanflytattoo.com

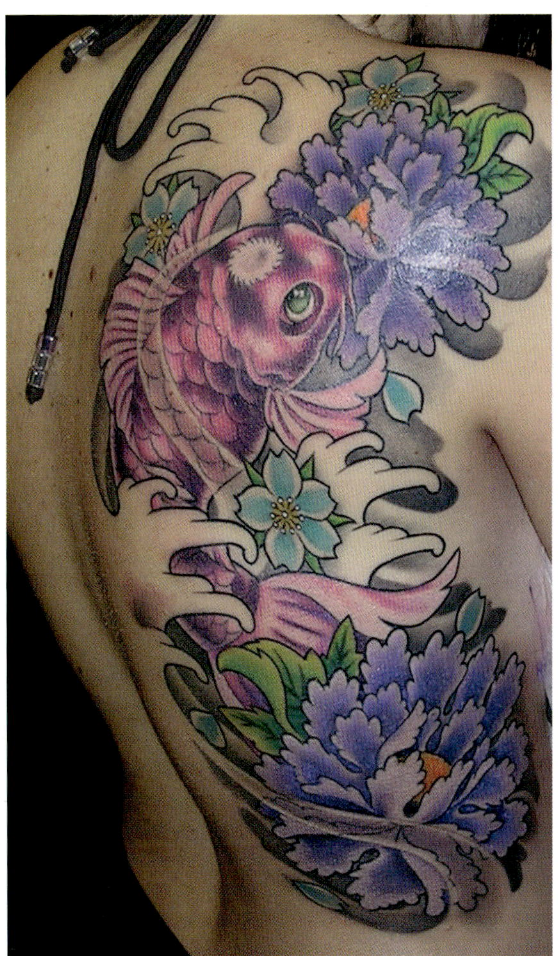

Joako
Human Fly Tattoo Studio
www.humanflytattoo.com

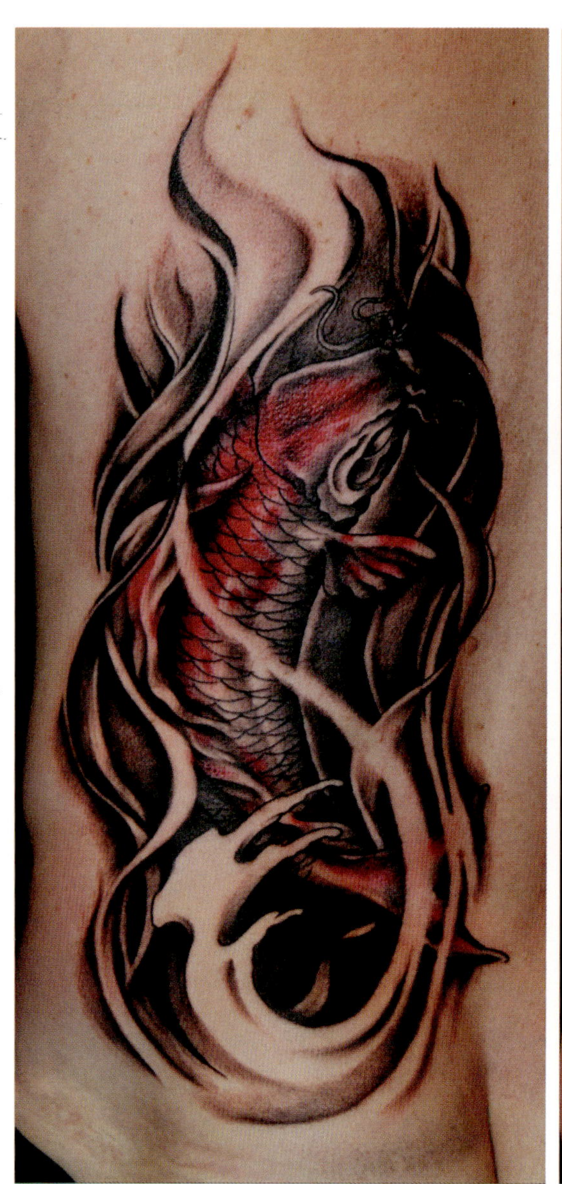

Jordi Pinzell
Brush Planet Tattoo
www.facebook/jordi.pinzell

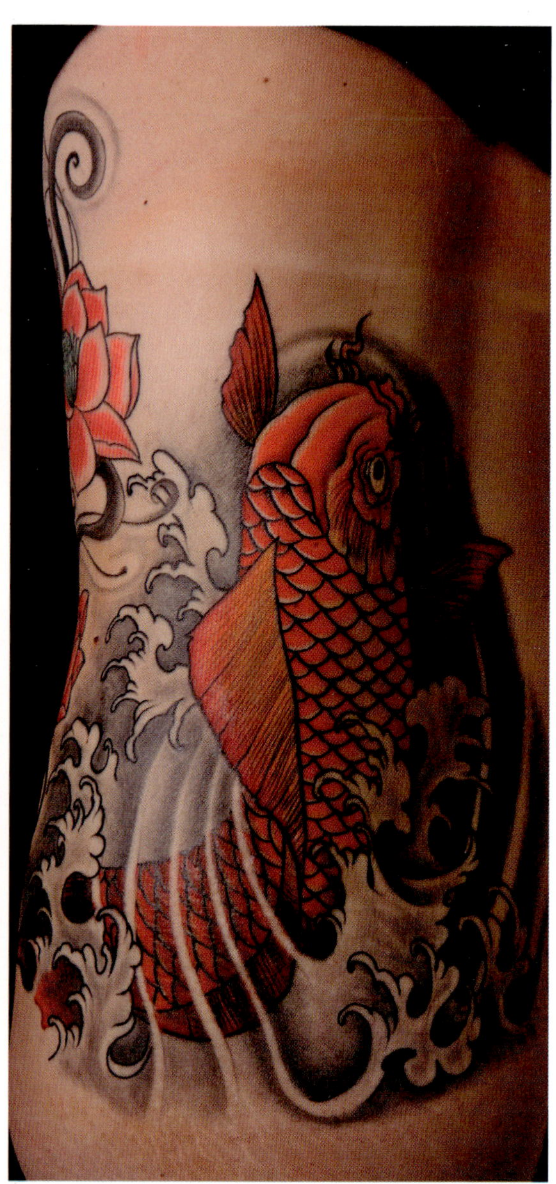

Javier Acero
Tattoo & Co. Miami
www.tattooandco.com

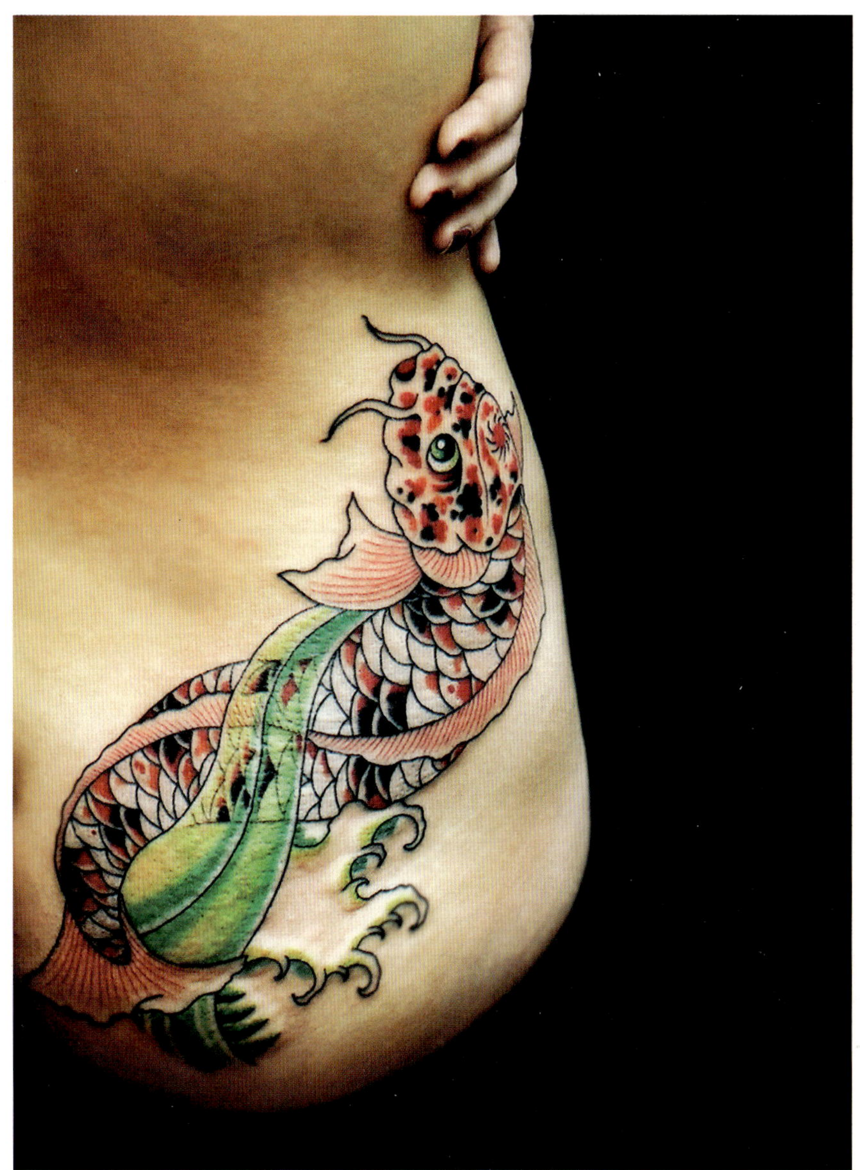

Horijin
Tatau Confort
tataucomfort@io.ocn.ne.jp

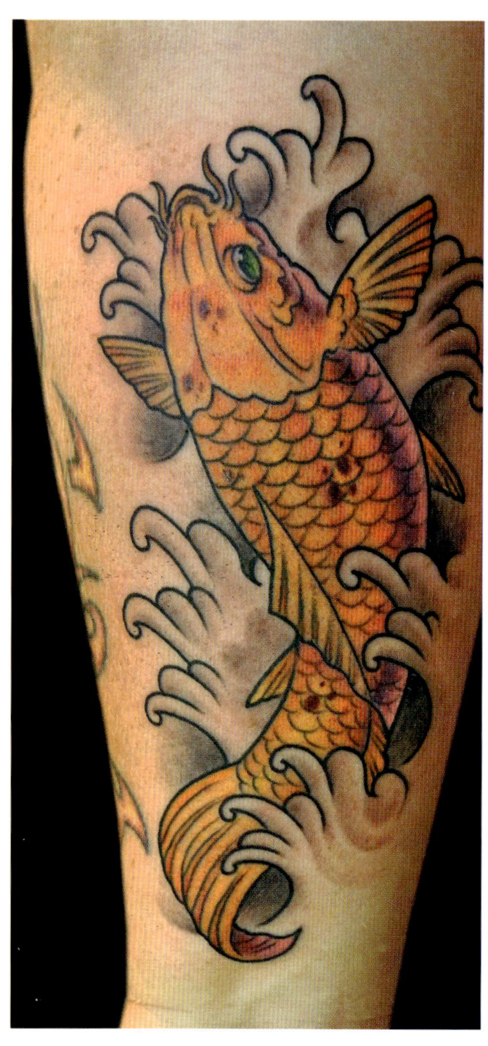

Joako
Human Fly Tattoo Studio
www.humanflytattoo.com

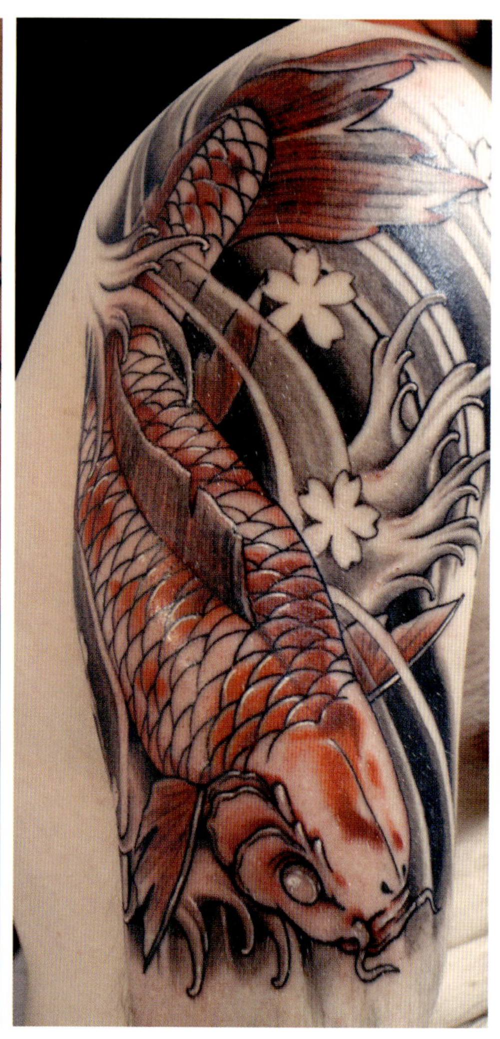

Satoshi Ohata
T3-Tattoos
www.t3-tattoos.com

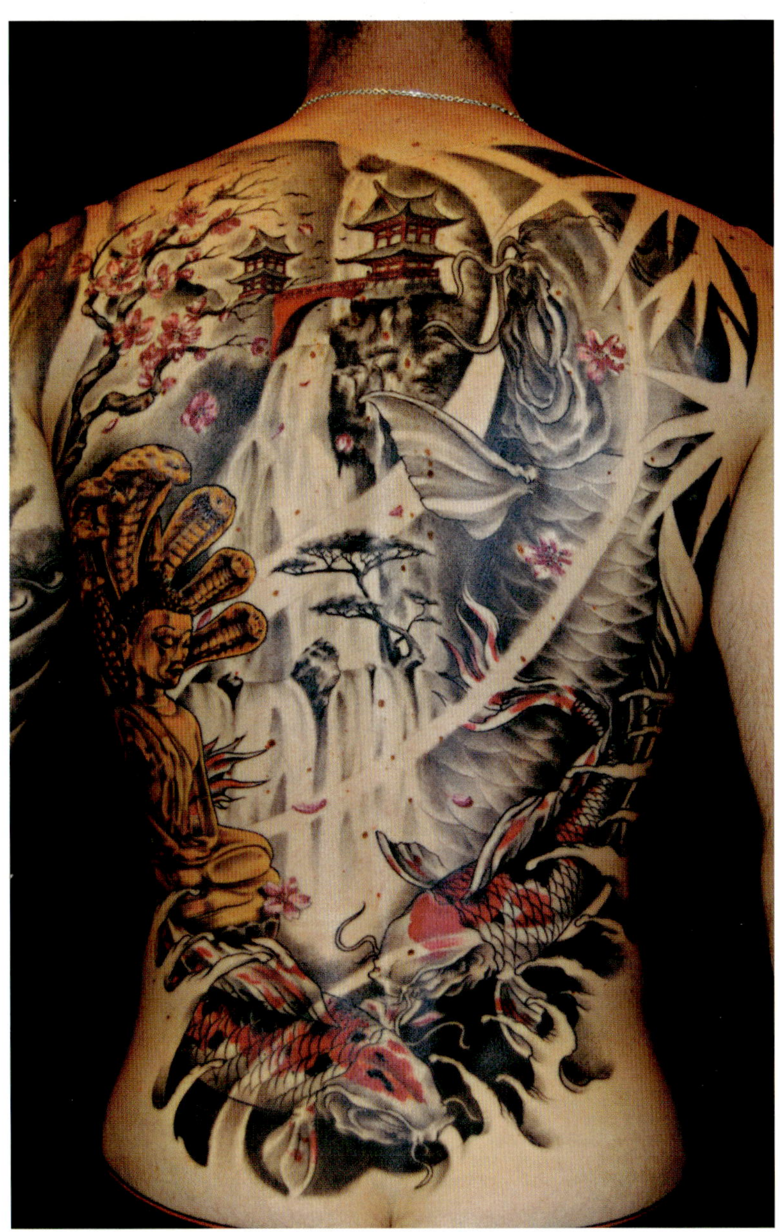

Jordi Pinzell
Brush Planet Tattoo
www.facebook/jordi.pinzell

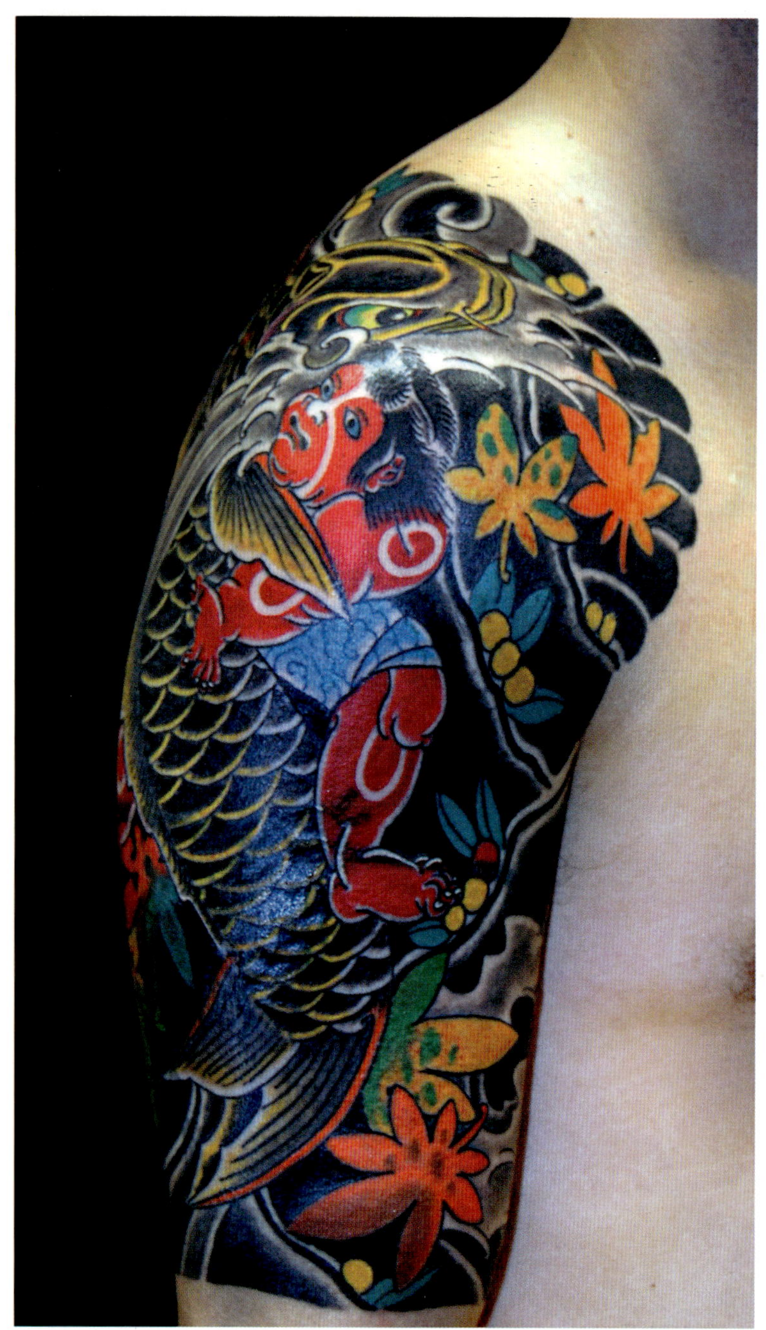

João Paulo Rodrigues
Acqua Santa Tattoo
www.jprodrigues.com

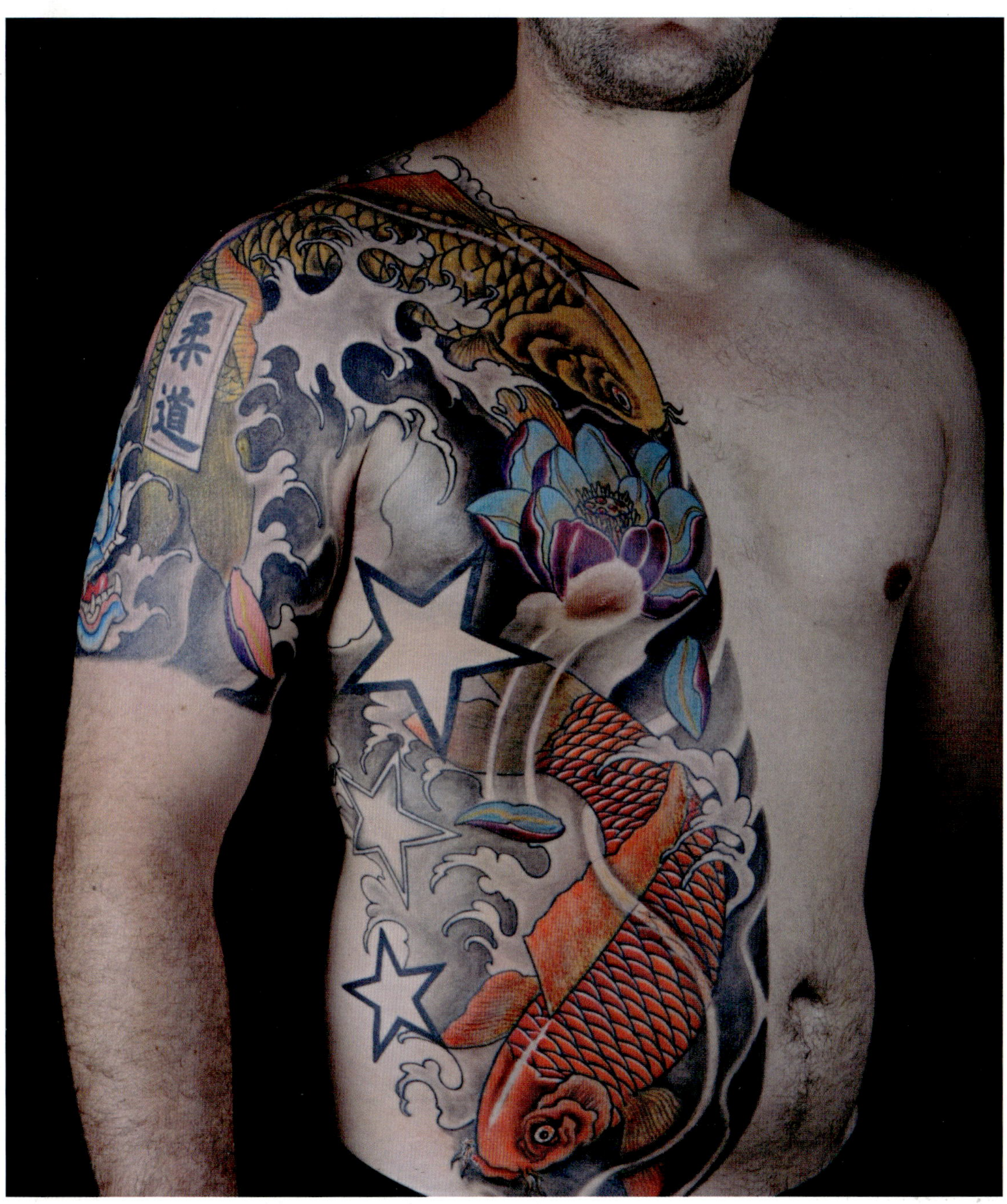

Javier Acero
Tattoo & Co. Miami
www.tattooandco.com

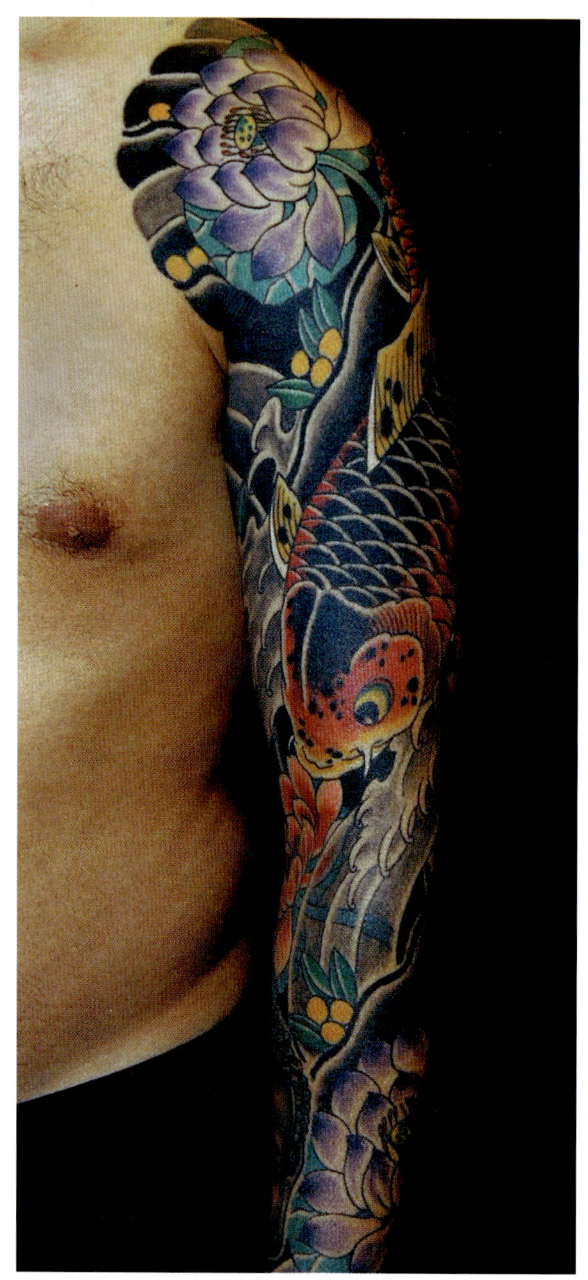

João Paulo Rodrigues
Acqua Santa Tattoo
www.jprodrigues.com

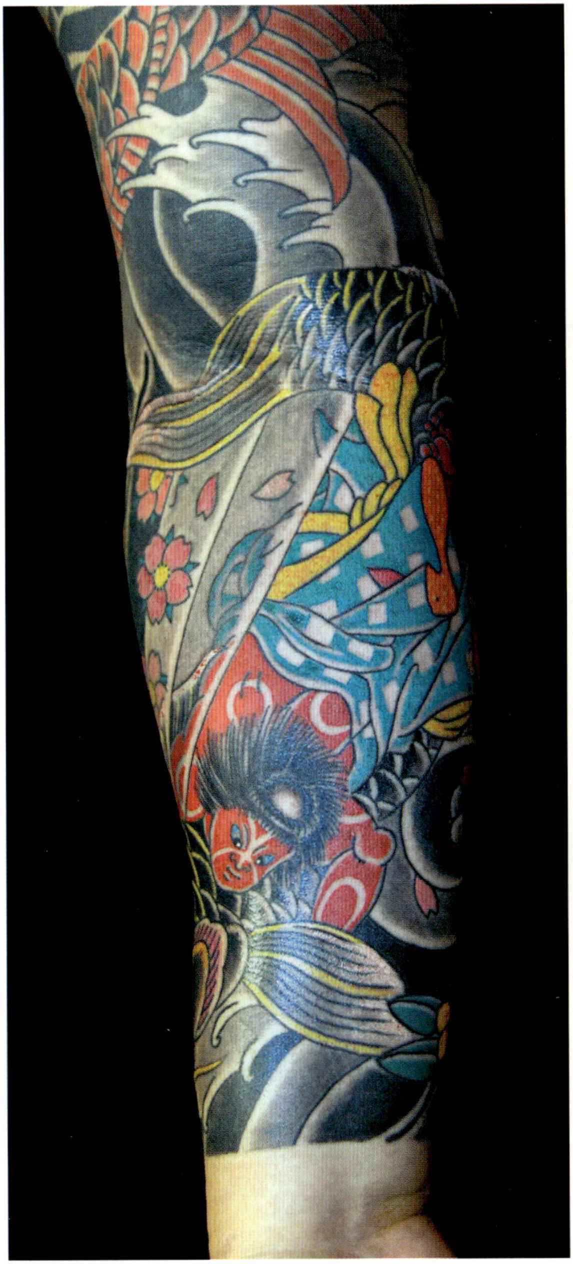

João Paulo Rodrigues
Acqua Santa Tattoo
www.jprodrigues.com

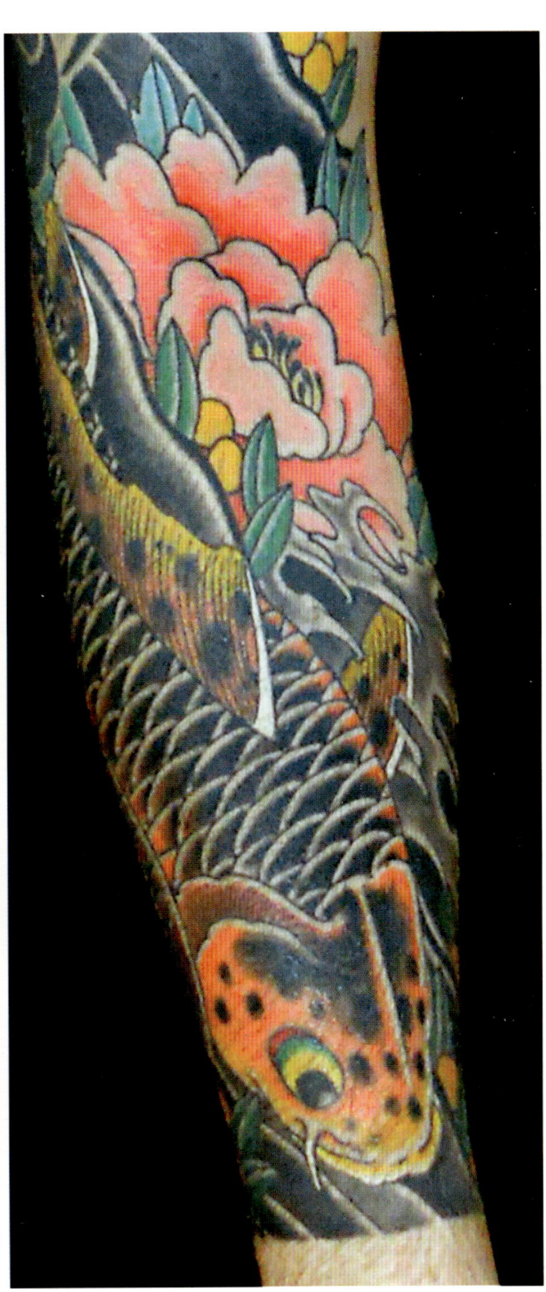

João Paulo Rodrigues
Acqua Santa Tattoo
www.jprodrigues.com

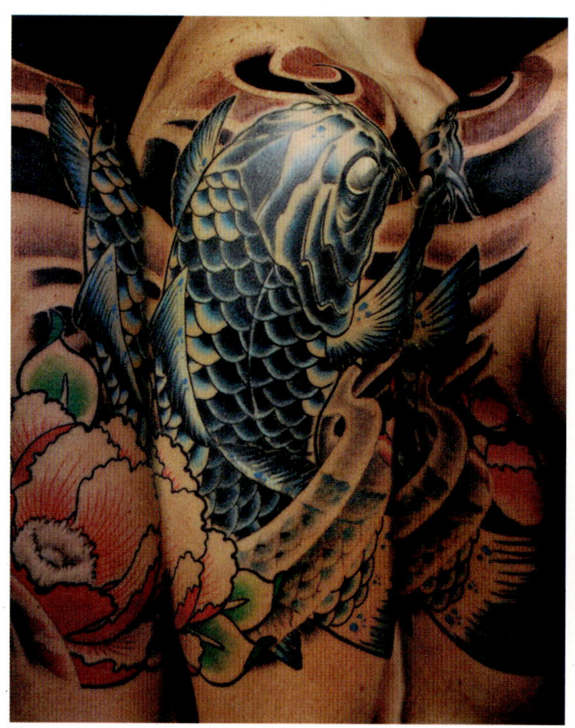

Joako
Human Fly Tattoo Studio
www.humanflytattoo.com

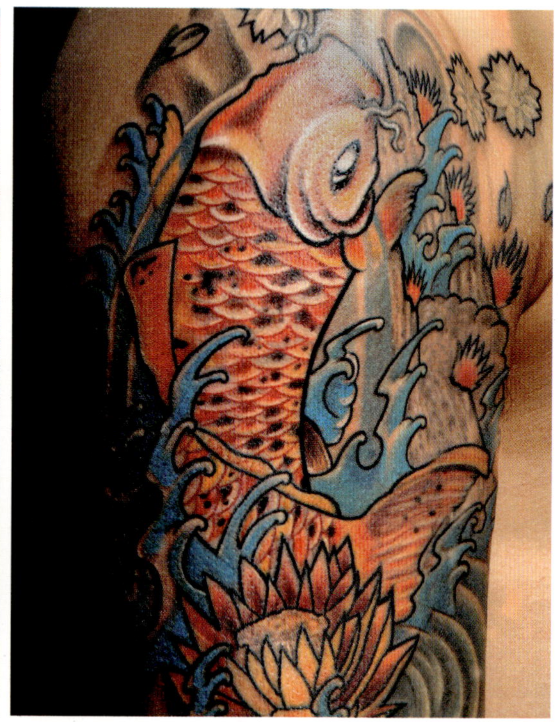

Alfonso Sánchez
Balinese Tattoo Studio
www.balinesetattoo.com

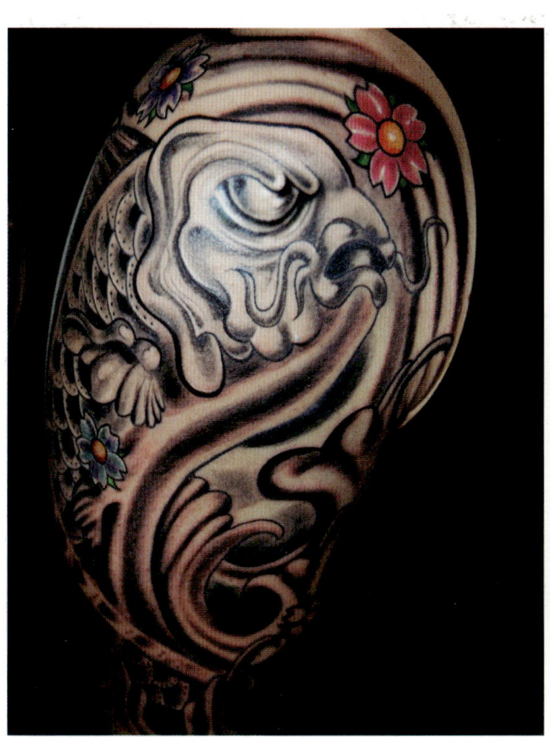

Alfonso Sánchez
Balinese Tattoo Studio
www.balinesetattoo.com

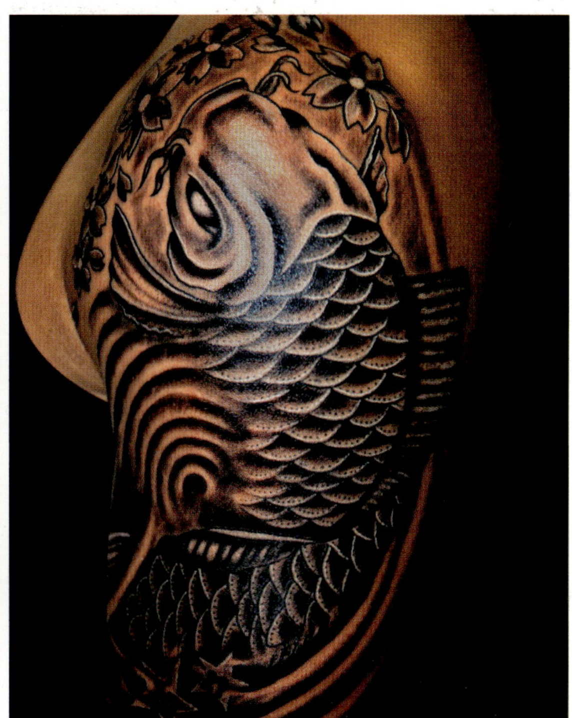

Alfonso Sánchez
Balinese Tattoo Studio
www.balinesetattoo.com

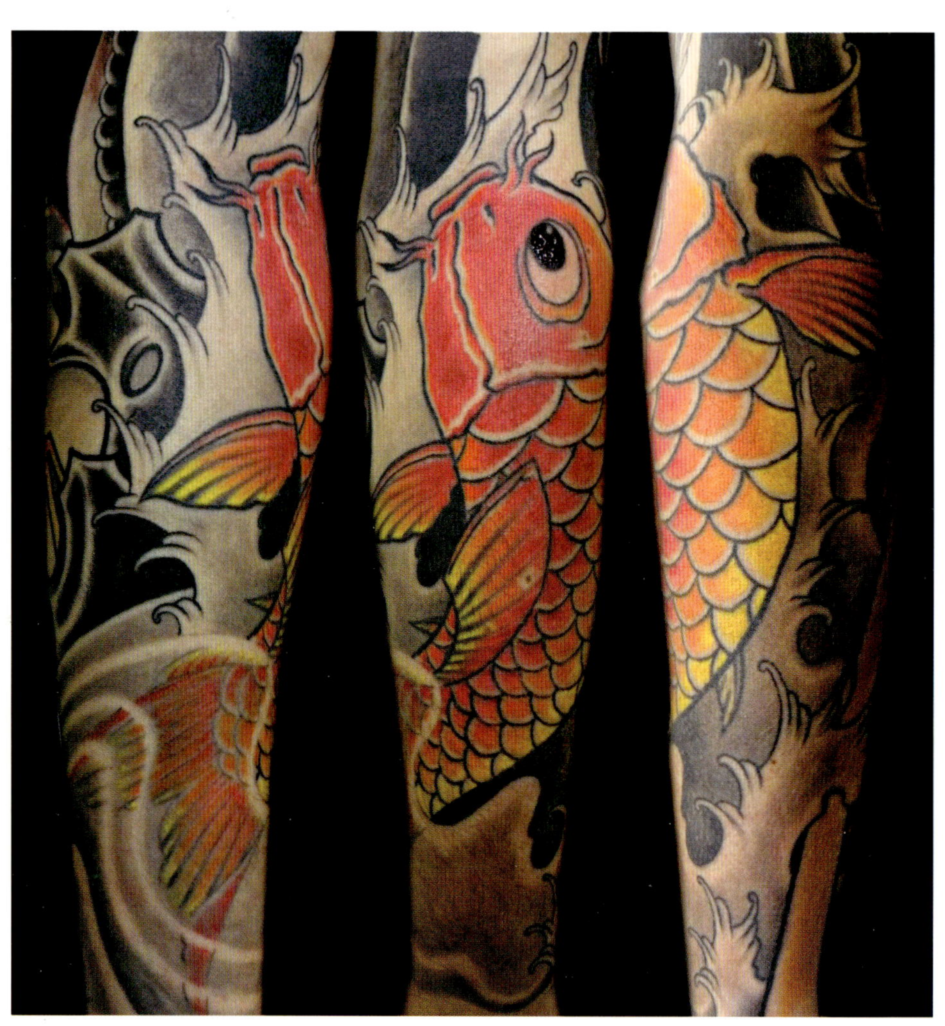

Vallekas Tattoo Zone

www.vallekastattoozone.es

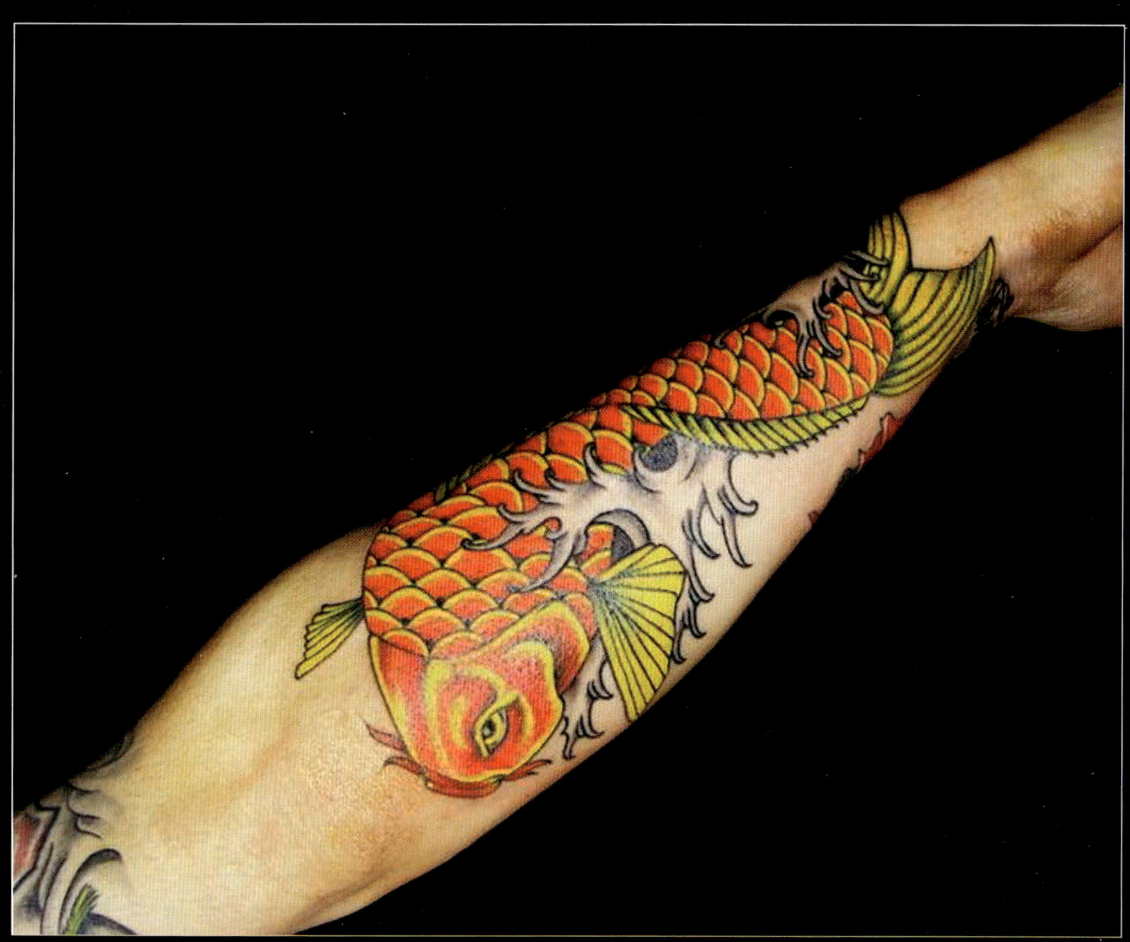

Vallekas Tattoo Zone
www.vallekastattoozone.es

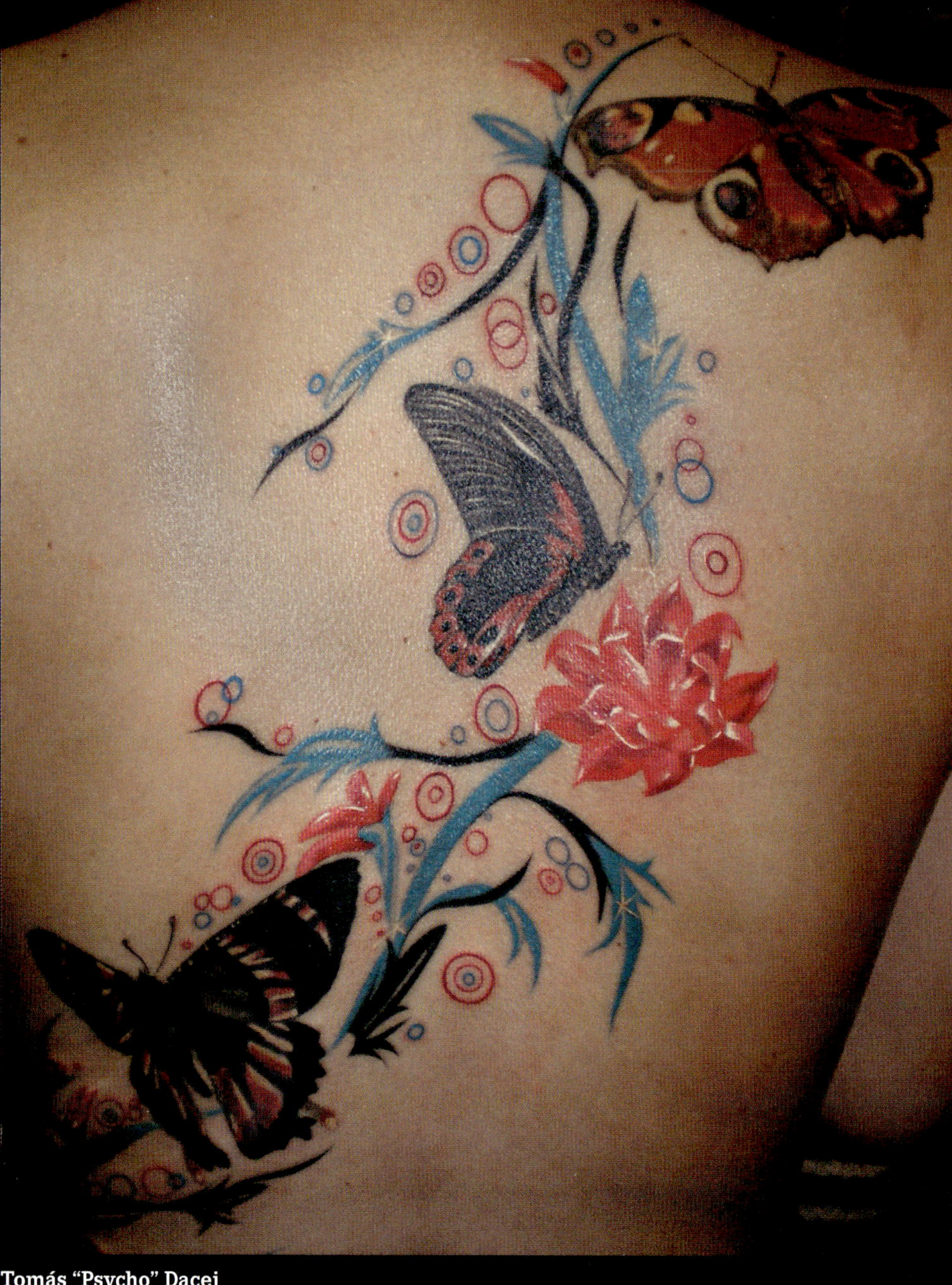

Tomás "Psycho" Dacej
Psycho Tattoo

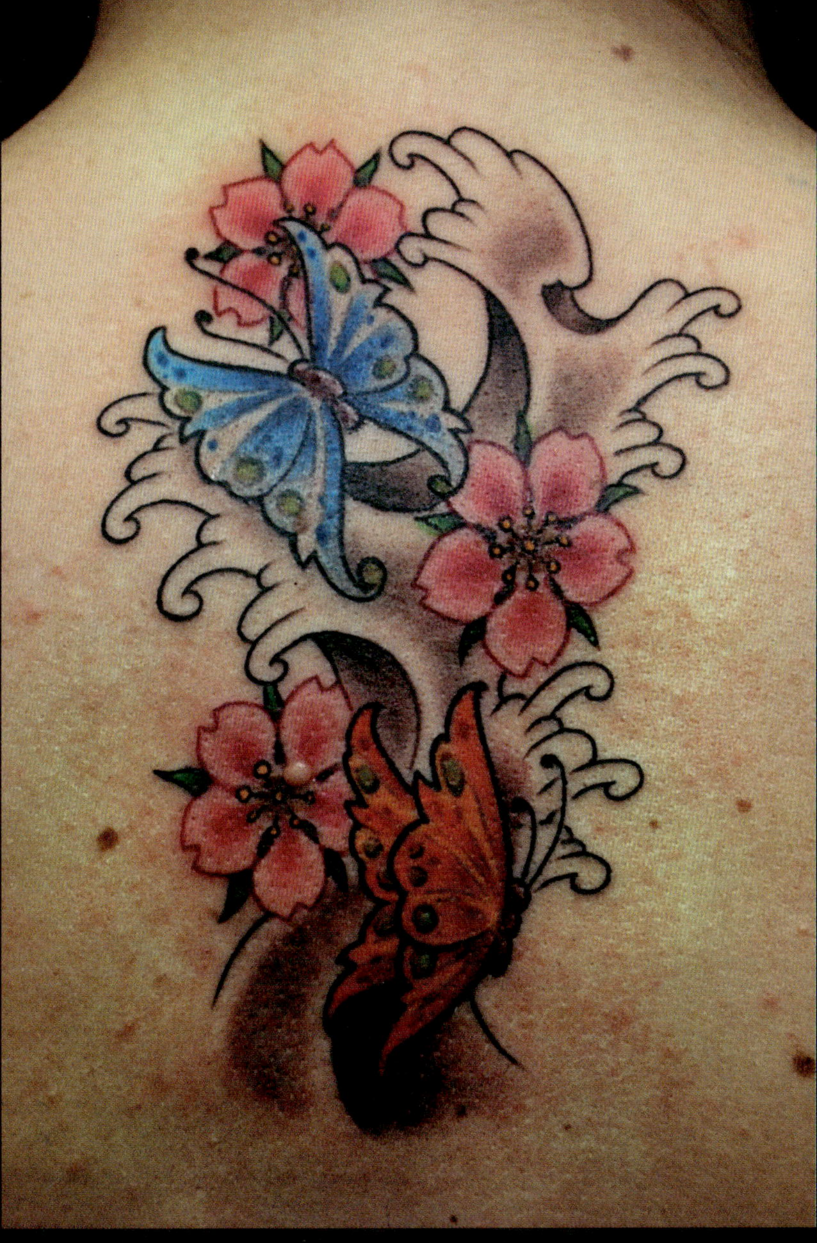

Joako

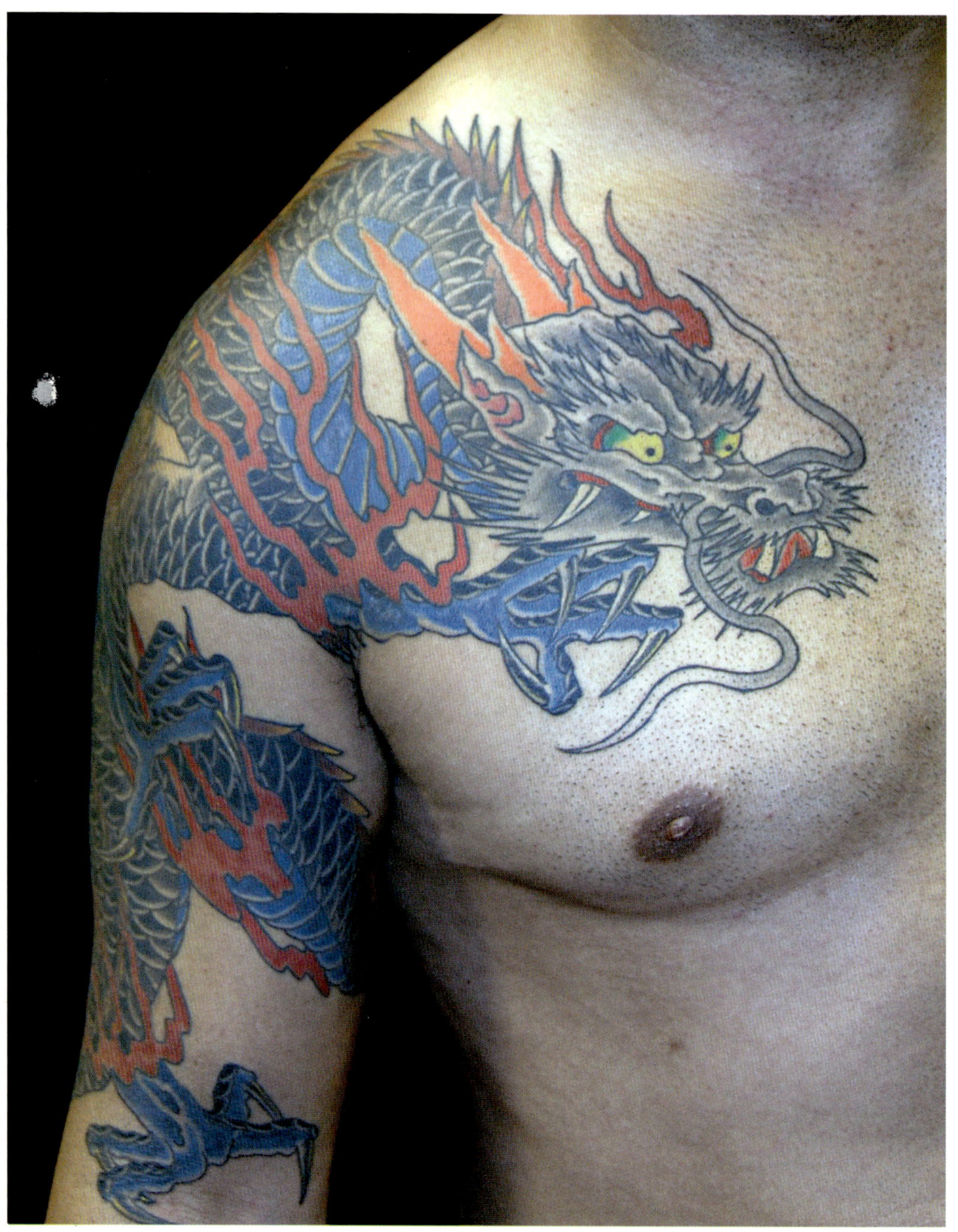

João Paulo Rodrigues
Acqua Santa Tattoo
www.jprodrigues.com

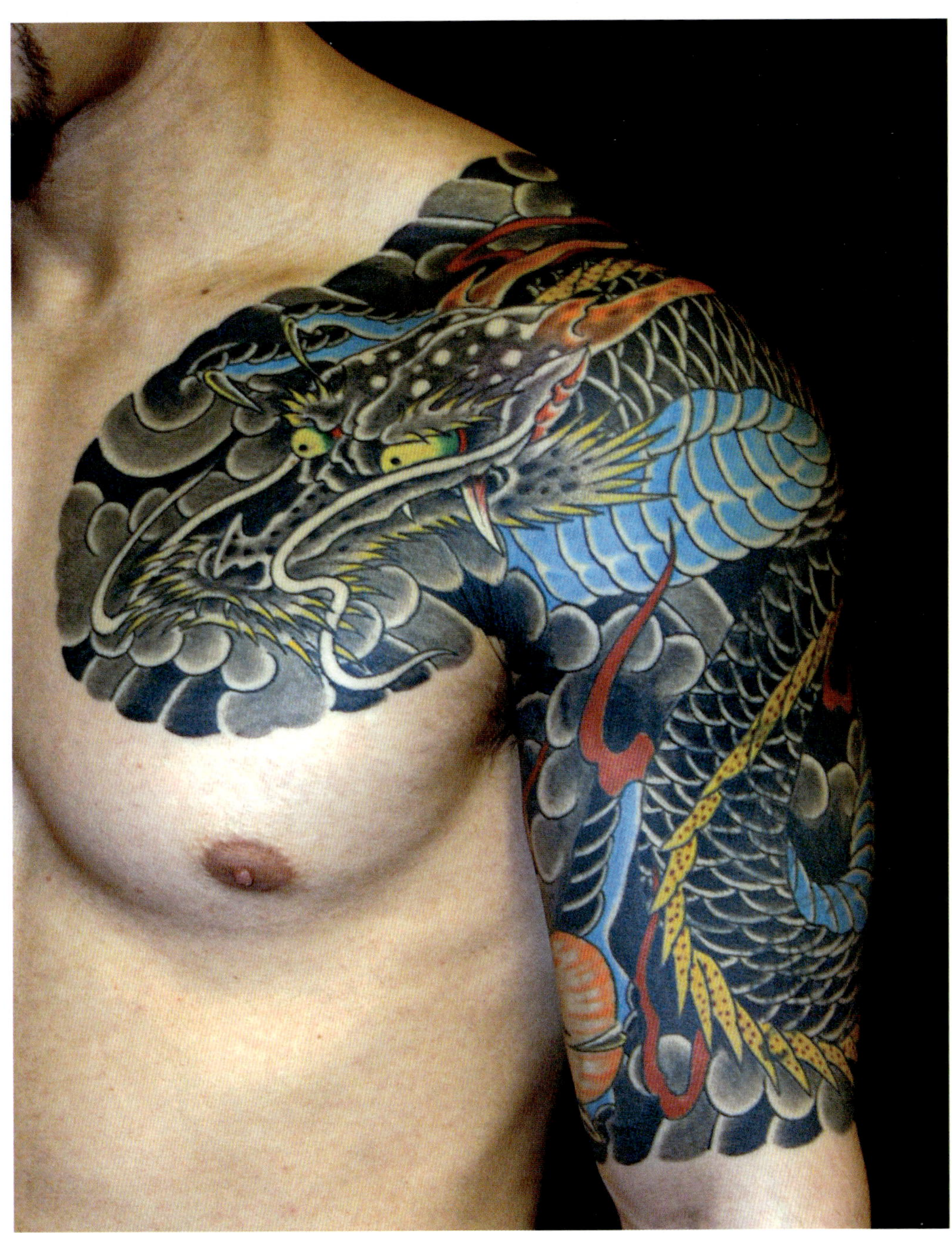

João Paulo Rodrigues
Acqua Santa Tattoo
www.jprodrigues.com

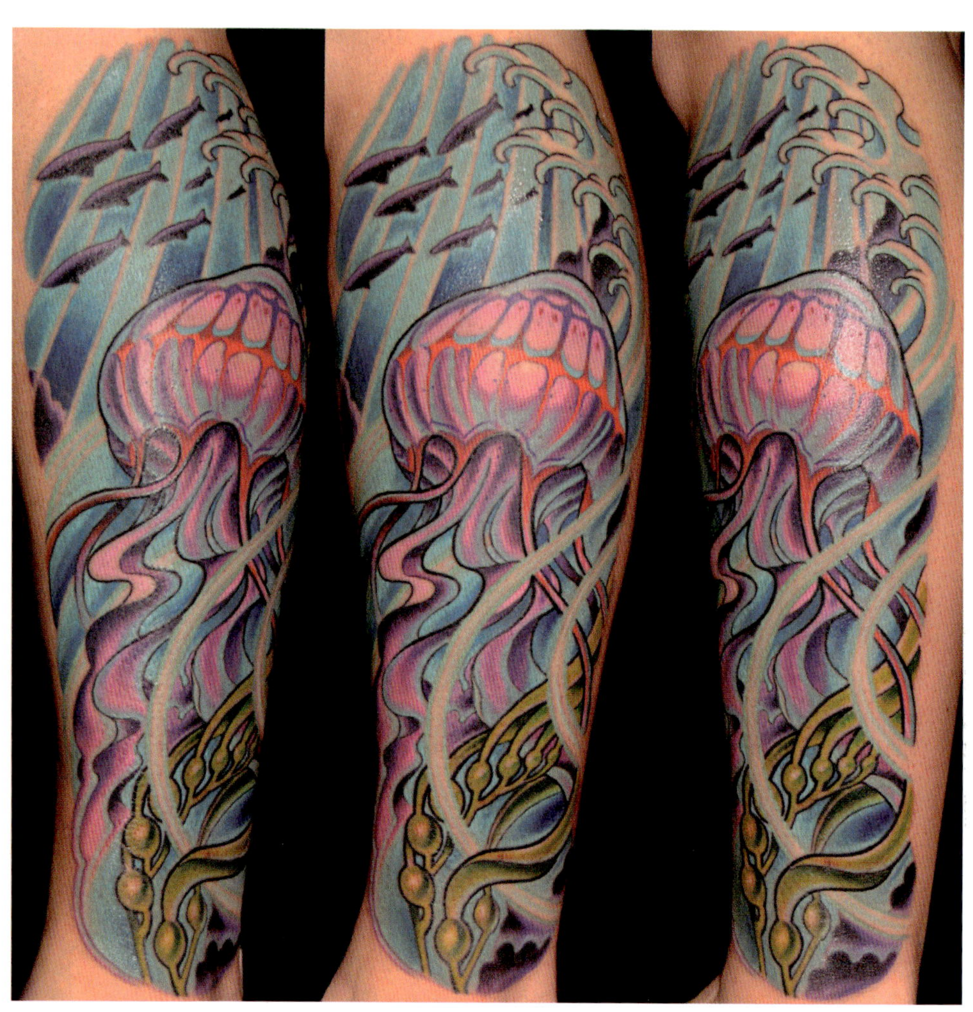

Terry Ribera
Remington Tattoo
www.terryribera.com

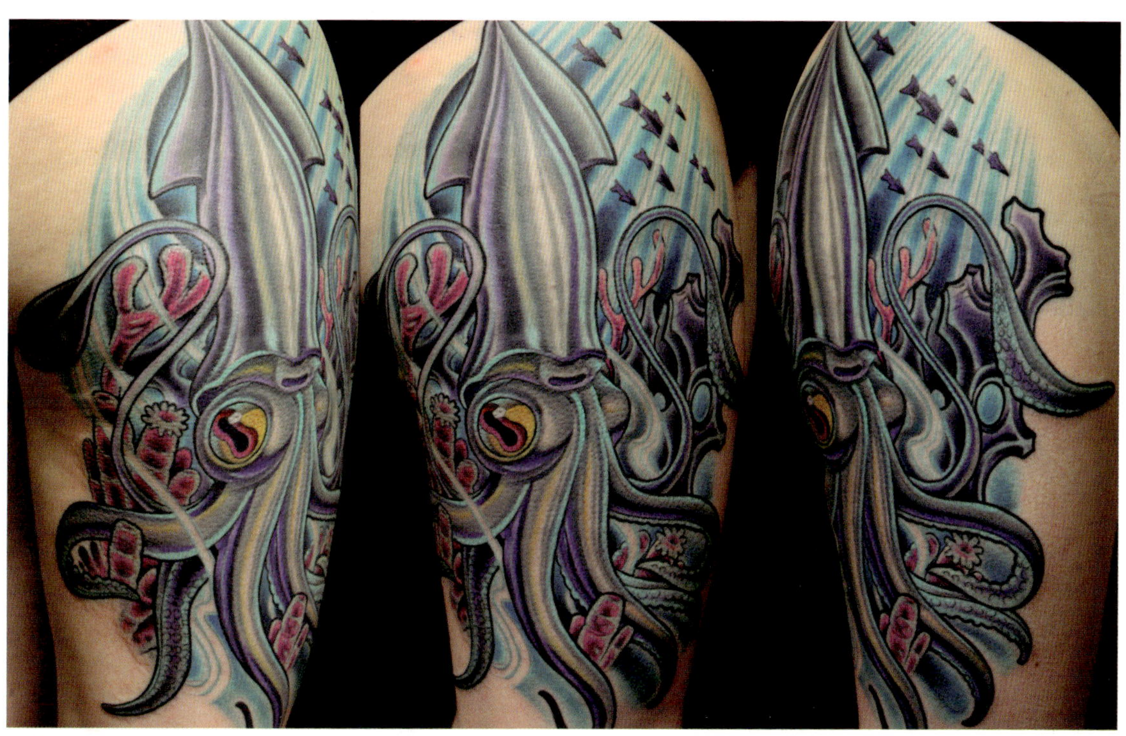

Terry Ribera
Remington Tattoo
www.terryribera.com

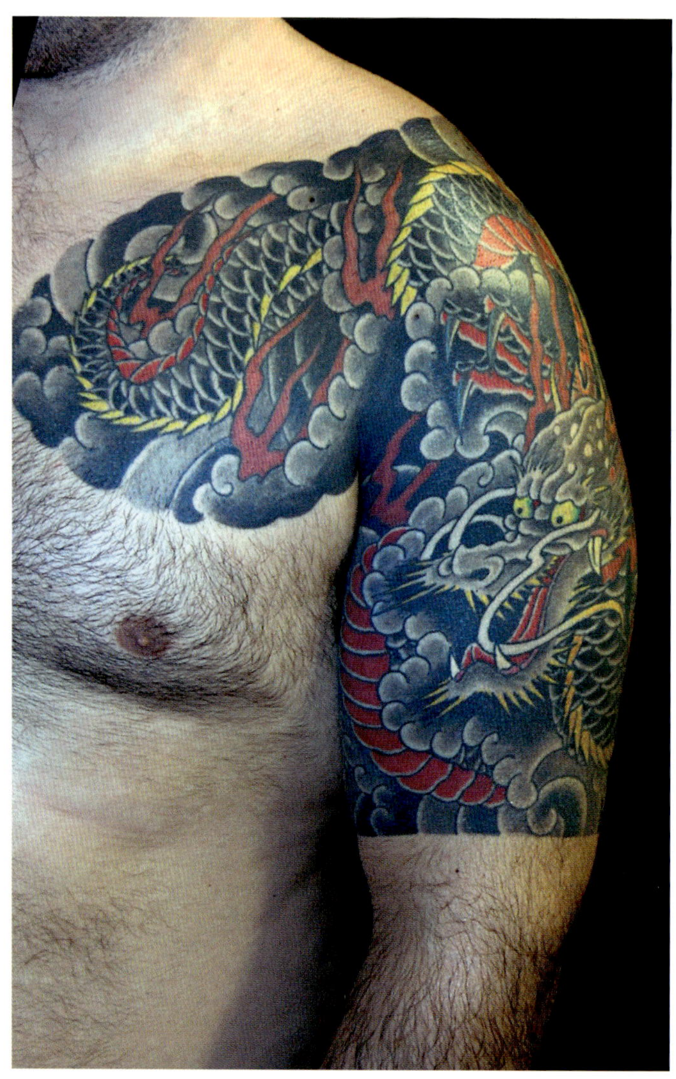

João Paulo Rodrigues
Acqua Santa Tattoo
www.jprodrigues.com

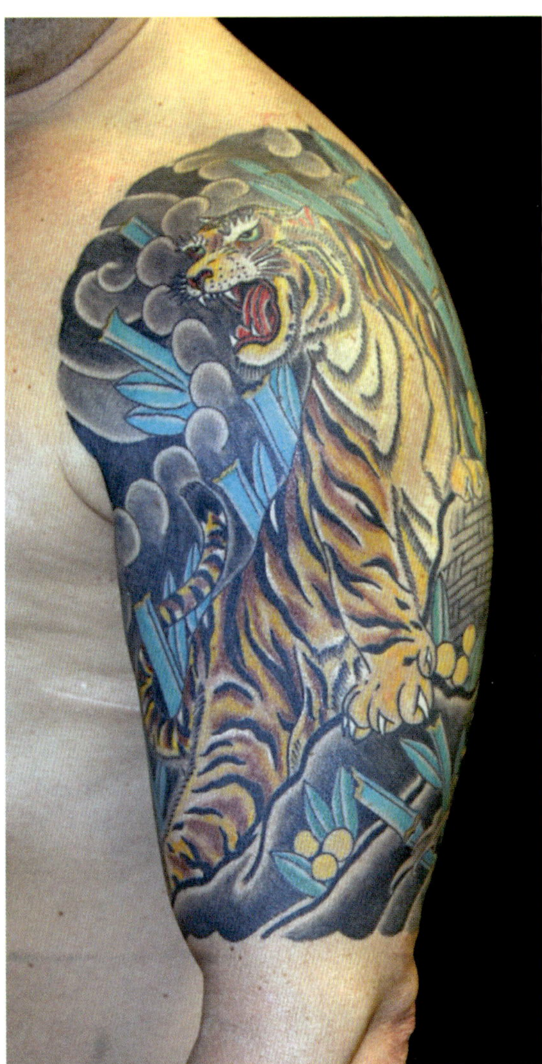

João Paulo Rodrigues
Acqua Santa Tattoo
www.jprodrigues.com

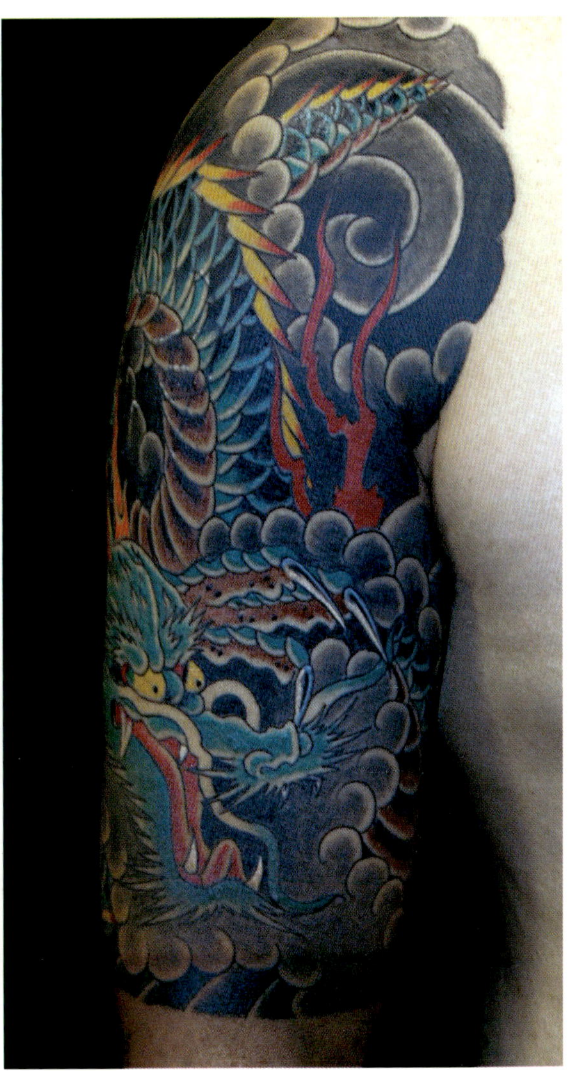

João Paulo Rodrigues
Acqua Santa Tattoo
www.jprodrigues.com

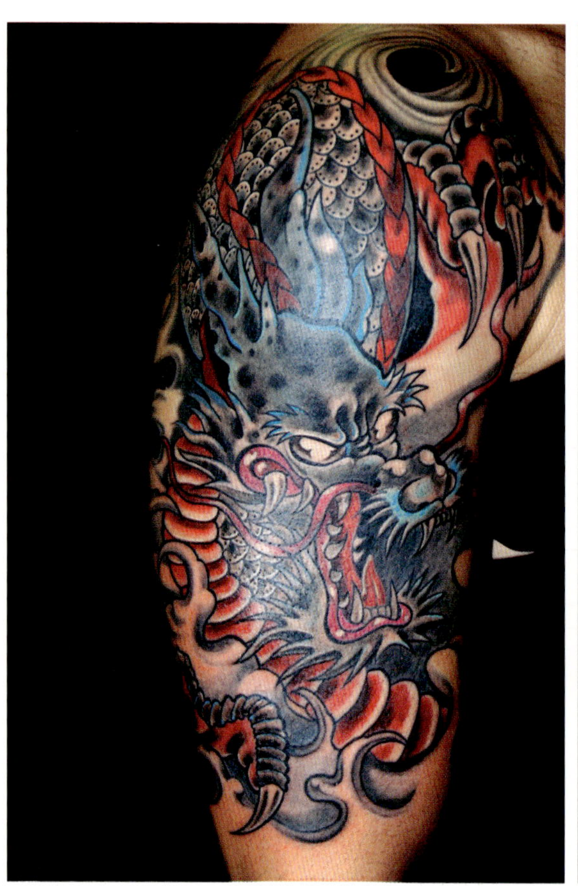

Alfonso Sánchez
Balinese Tattoo Studio
www.balinesetattoo.com

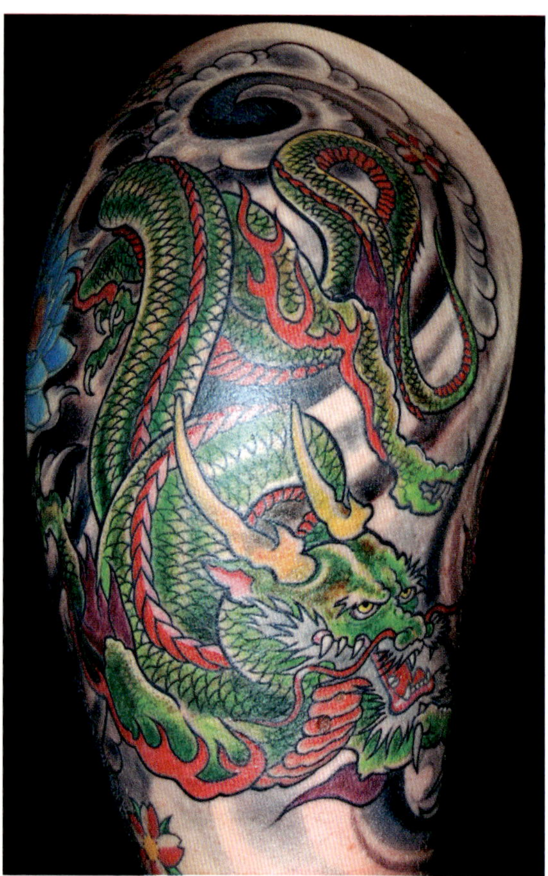

Alfonso Sánchez
Balinese Tattoo Studio
www.balinesetattoo.com

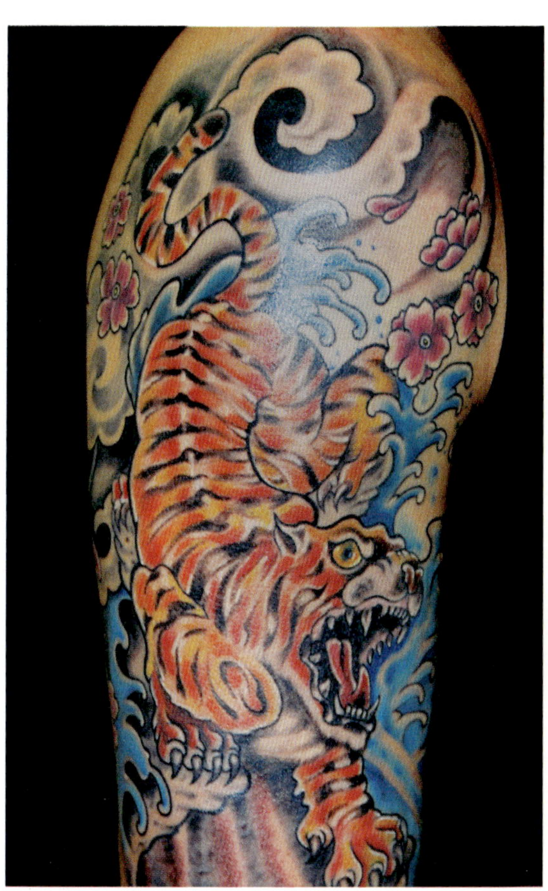

Alfonso Sánchez
Balinese Tattoo Studio
www.balinesetattoo.com

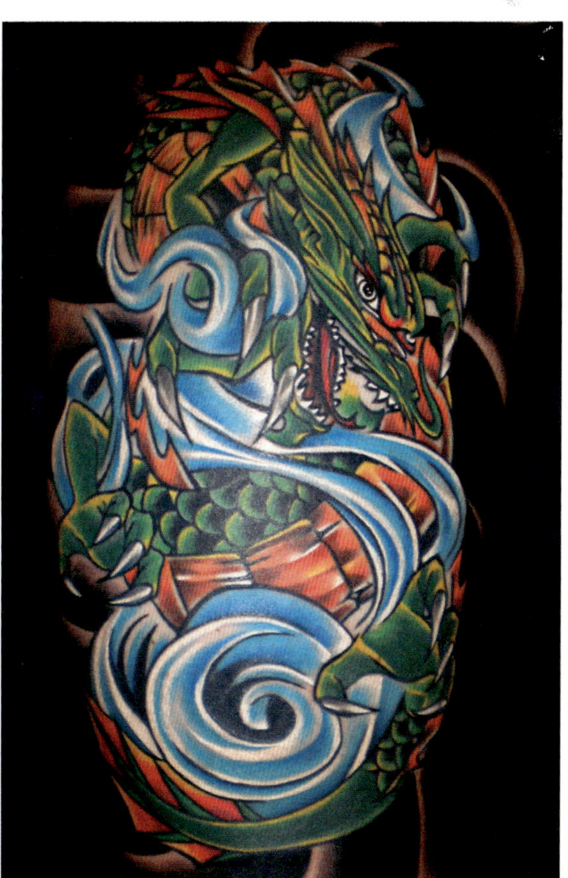

Tomás "Psycho" Dacej
Psycho Tattoo
www.facebook.com/tomas.dacej

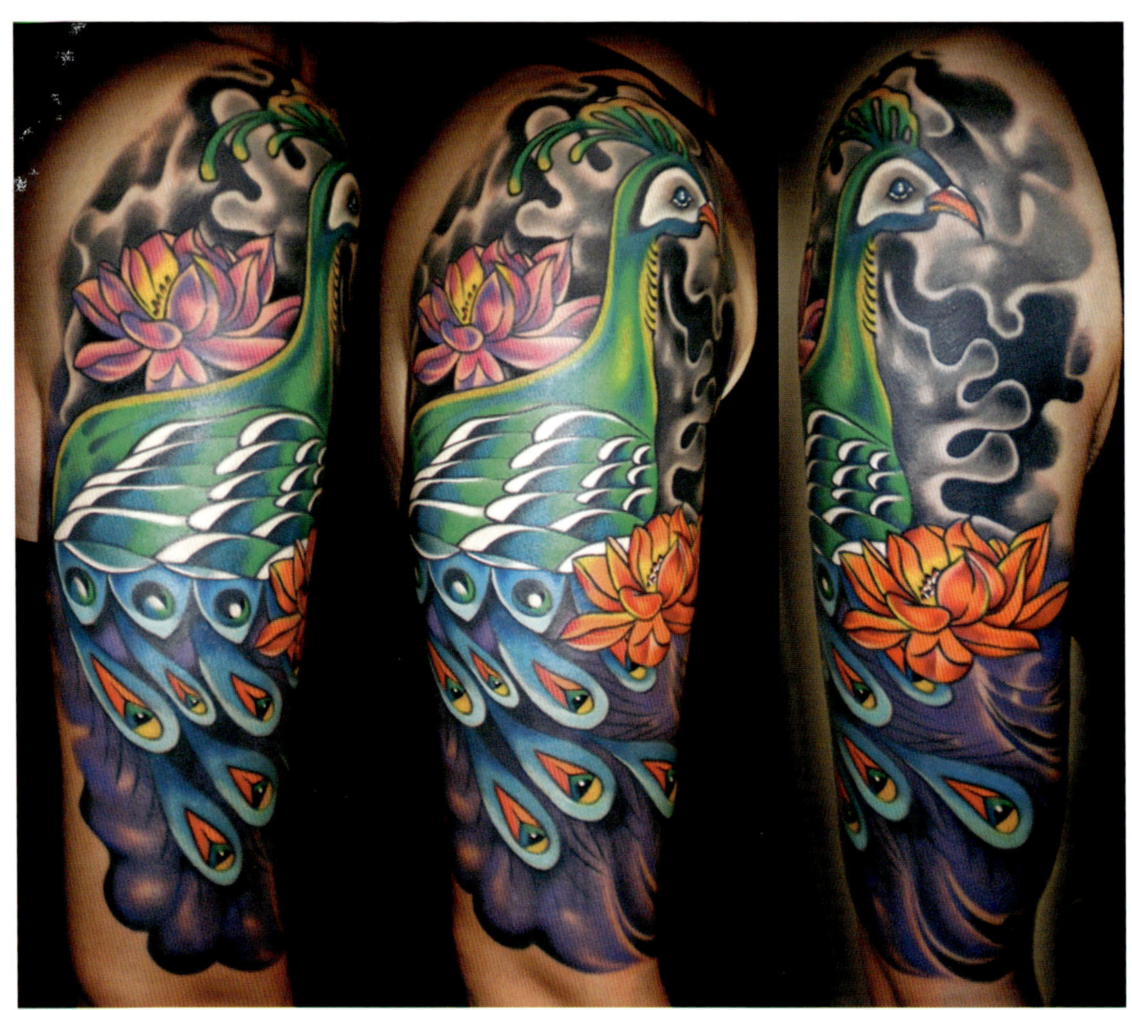

Tomás "Psycho" Dacej
Psycho Tattoo
www.facebook.com/tomas.dacej

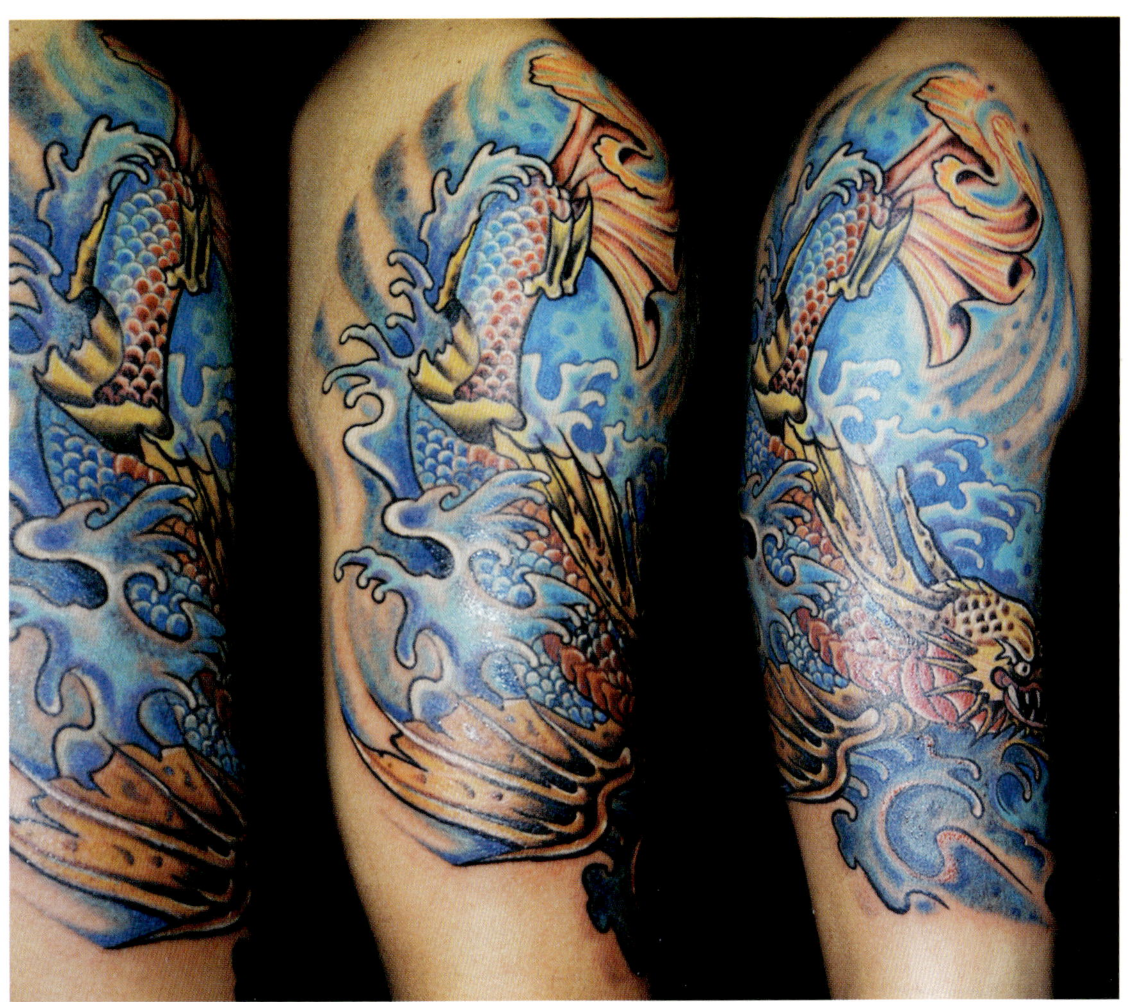

Alfonso Sánchez
Balinese Tattoo Studio
www.balinesetattoo.com

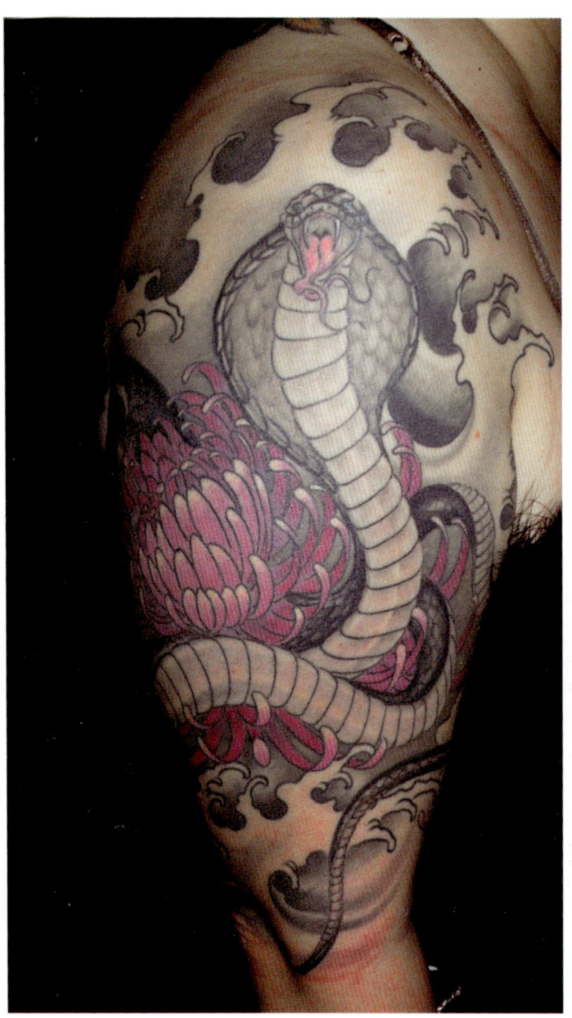

Bill Funk
Body Graphics
www.bodygraphics.com

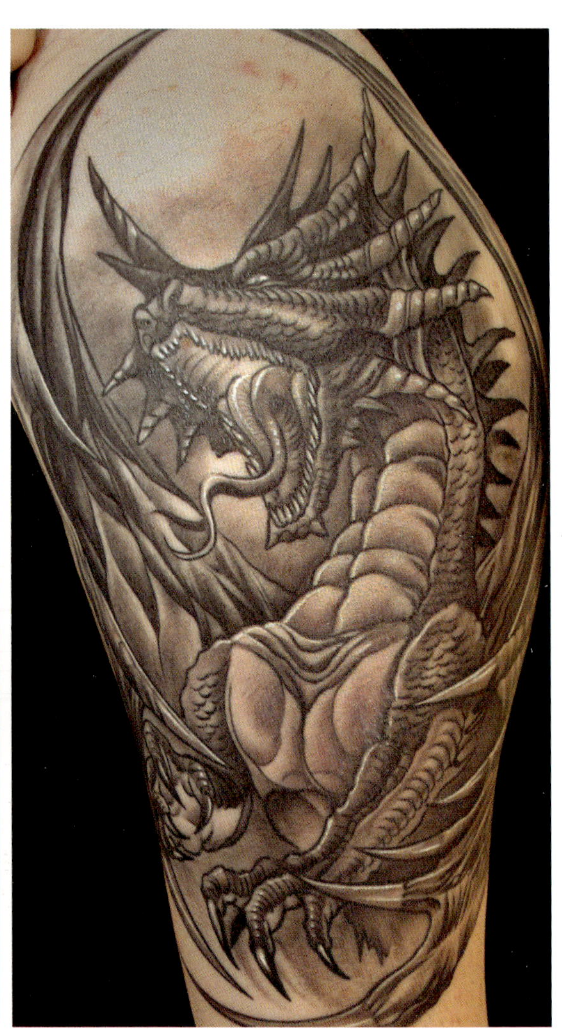

Mariano Wheeler
Estudio Ancient Fantasy
www.ancientfantasy.com.ar

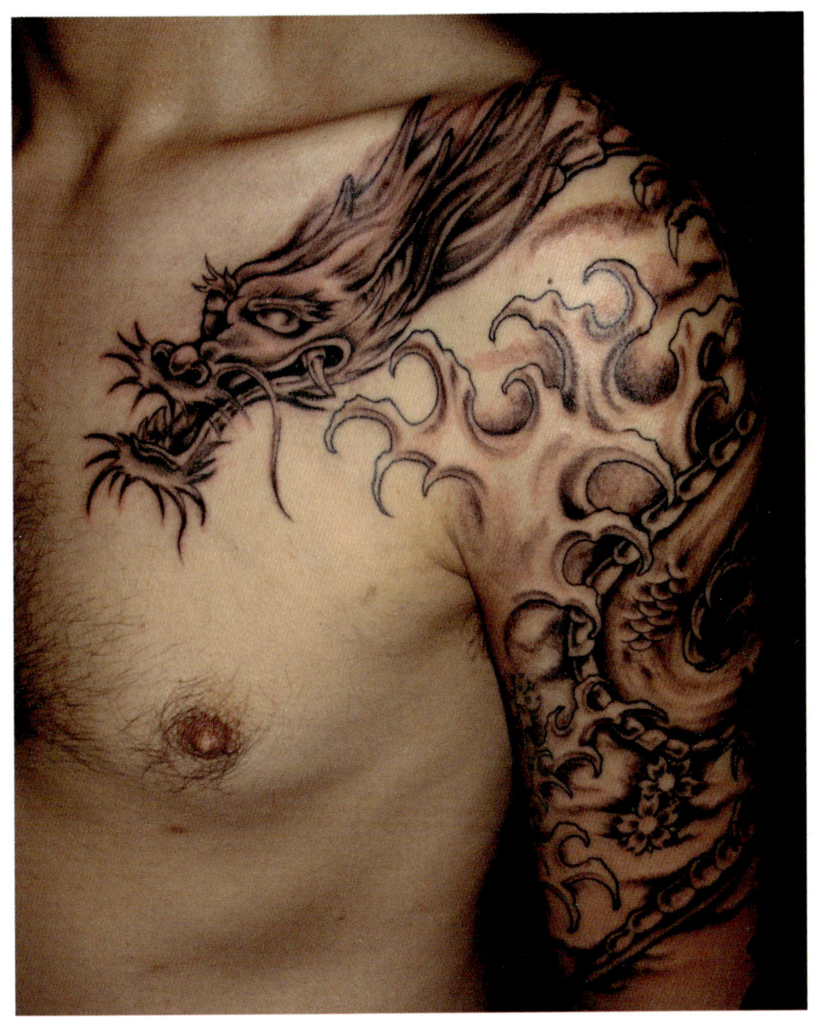

Falke
Pro-Arts Tattoo
www.pro-arts.com

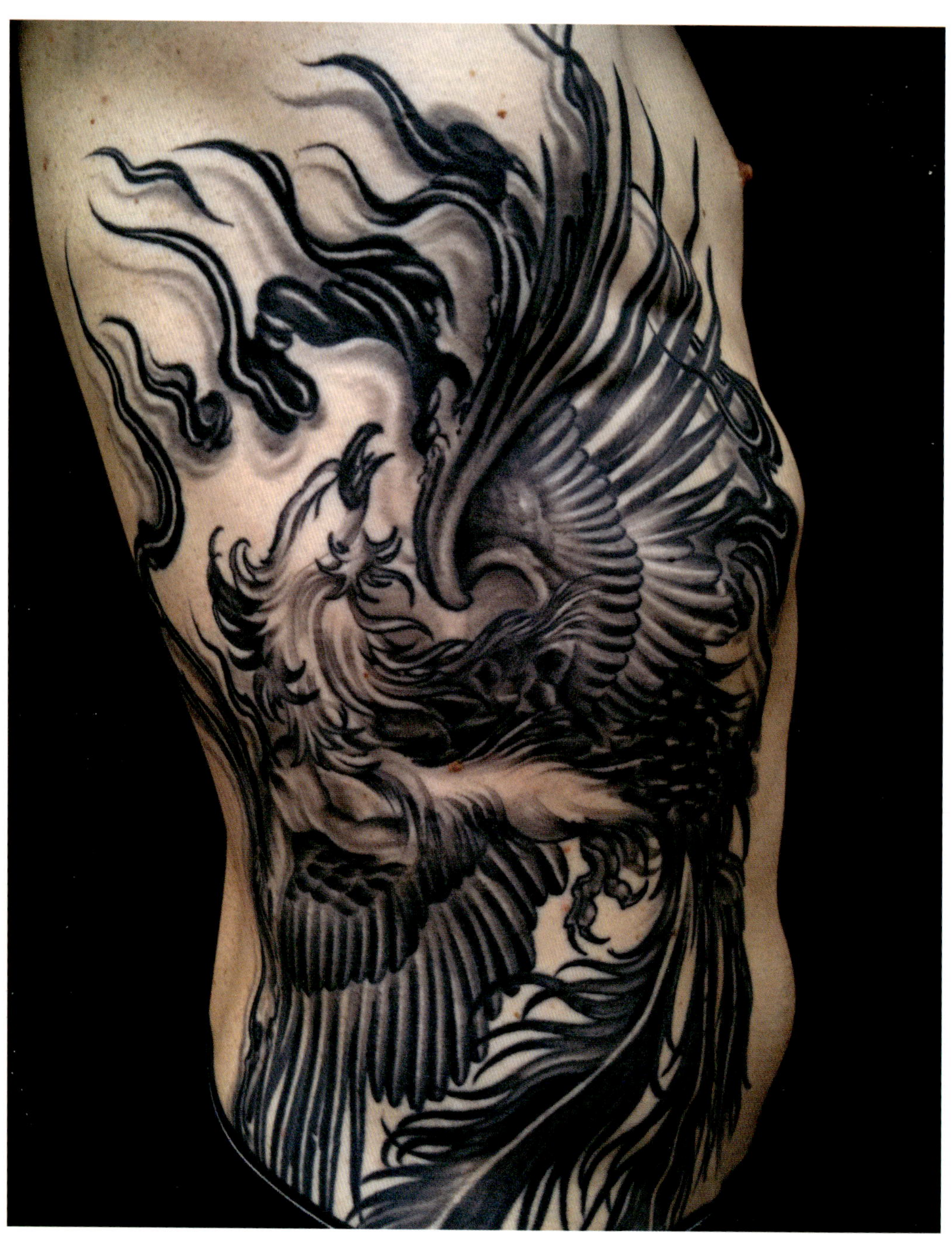

Bill Funk
Body Graphics
www.bodygraphics.com

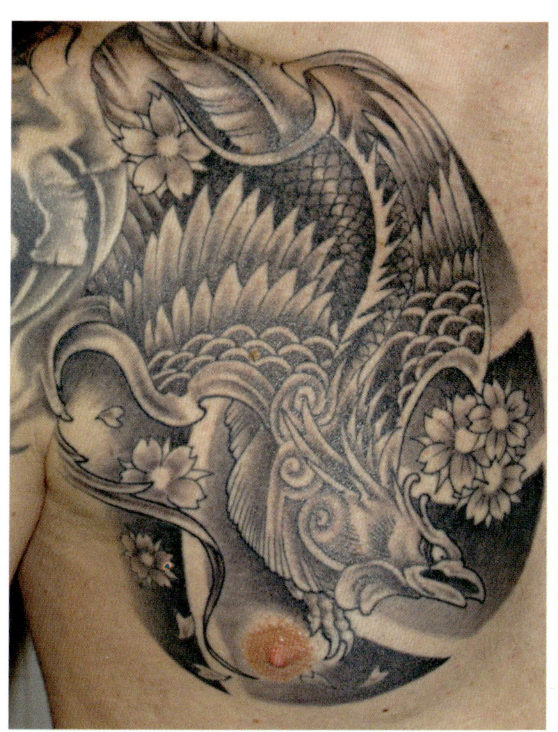

Voodoo
Voodoo Tattoo Barcelona
www.voodootattoo.com

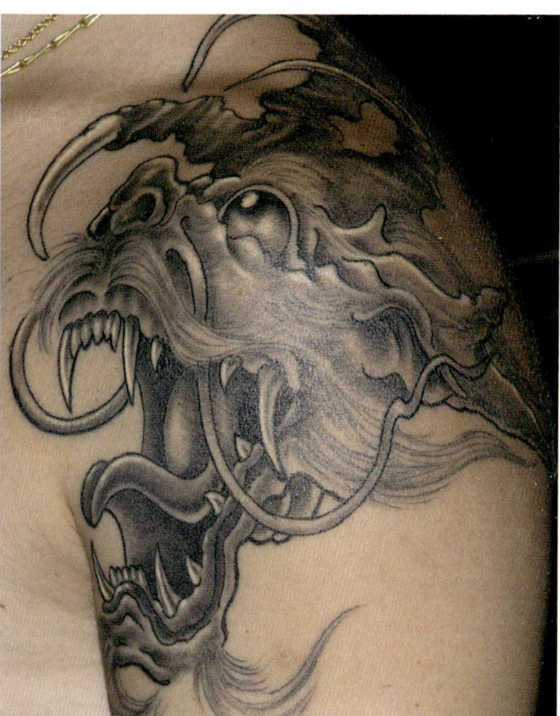

Voodoo
Voodoo Tattoo Barcelona
www.voodootattoo.com

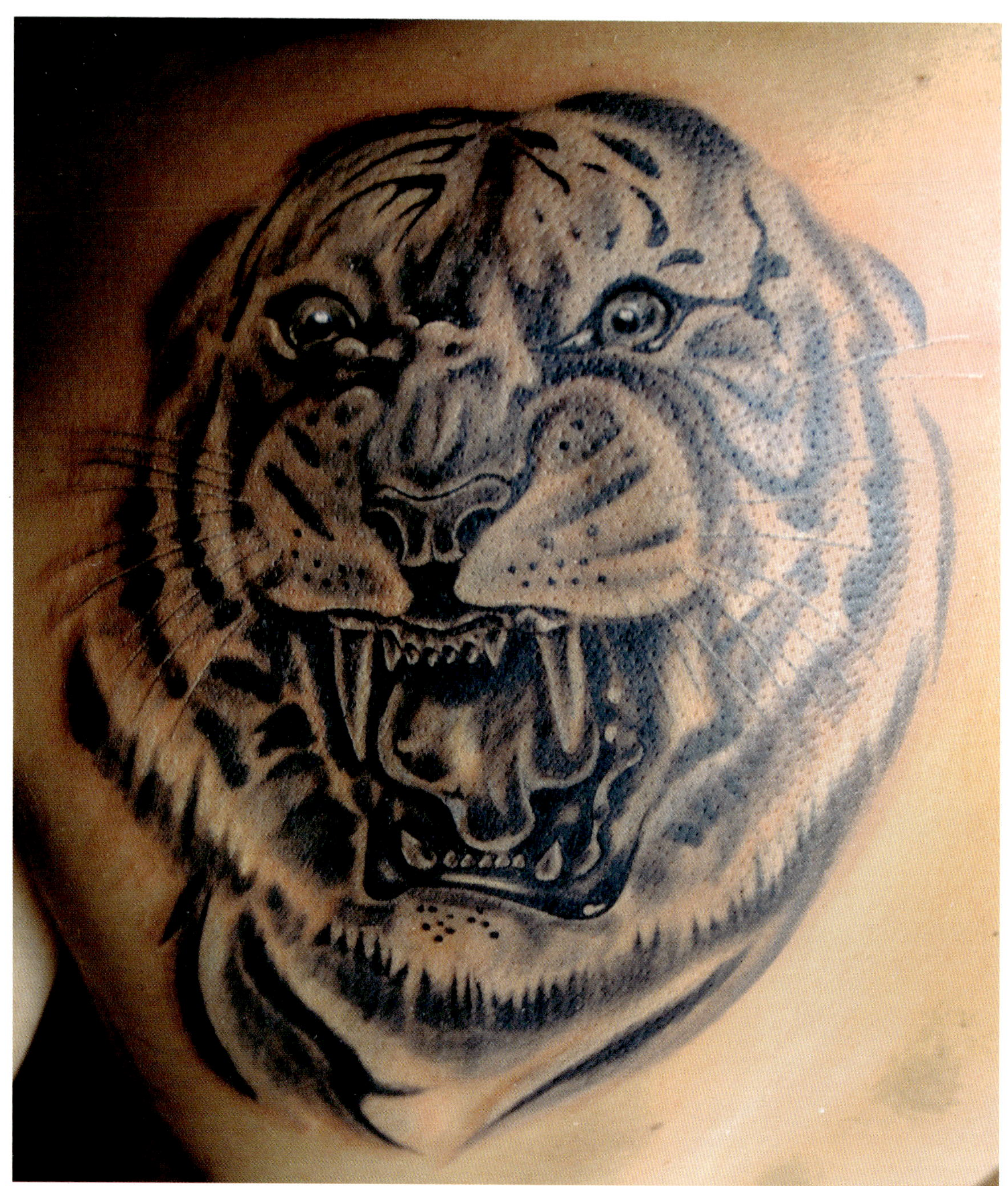

Alfonso Sánchez
Balinese Tattoo Studio
www.balinesetattoo.com

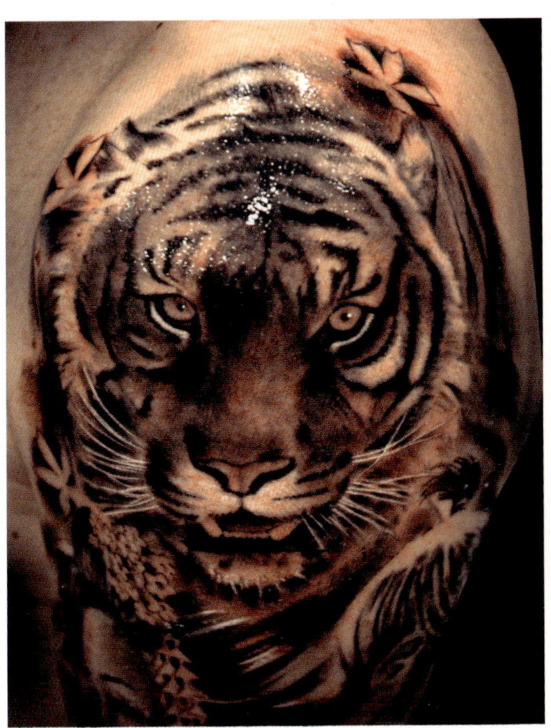

Miguel Angel Bohigues
V Tattoo
www.vtattoo.es

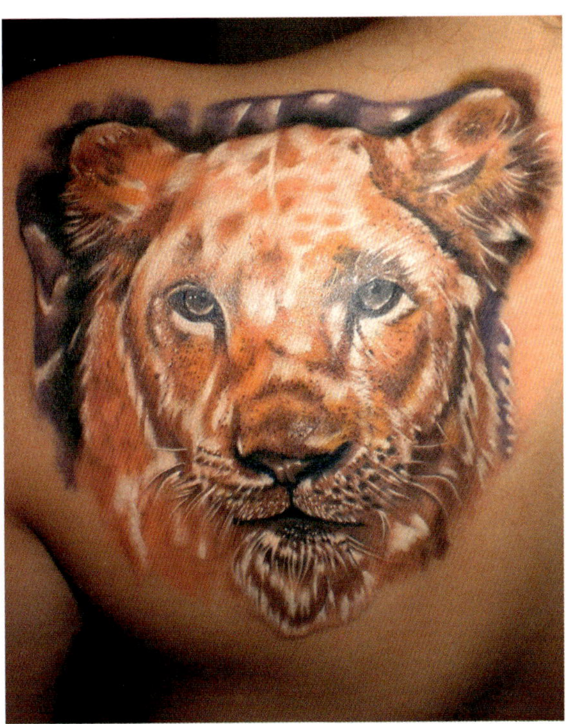

Tomás "Psycho" Dacej
Psycho Tattoo
www.facebook.com/tomas.dacej

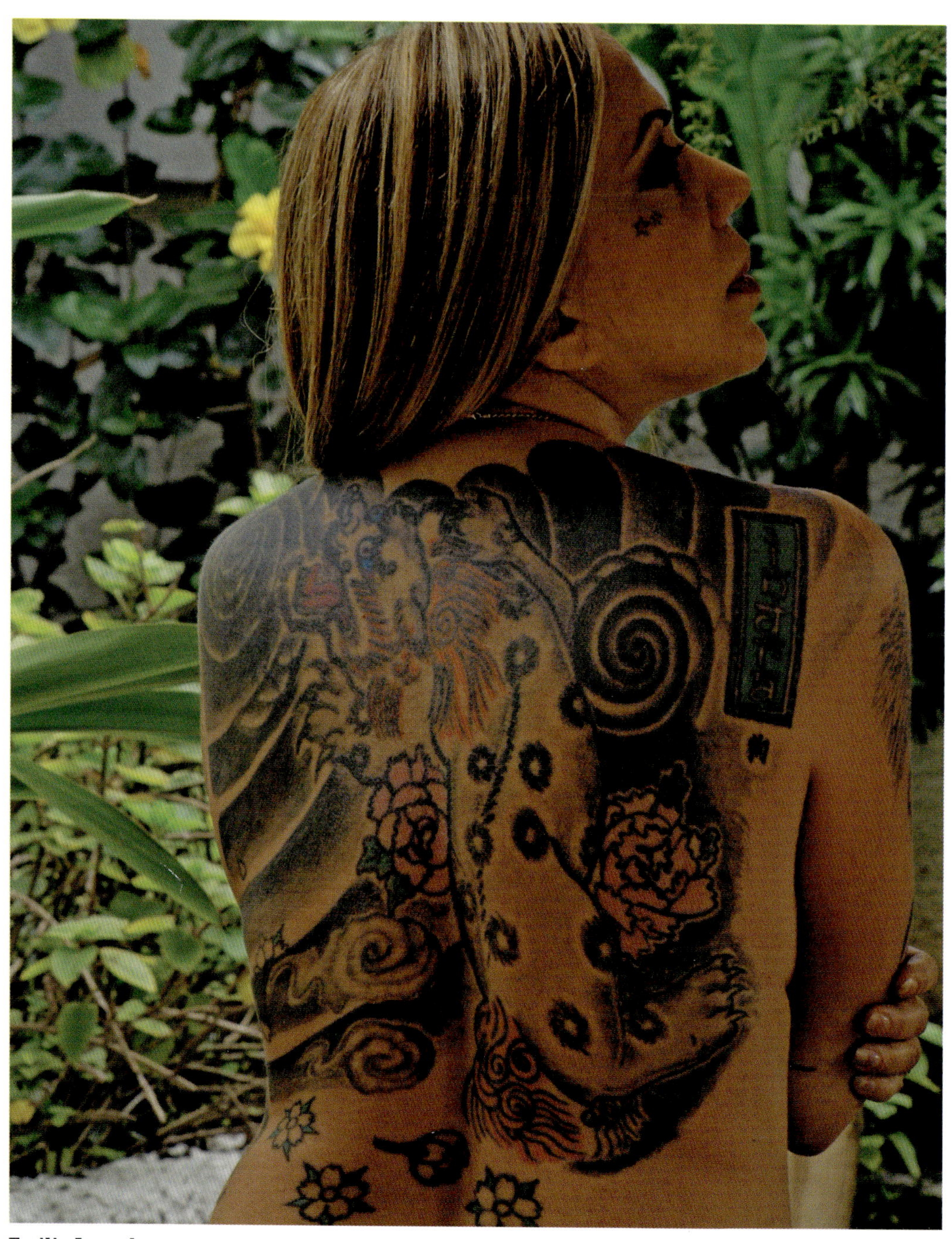

Emilia Laurel

www.emiliatattooart.com

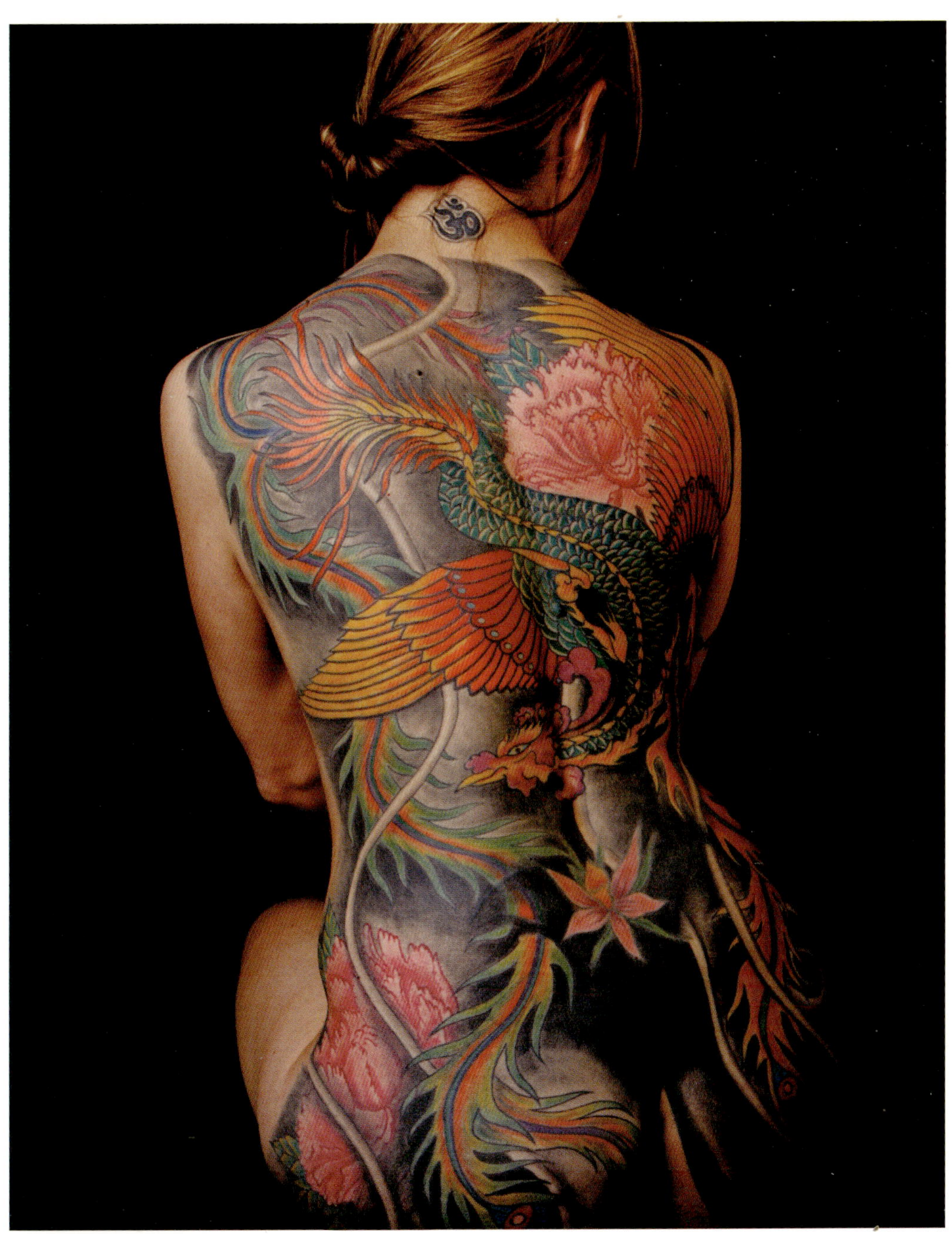

Javier Acero
Tattoo & Co. Miami
www.tattooandco.com

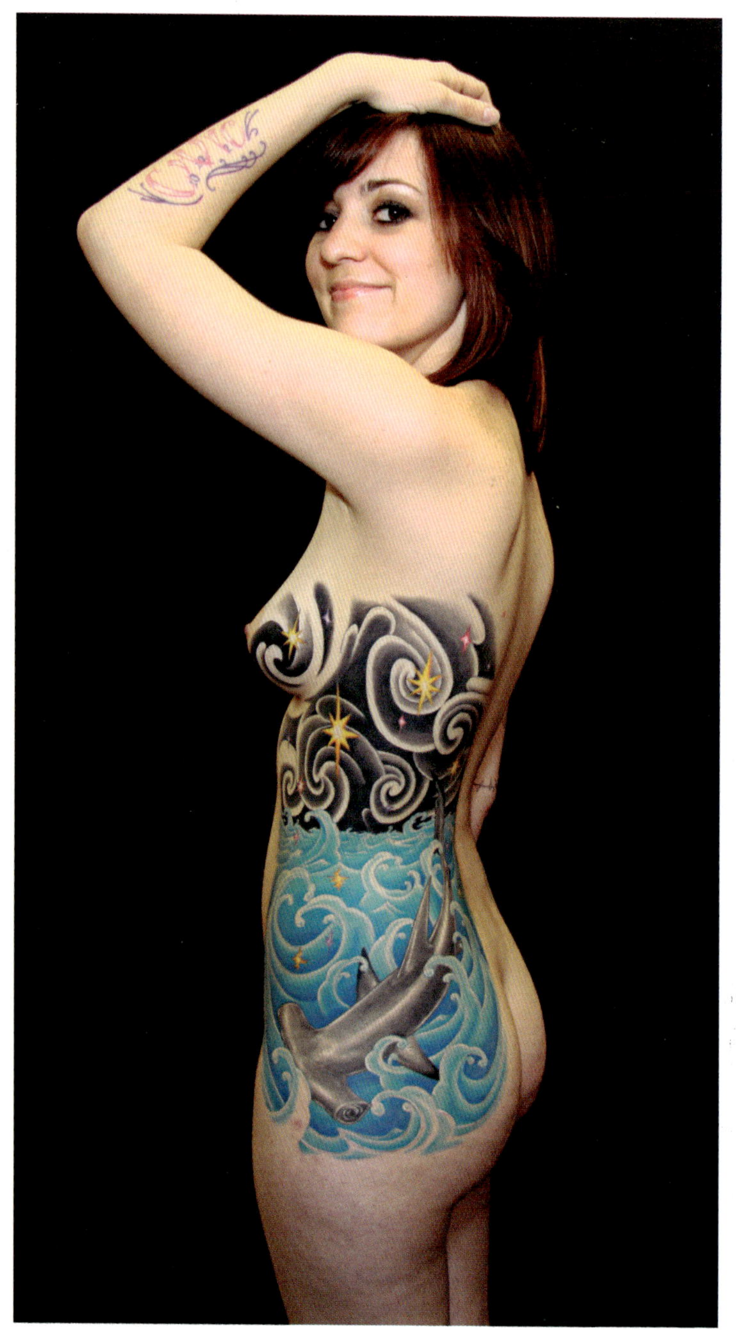

Jesse Neese
Nuclear Ink Custom Tattoo & Piercing
www.nuclear-ink.com

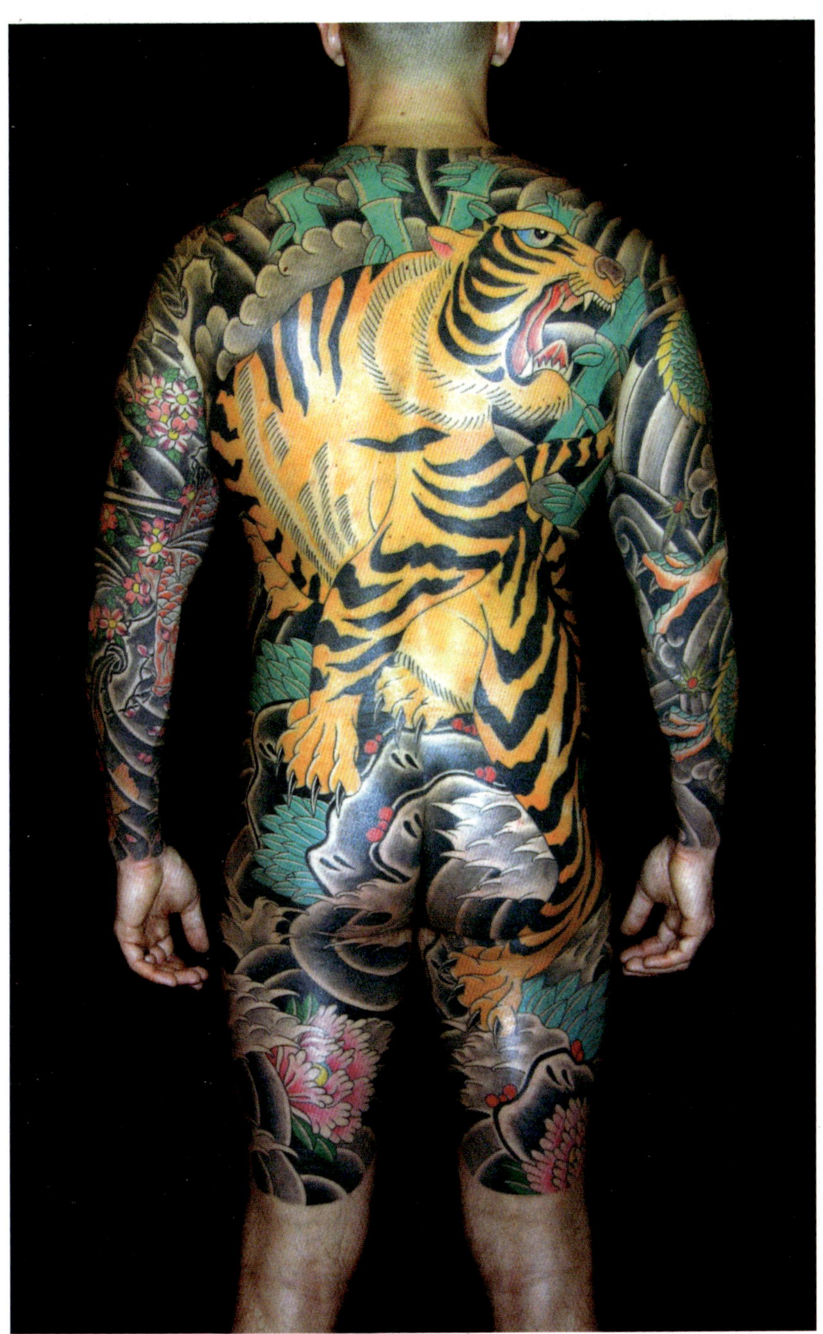

João Paulo Rodrigues
Acqua Santa Tattoo
www.jprodrigues.com

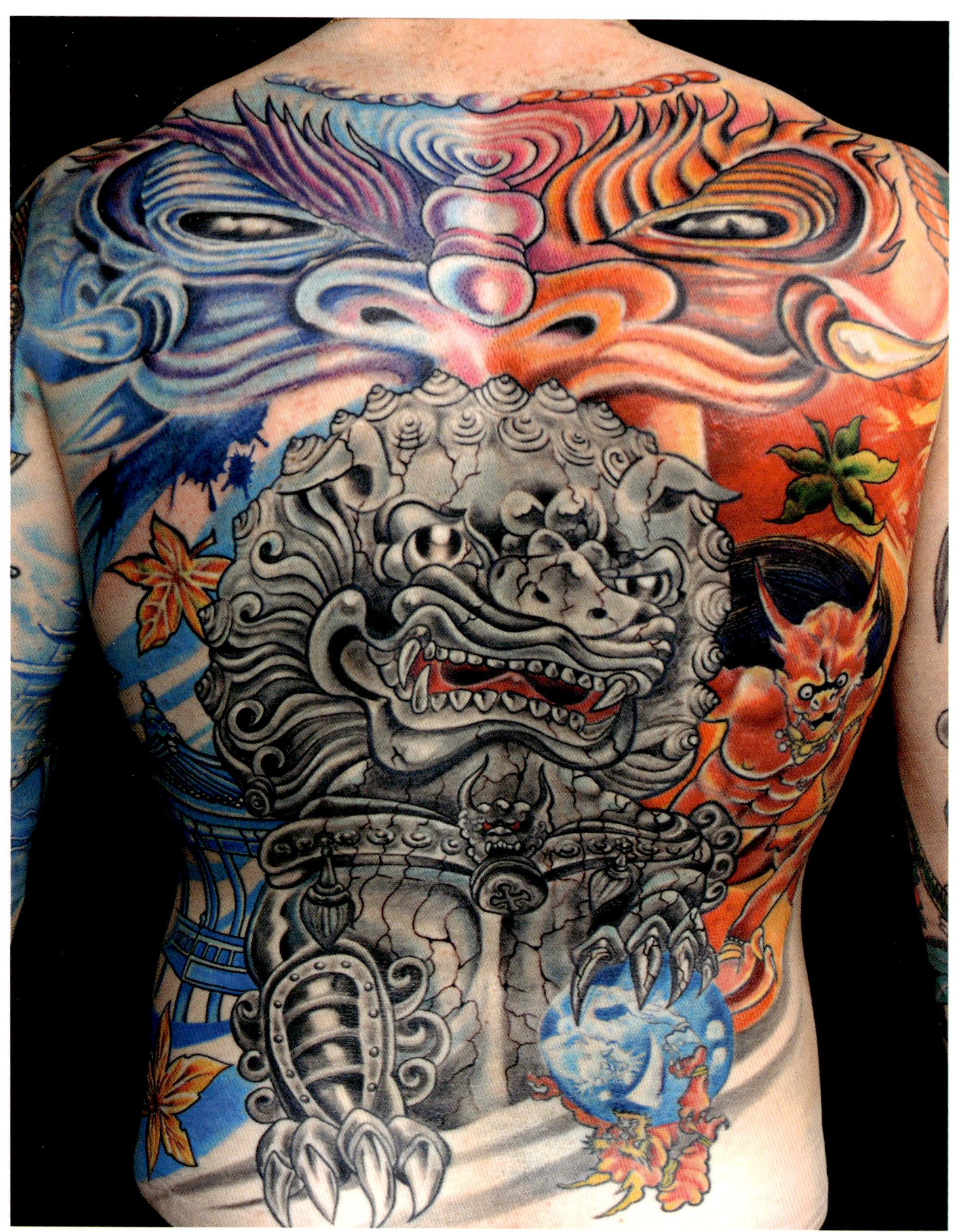

Alfonso Sánchez
Balinese Tattoo Studio
www.balinesetattoo.com

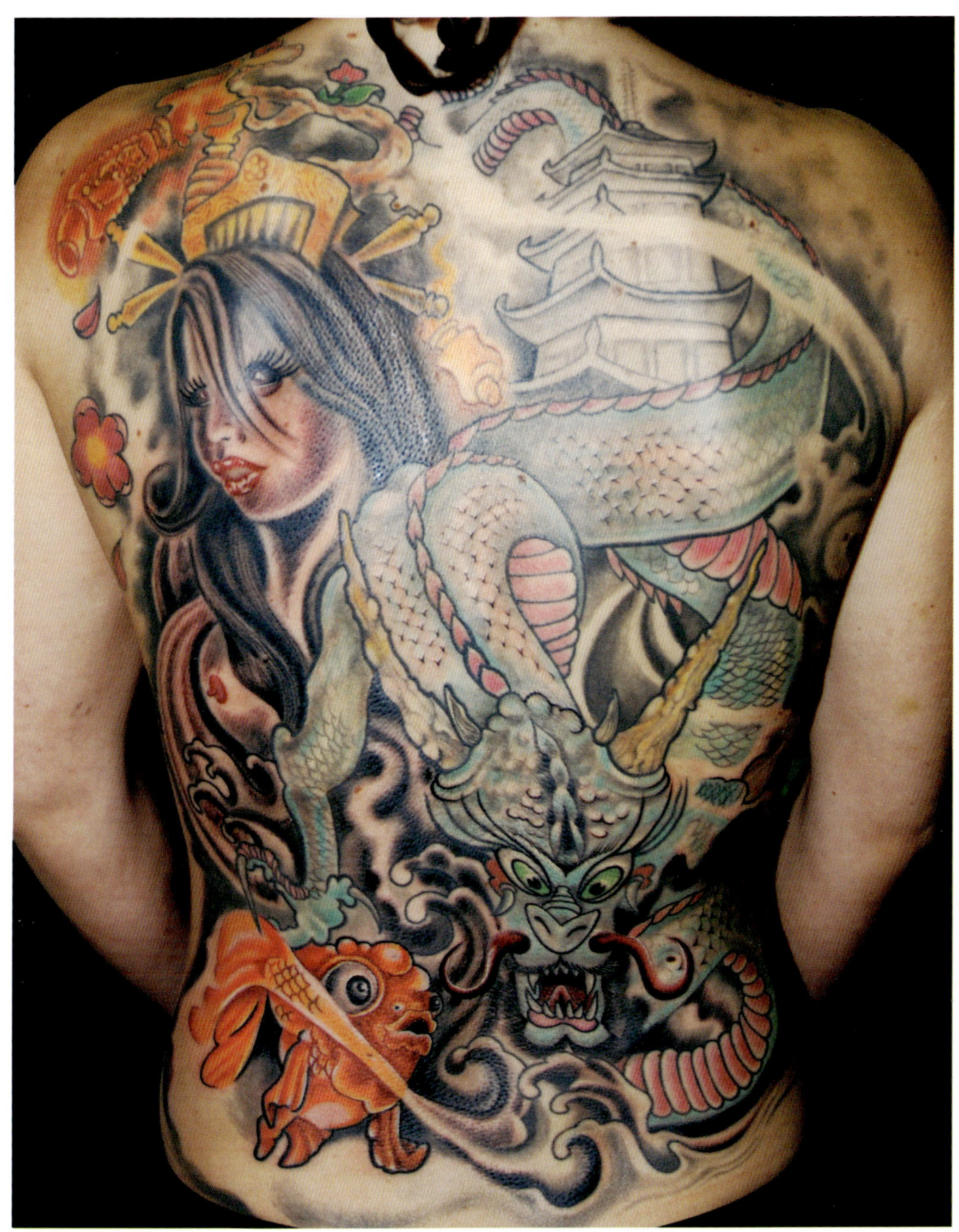

Alfonso Sánchez
Balinese Tattoo Studio
www.balinesetattoo.com

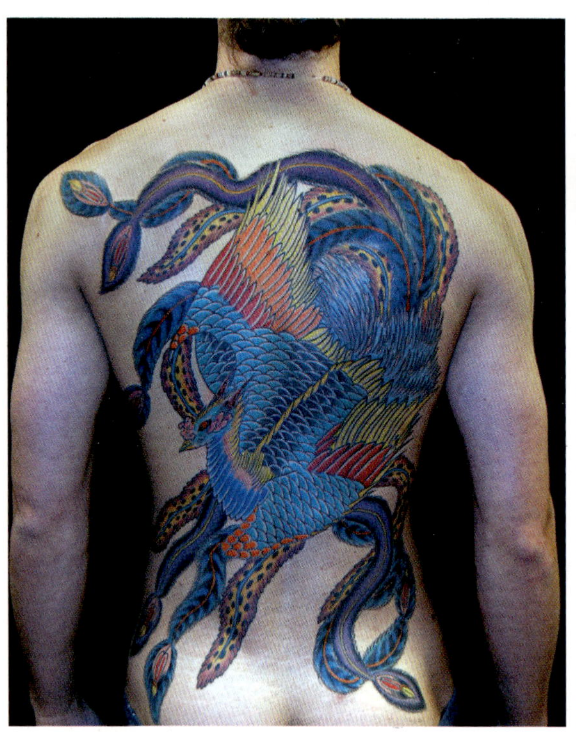

João Paulo Rodrigues
Acqua Santa Tattoo
www.jprodrigues.com

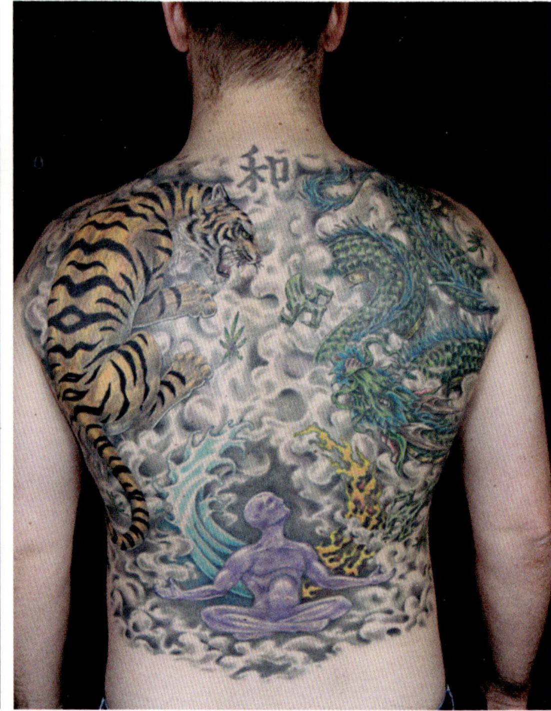

Jesse Neese
Nuclear Ink Custom Tattoo & Piercing
www.nuclear-ink.com

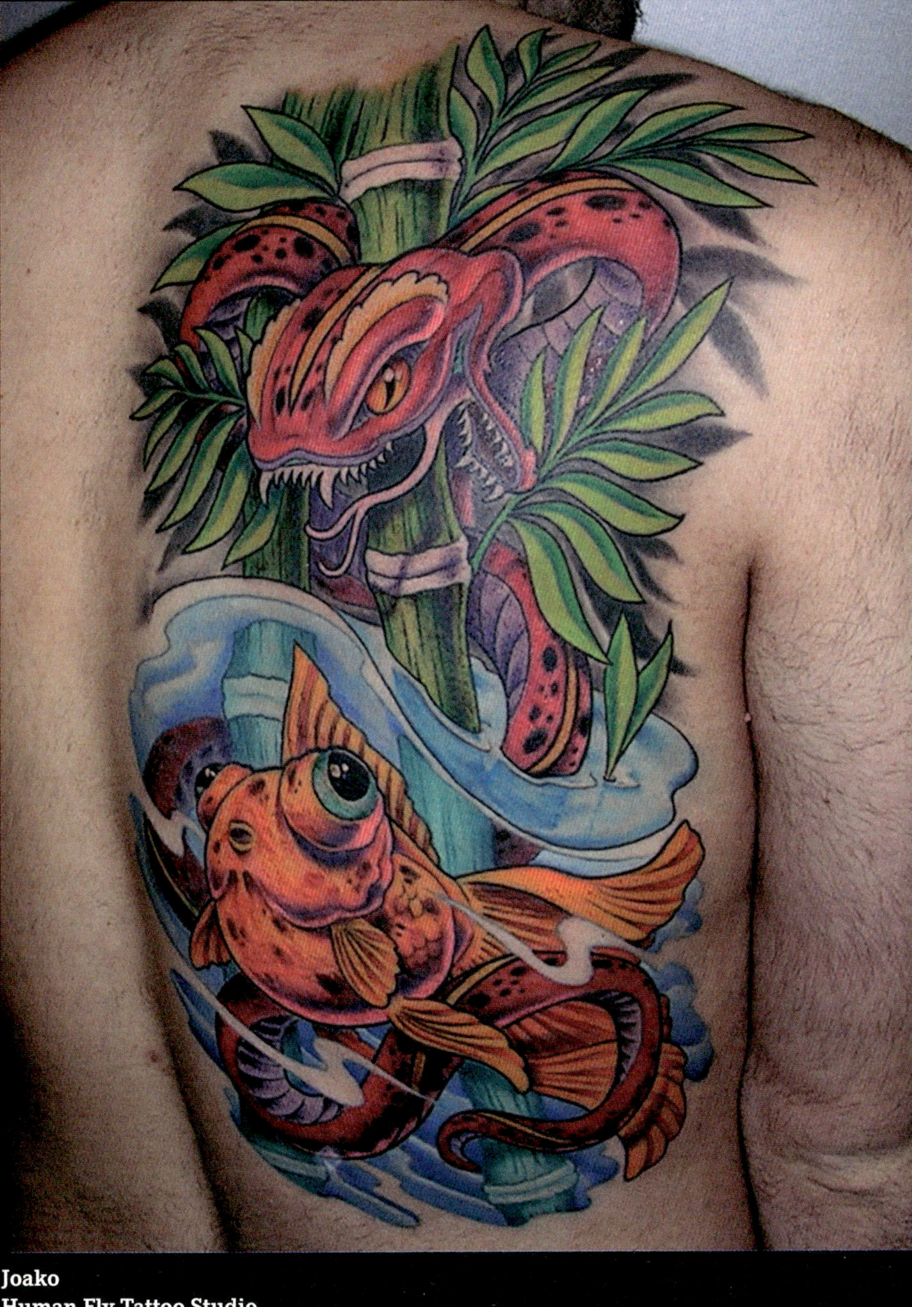

Joako
Human Fly Tattoo Studio
www.humanflytattoo.com

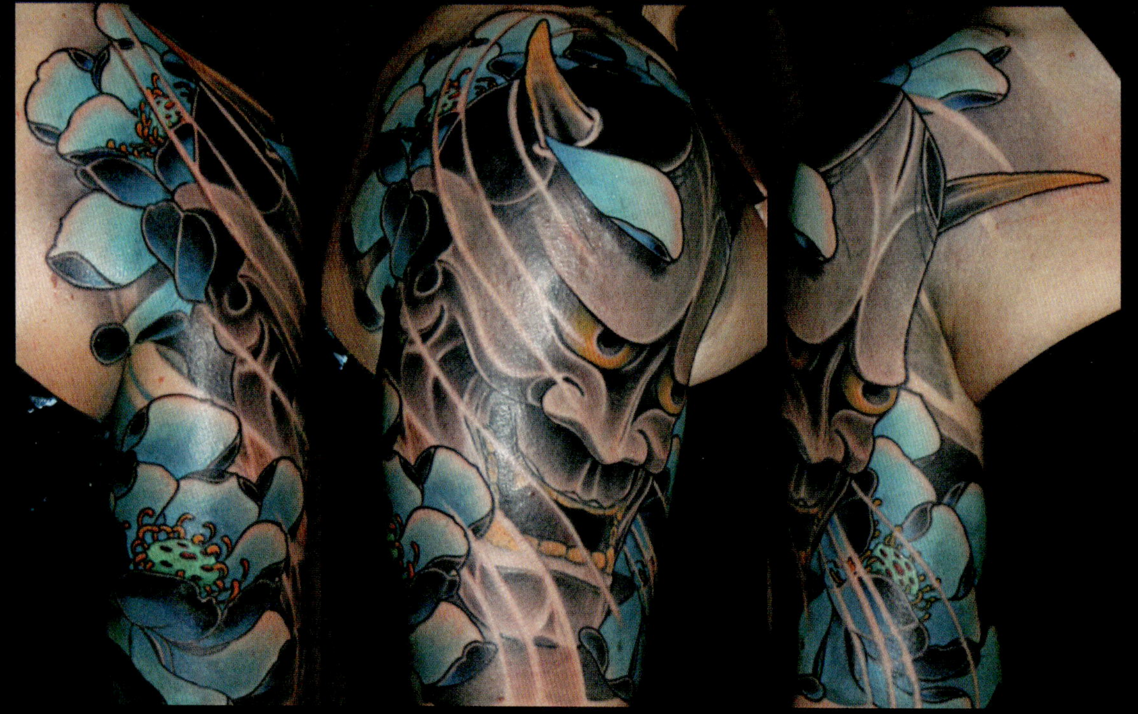

Carl Corson
Studio King Carlos Tattoo
www.kingcarlostattoo.com

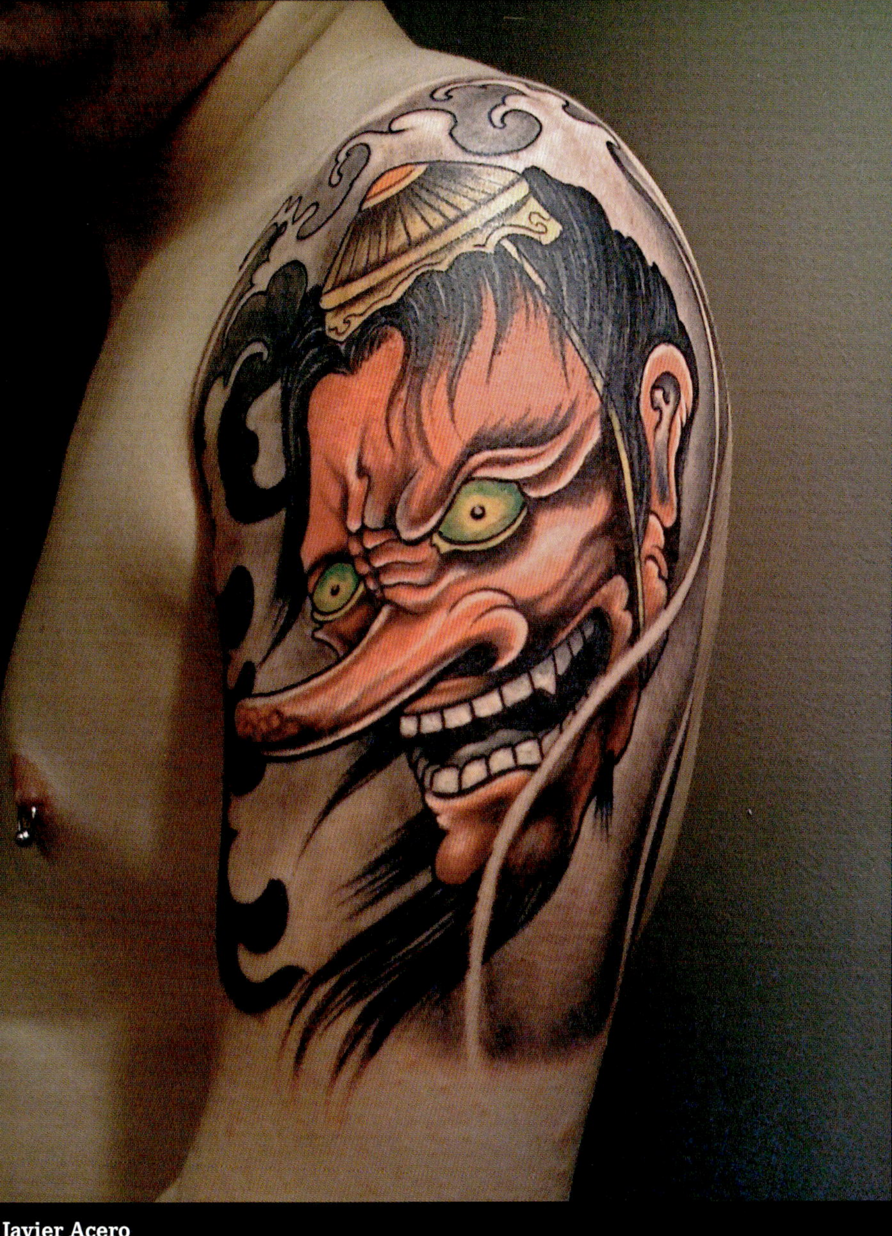

Javier Acero
Tattoo & Co. Miami

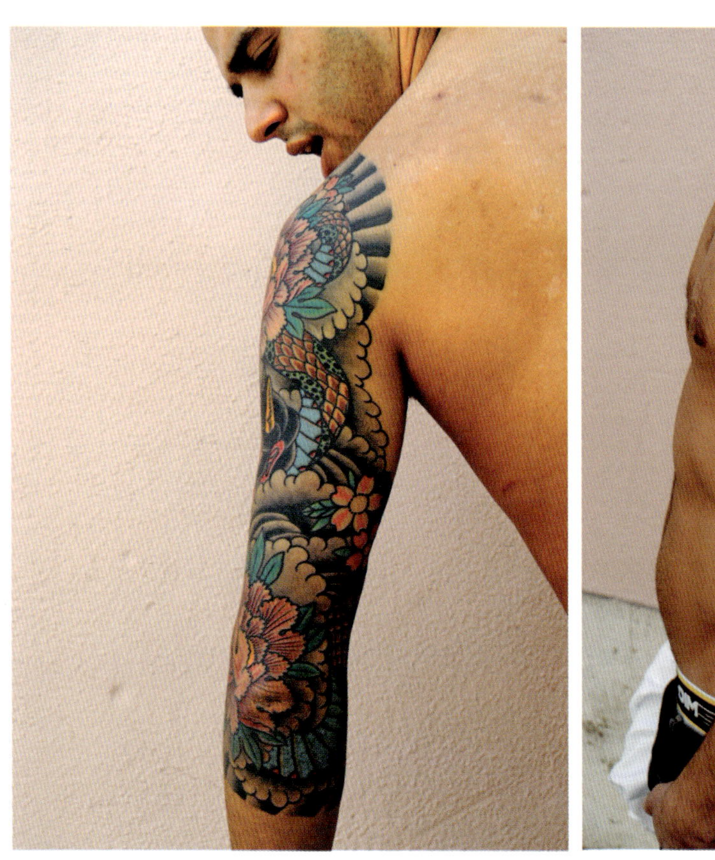

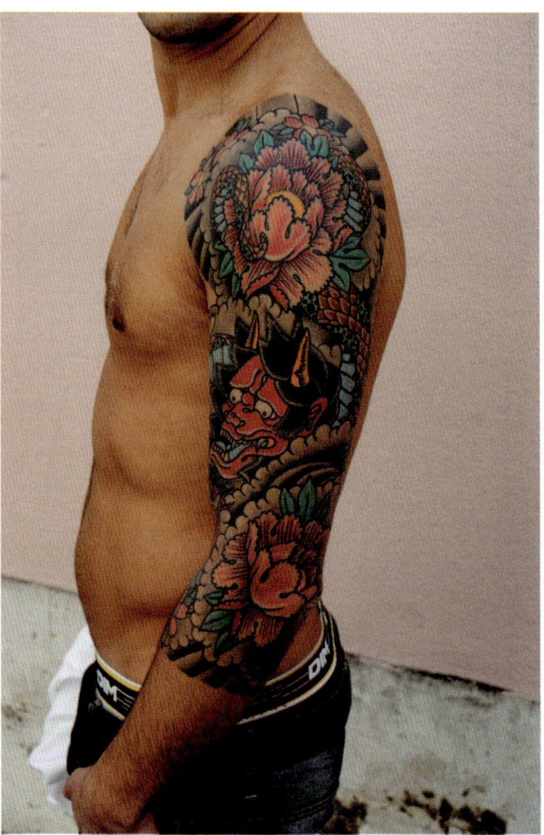

Pedro.soos
Ohana Tattoo Company
www.tattoosbypedro.org

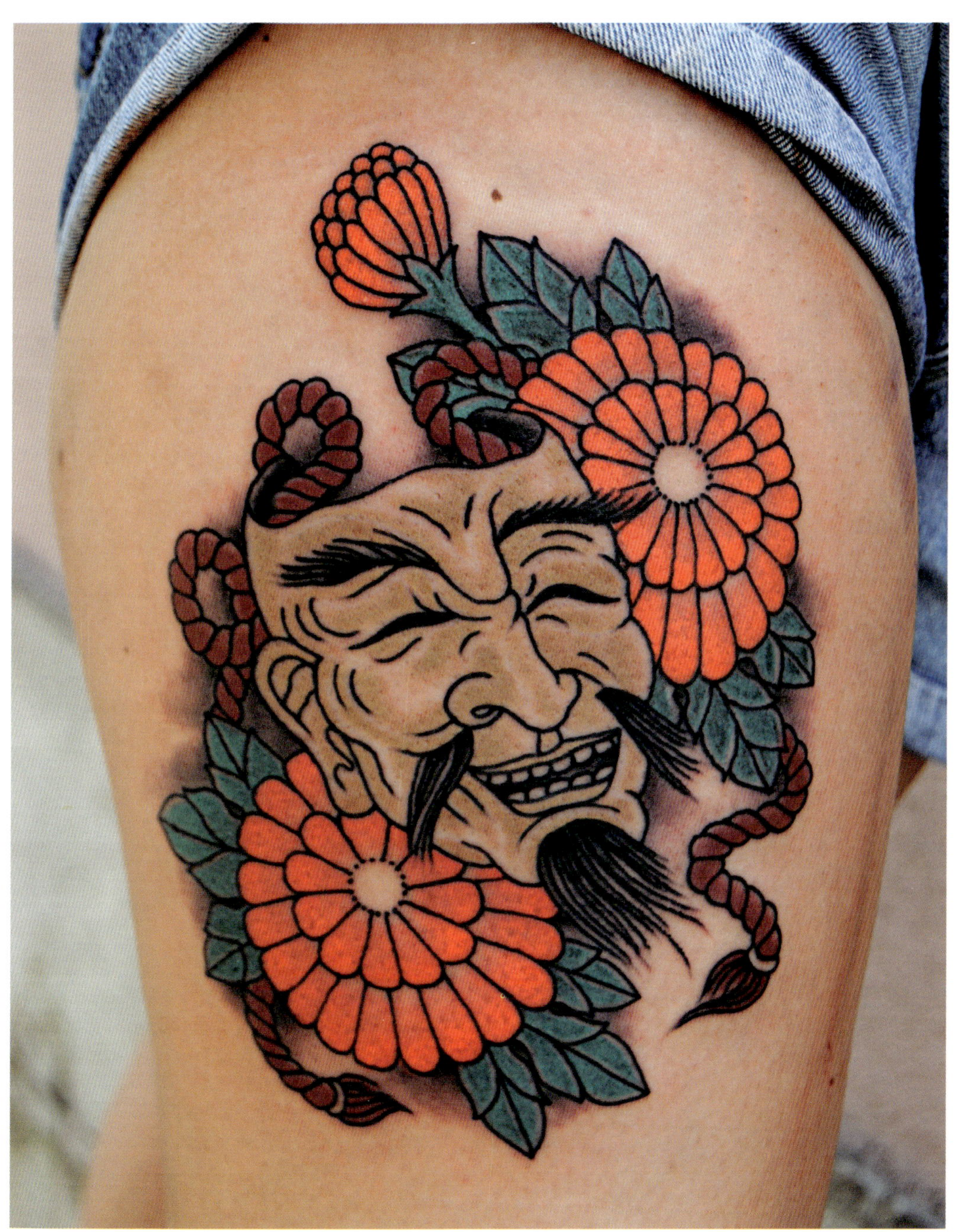

Pedro.soos
Ohana Tattoo Company
www.tattoosbypedro.org

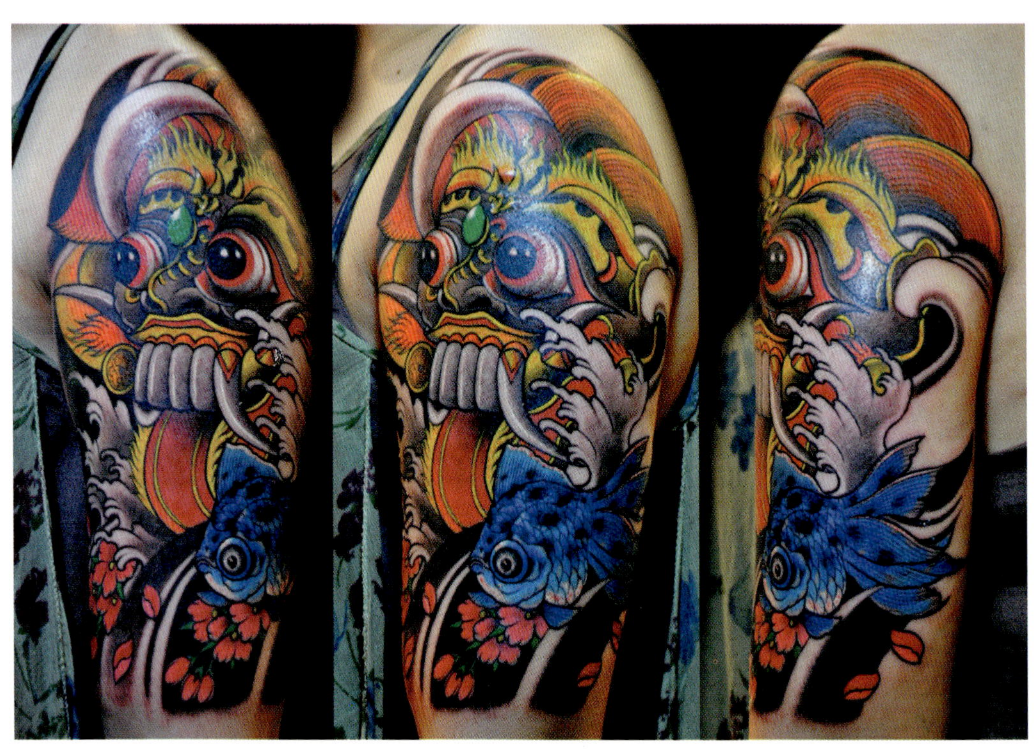

Tang Ping
Zi You Tattoo
www.myspace.com/ziyoutattoo

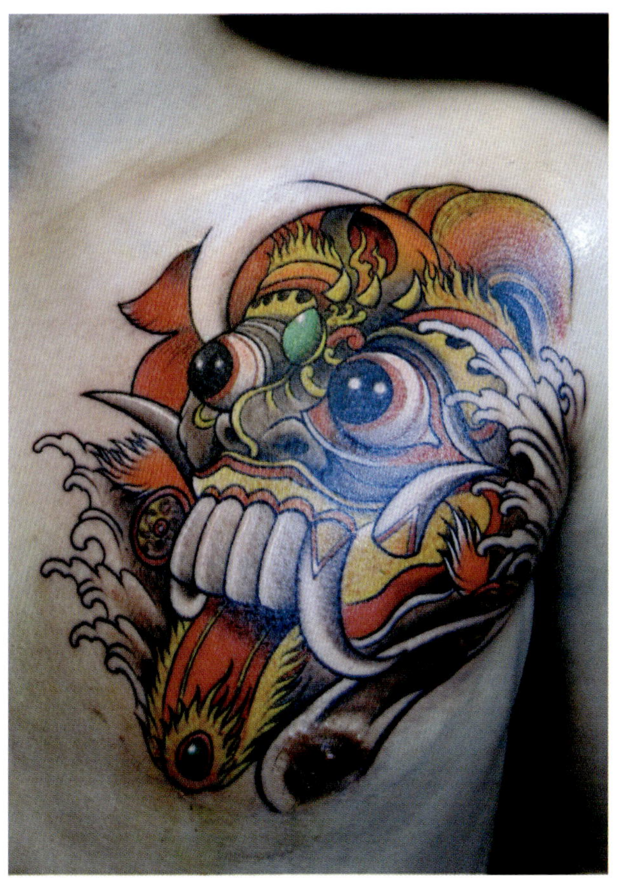

Tang Ping
Zi You Tattoo
www.myspace.com/ziyoutattoo

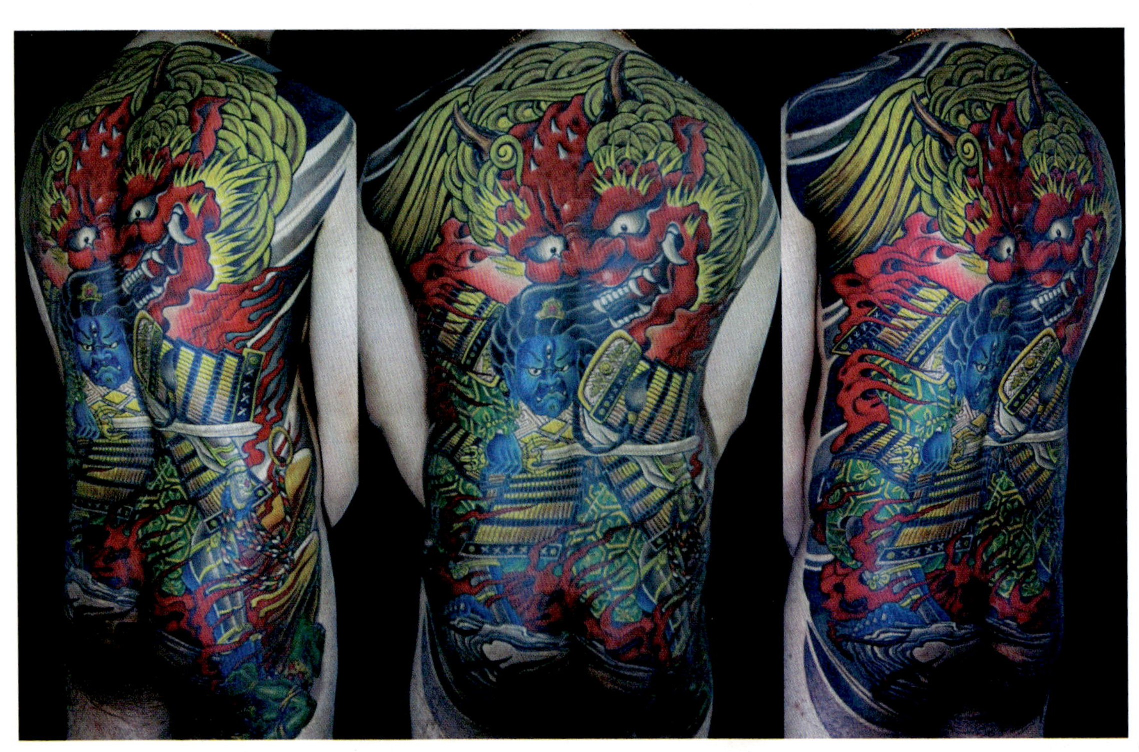

Tang Ping
Zi You Tattoo
www.myspace.com/ziyoutattoo

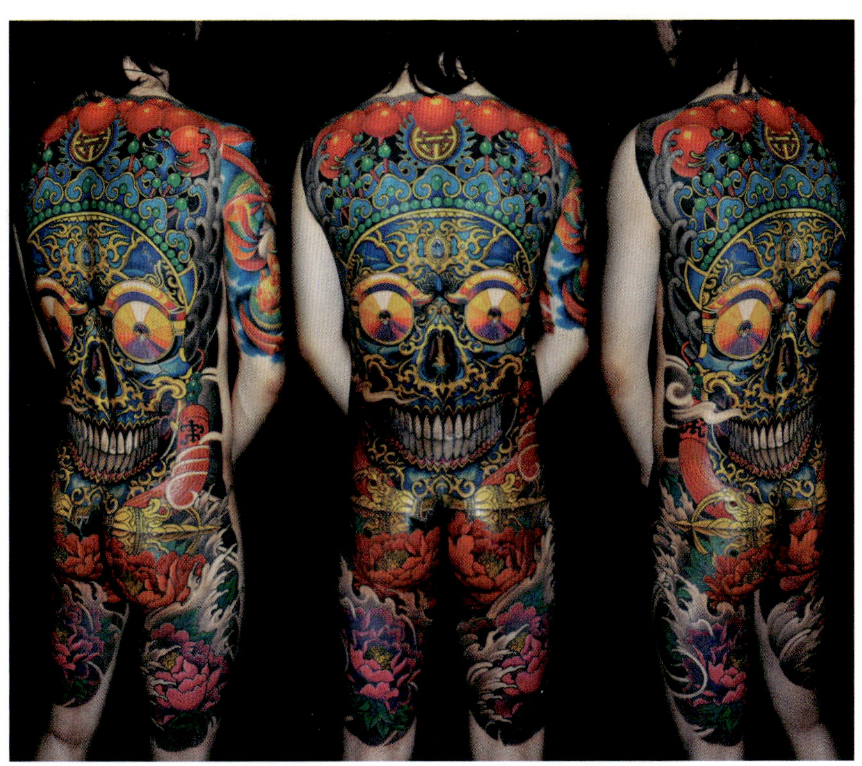

Tang Ping
Zi You Tattoo
www.myspace.com/ziyoutattoo

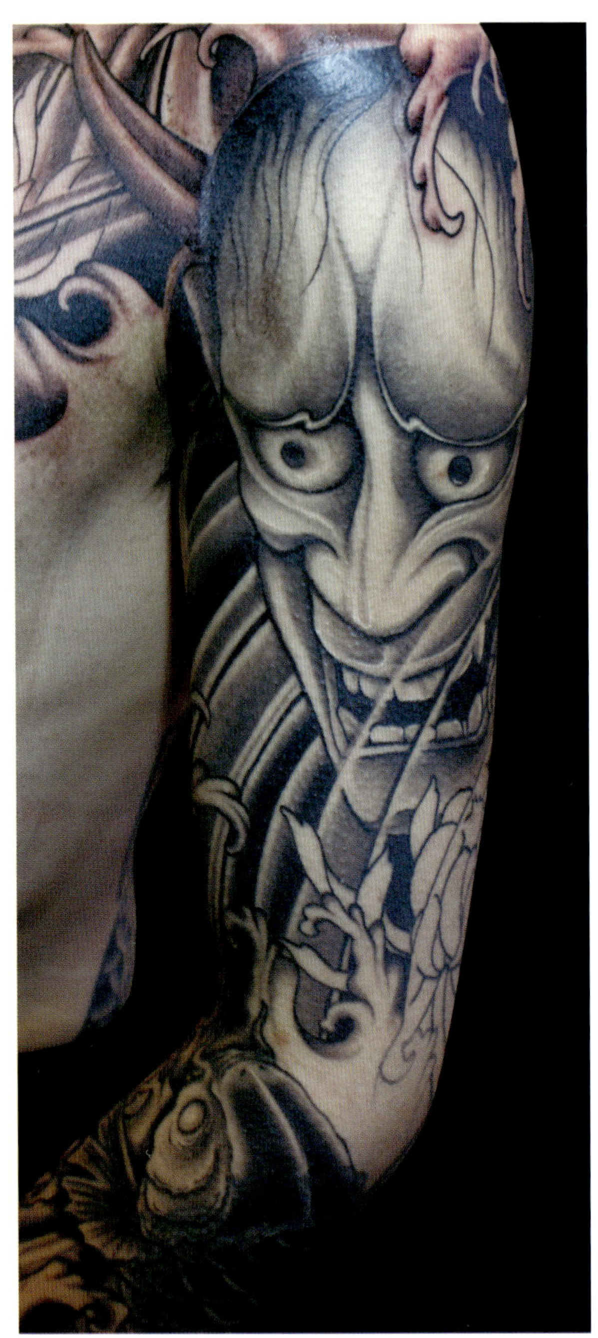

Satoshi Ohata
T3-Tattoos
www.t3-tattoos.com

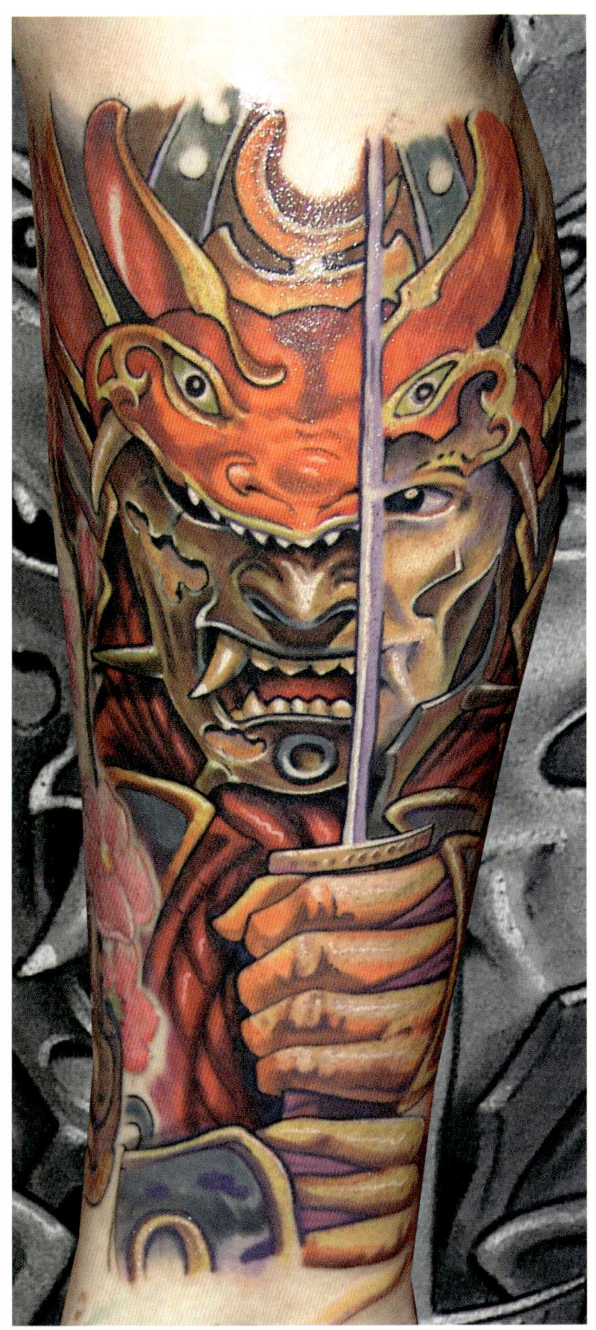

Zsolt
Dark Art Tattoo
www.darkart.hu

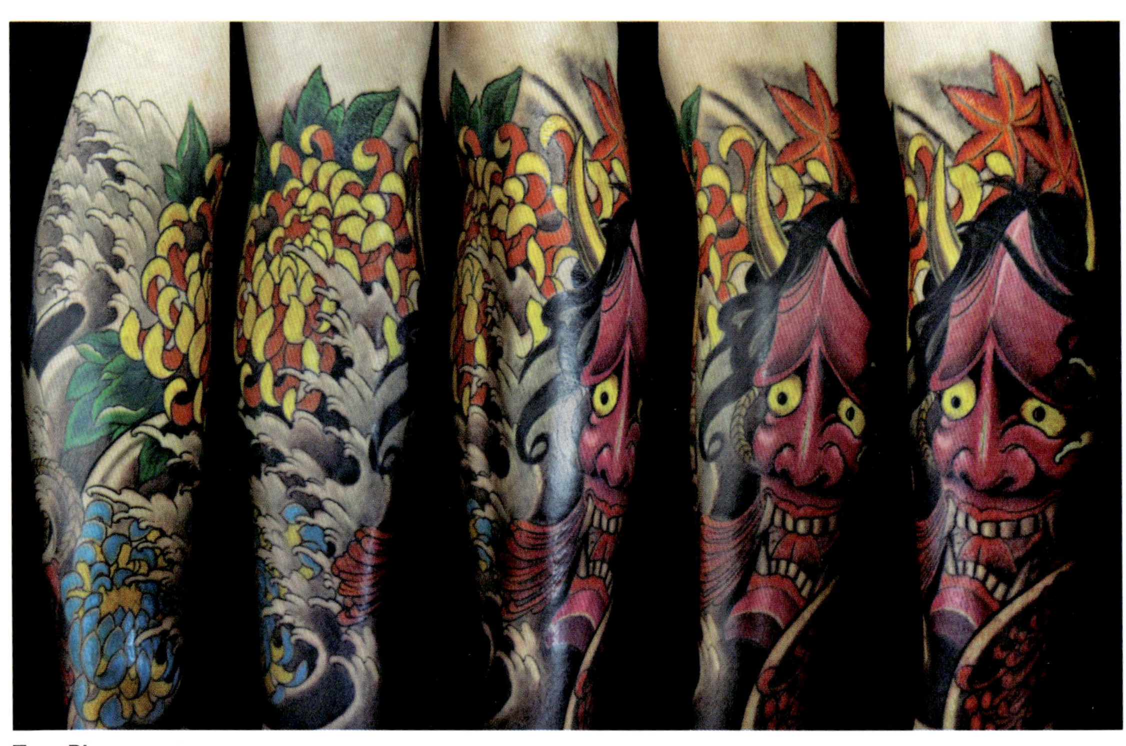

Tang Ping
Zi You Tattoo
www.myspace.com/ziyoutattoo

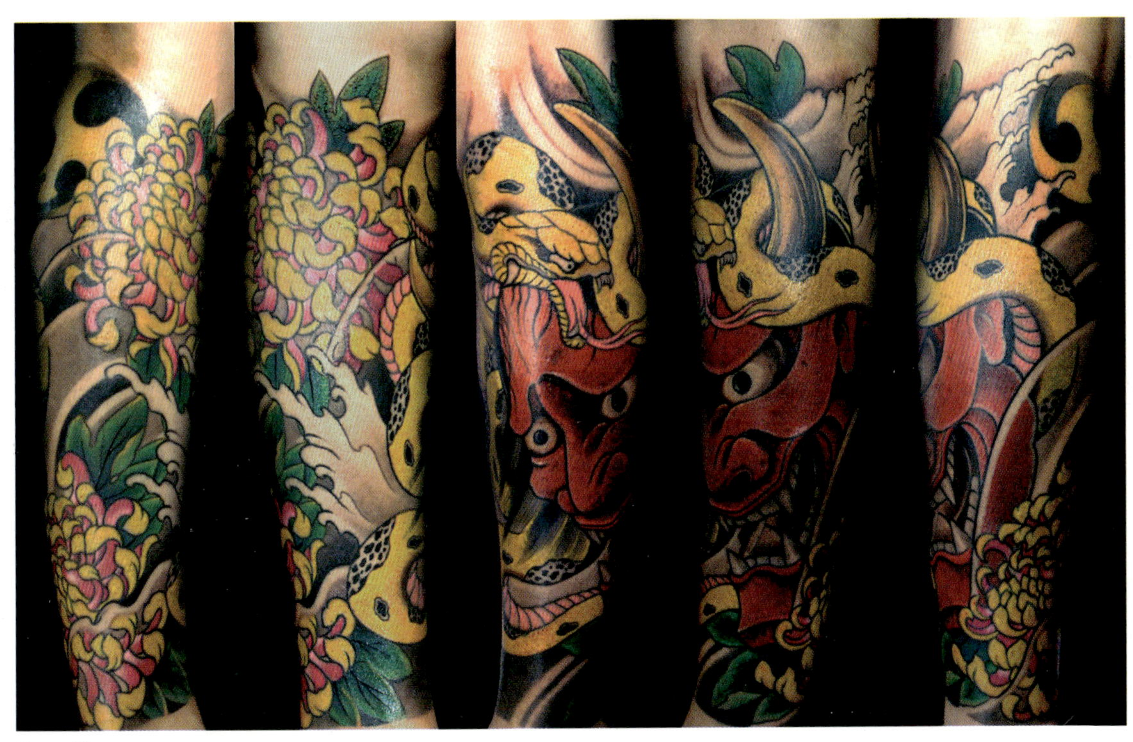

Tang Ping
Zi You Tattoo
www.myspace.com/ziyoutattoo

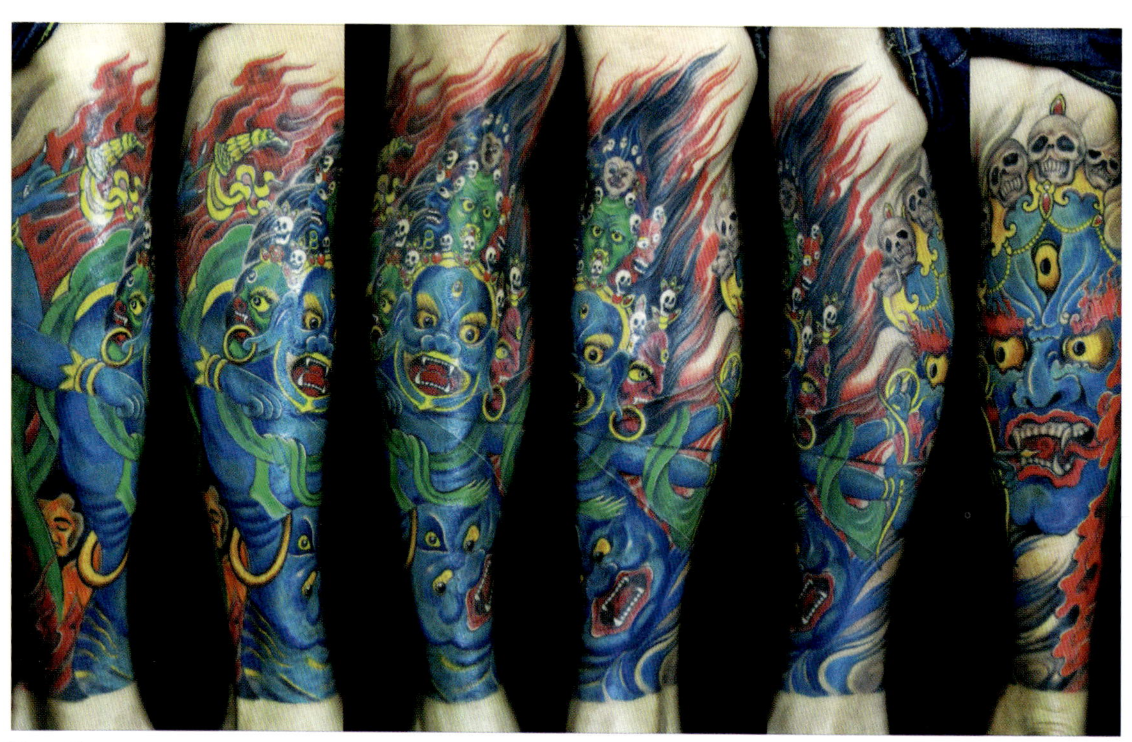

Tang Ping
Zi You Tattoo
www.myspace.com/ziyoutattoo

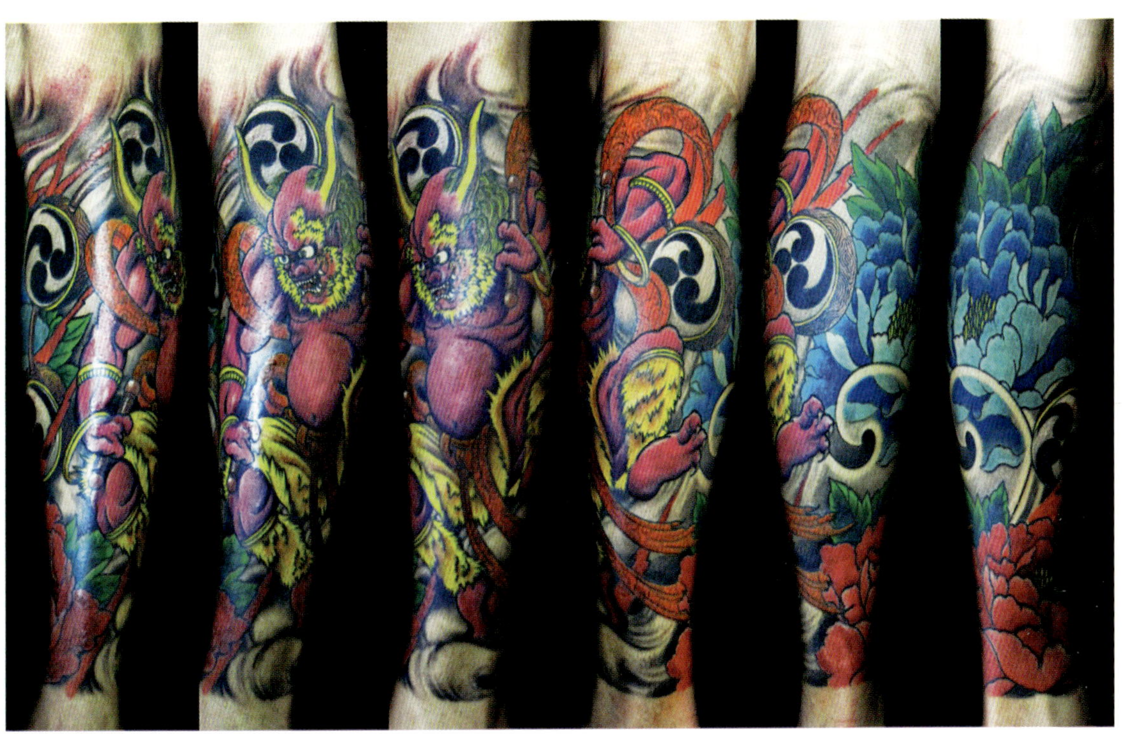

Tang Ping
Zi You Tattoo
www.myspace.com/ziyoutattoo

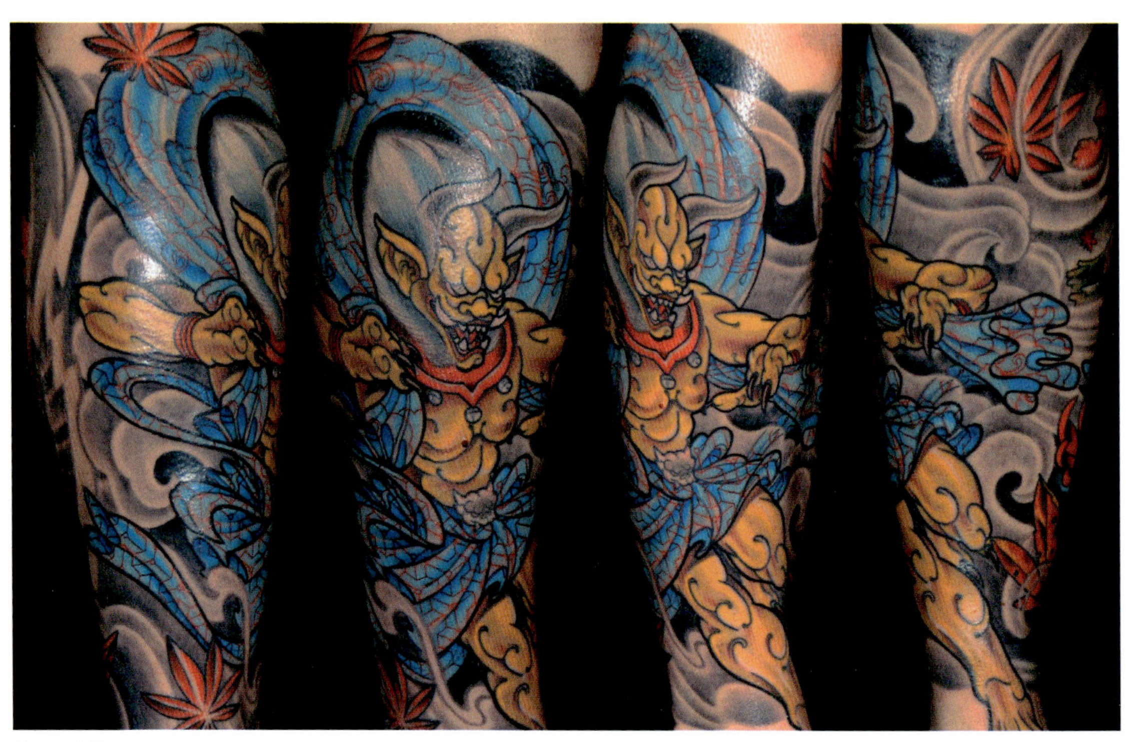

Terry Ribera
Remington Tattoo
www.terryribera.com

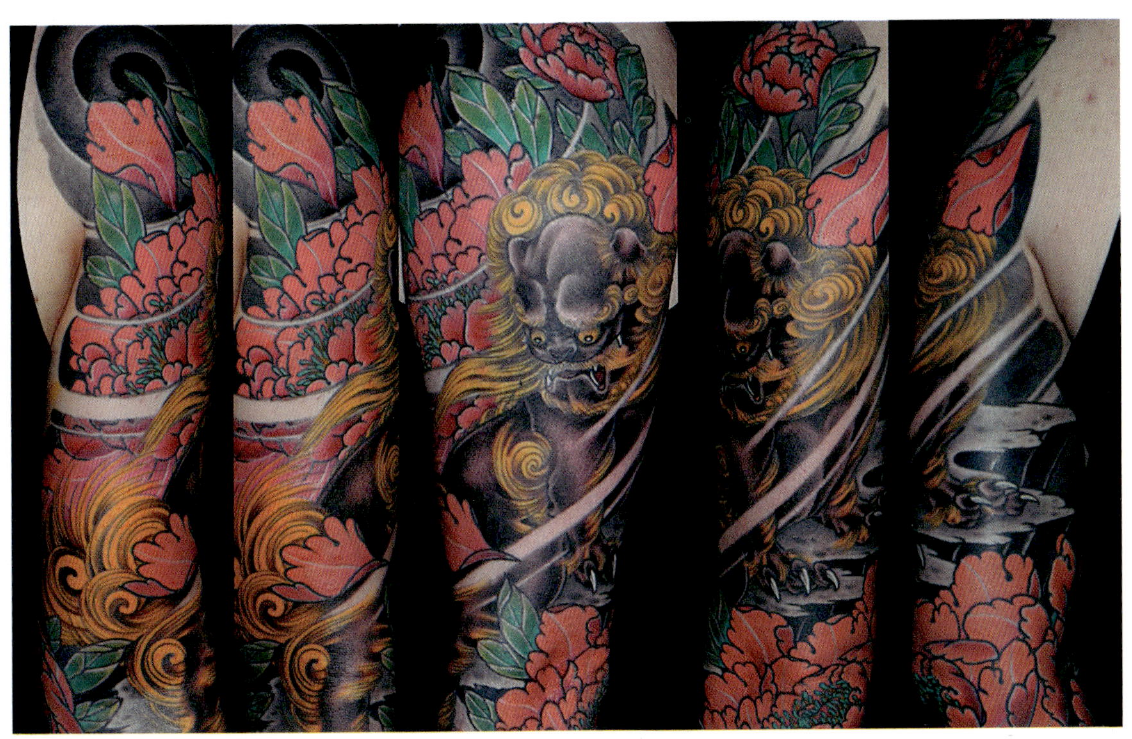

Carl Corson
Studio King Carlos Tattoo
www.kingcarlostattoo.com

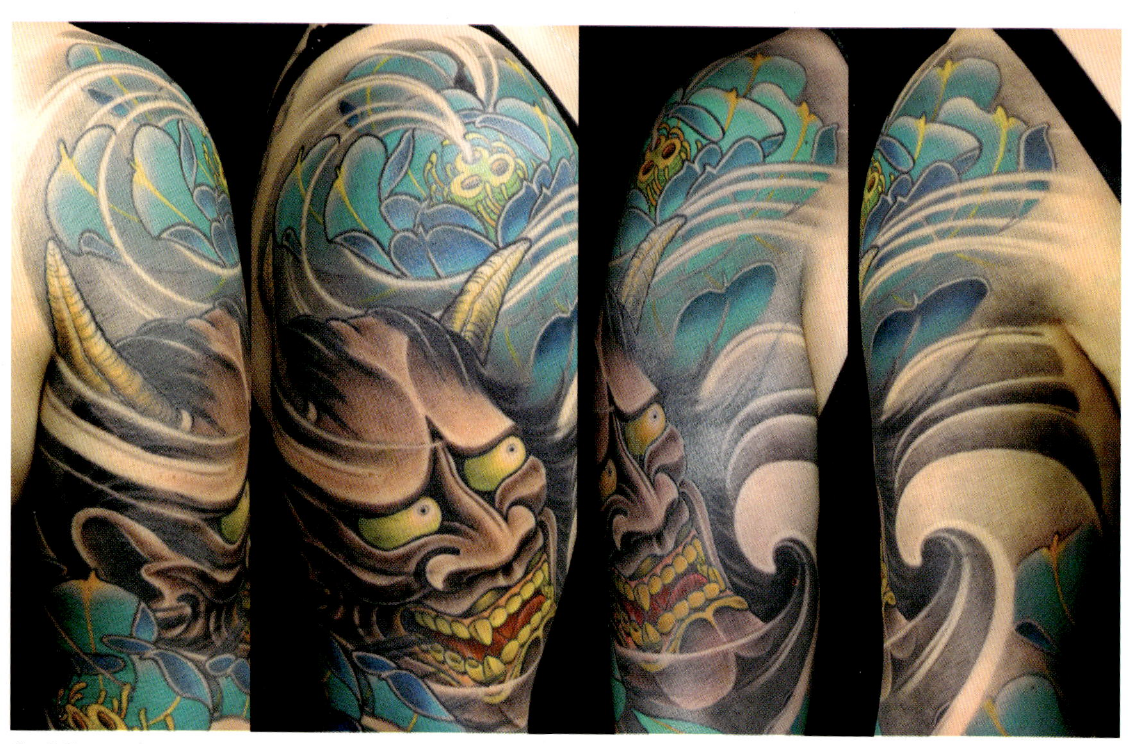

Carl Corson
Studio King Carlos Tattoo
www.kingcarlostattoo.com

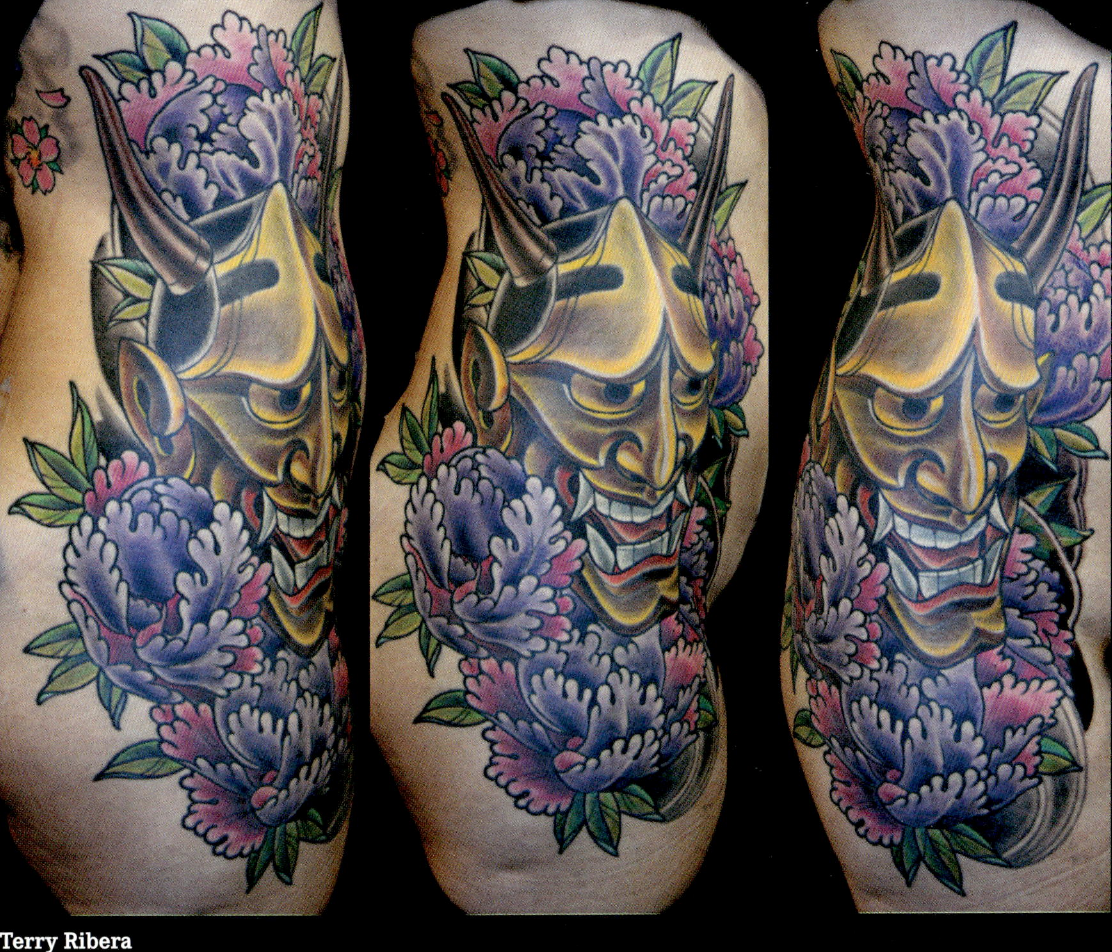

Terry Ribera
Remington Tattoo

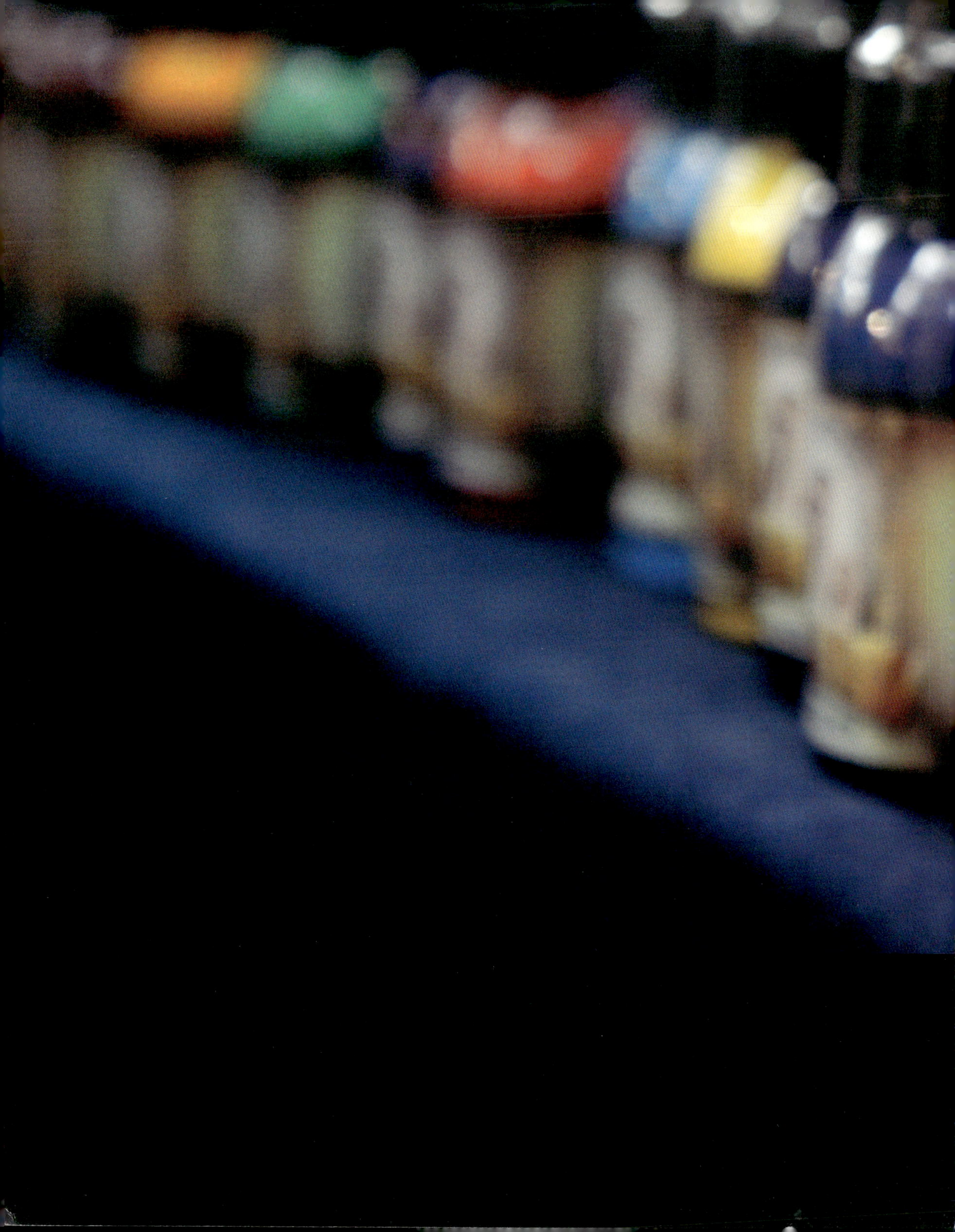

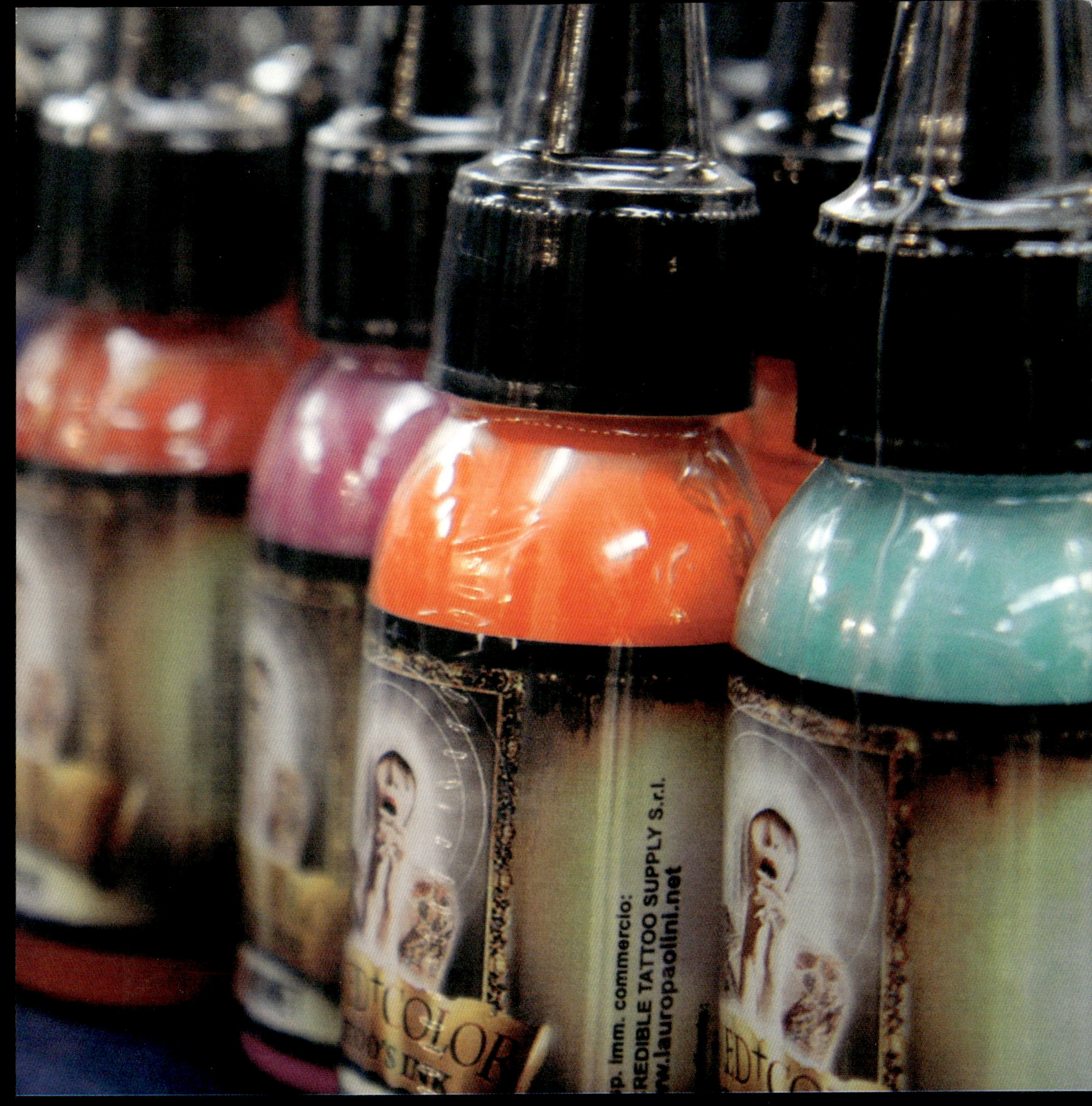

PHOTOGRAPHES

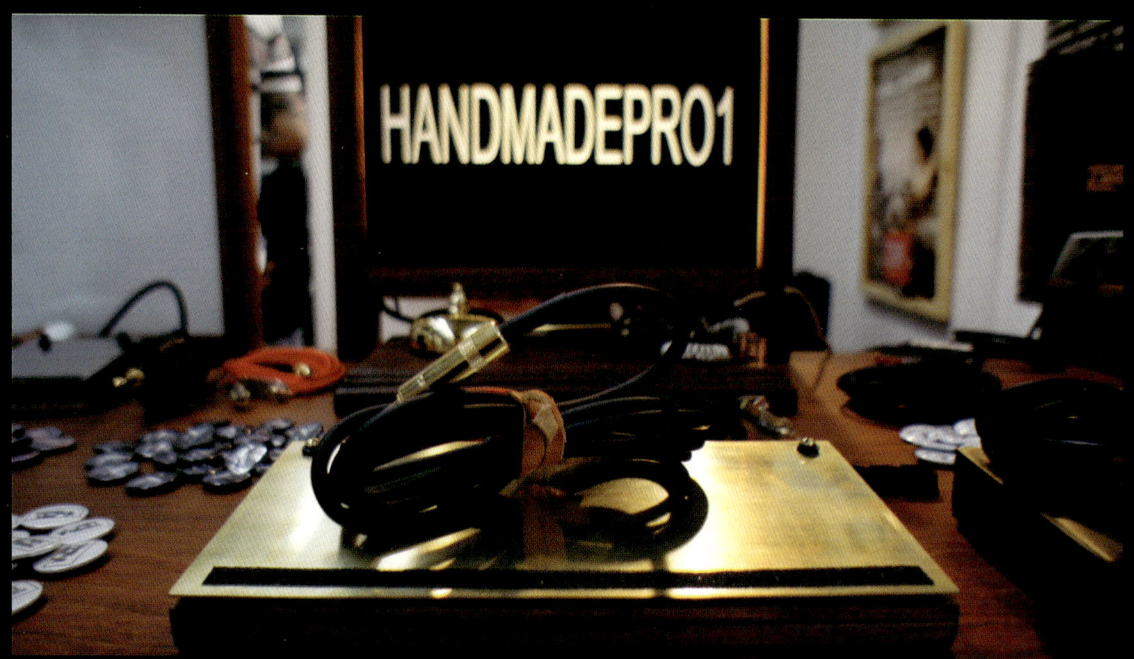

Louise Brix

www.linkedin.com/pub/louise-brix/1/786/36a

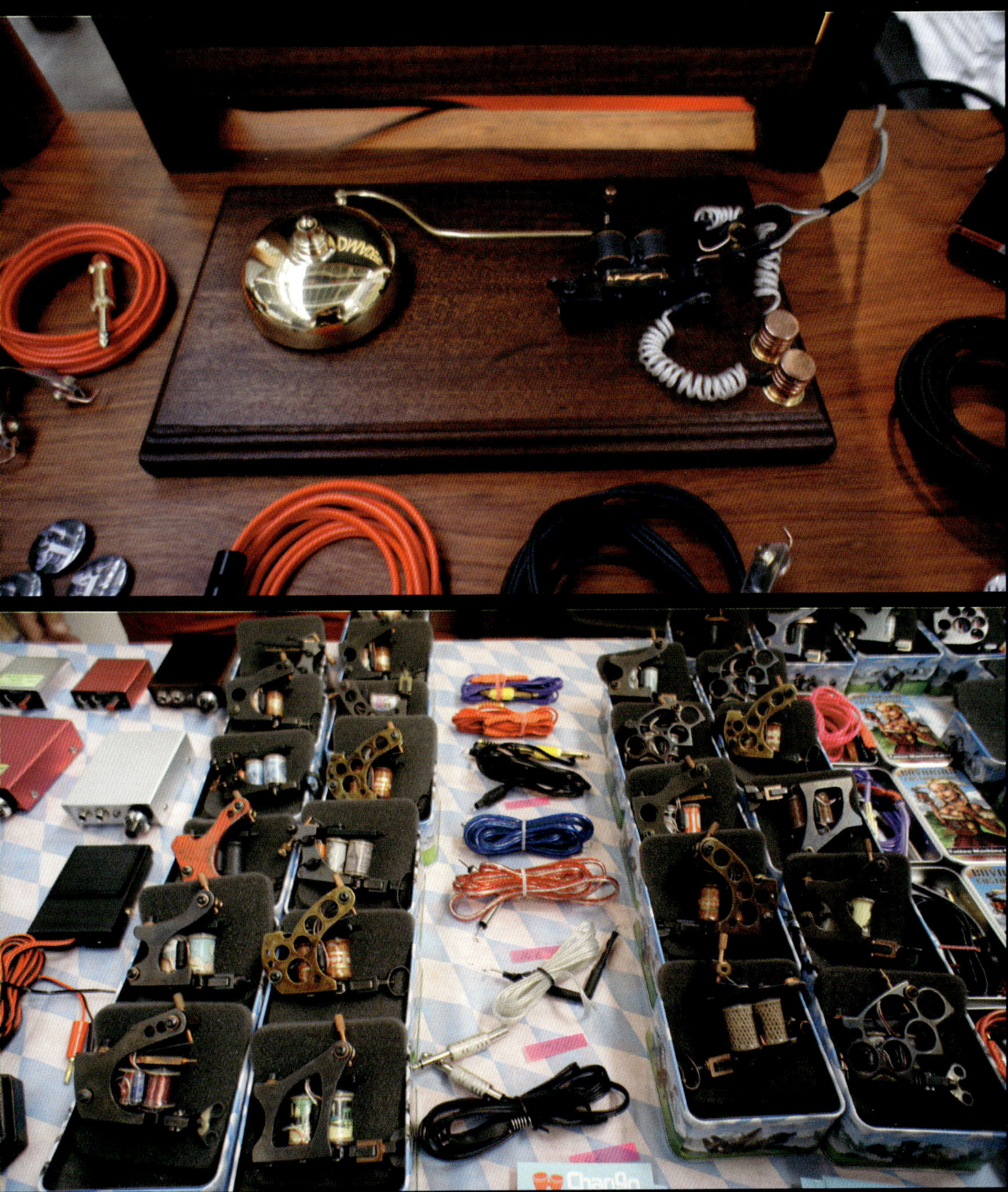

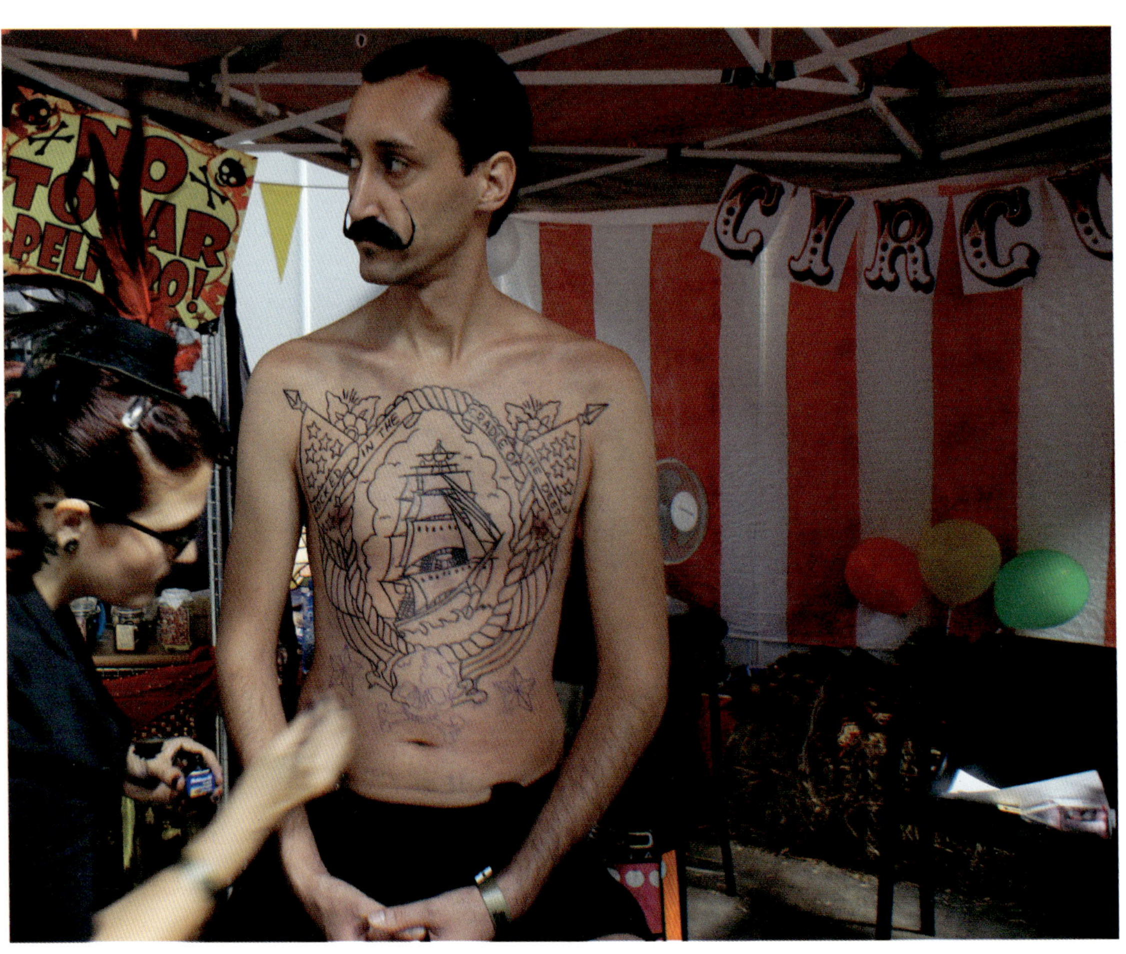
NO
CIRC

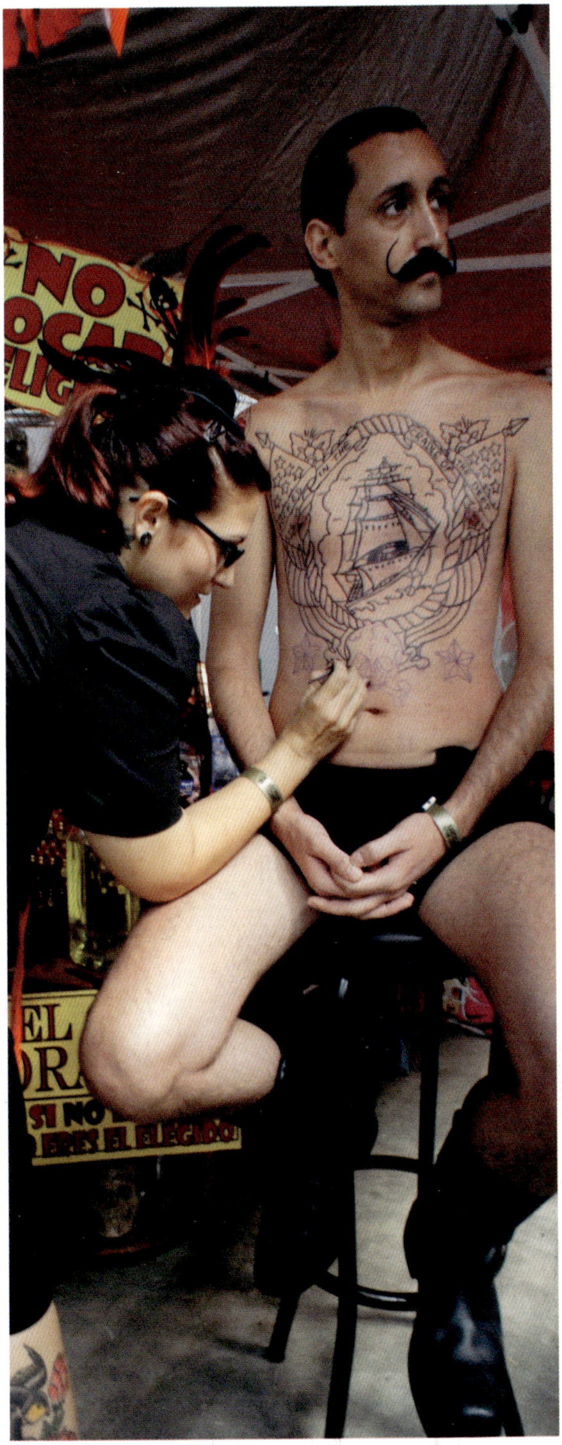

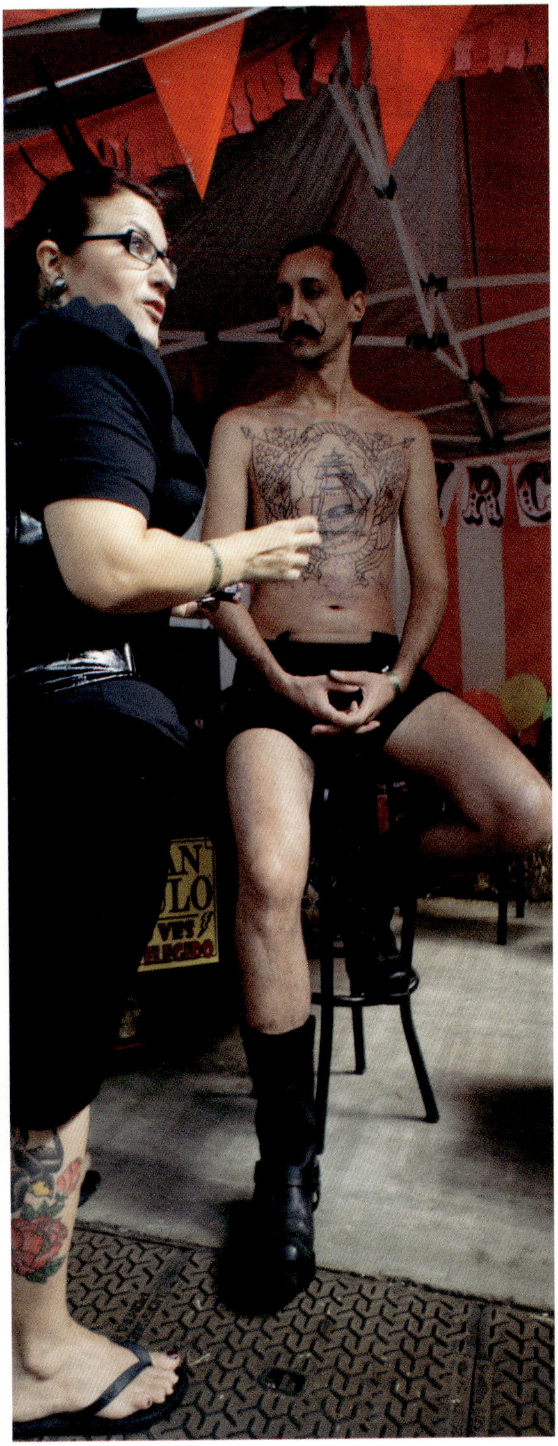

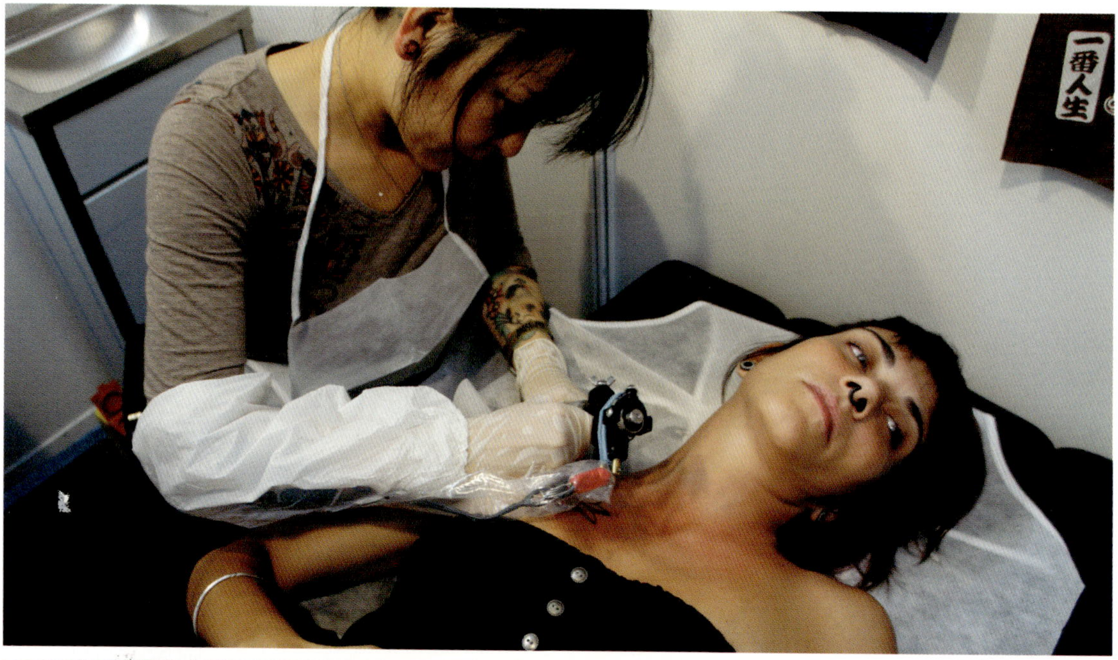

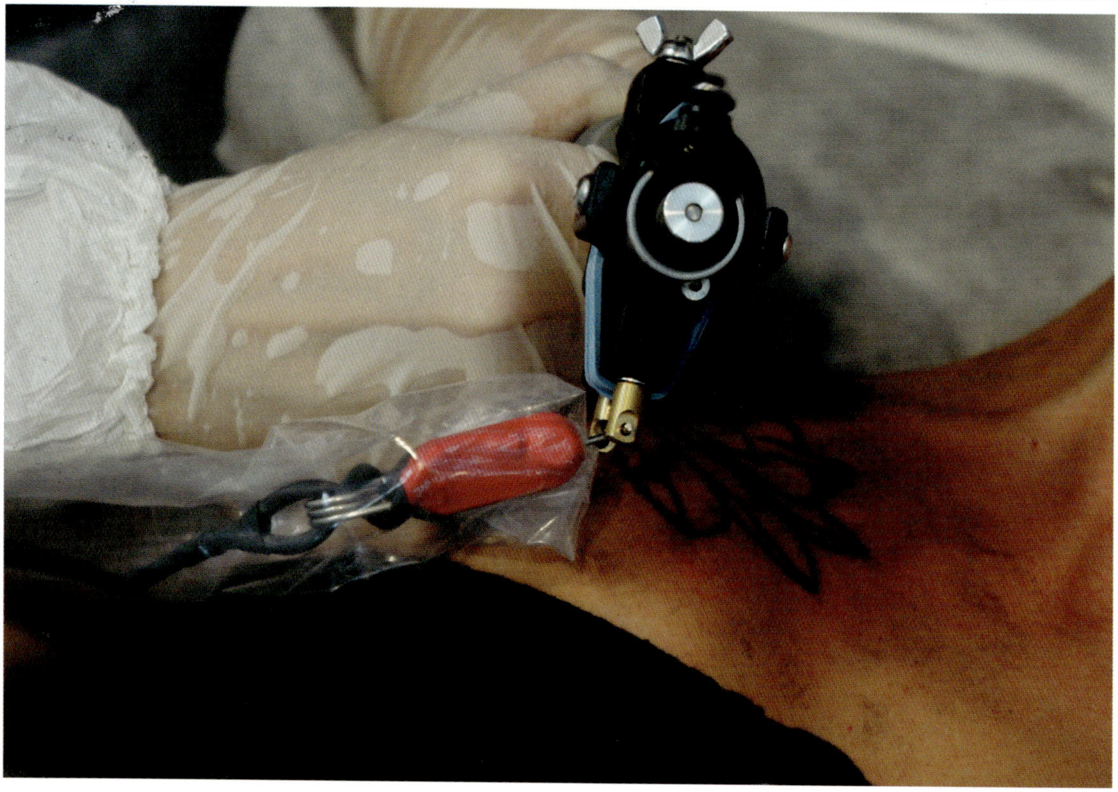

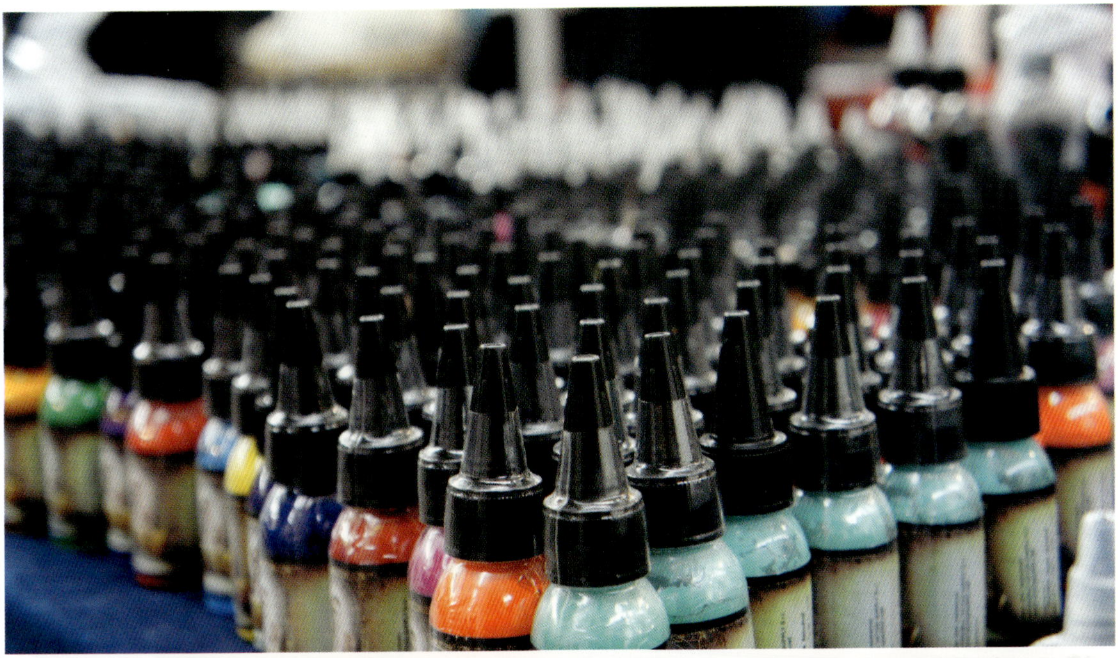

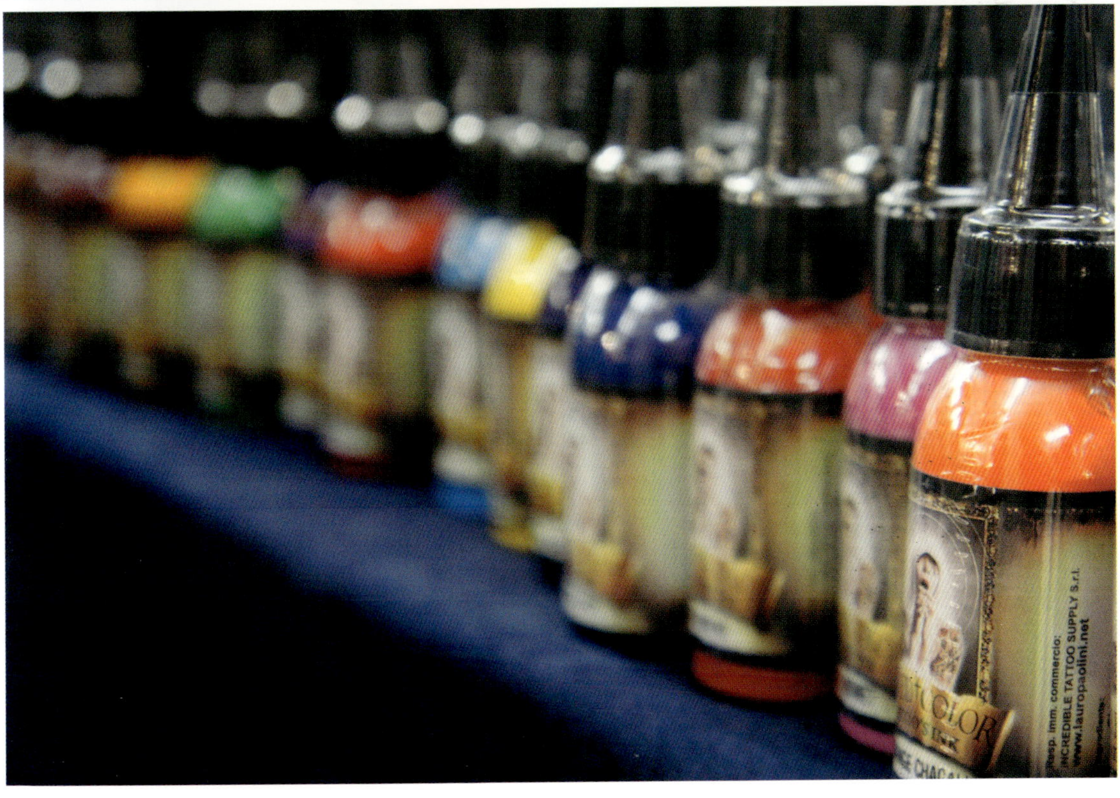

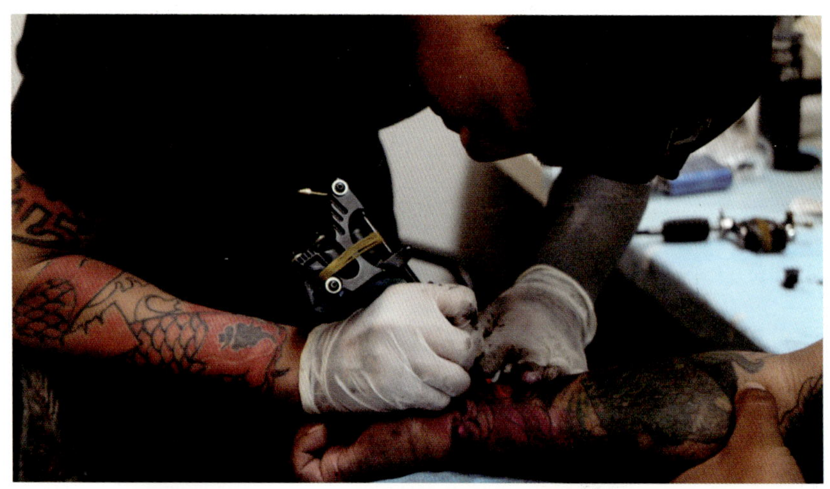

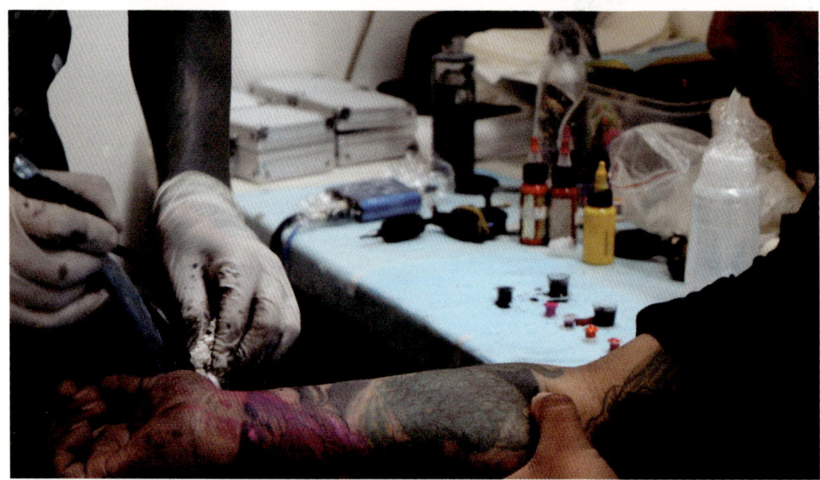

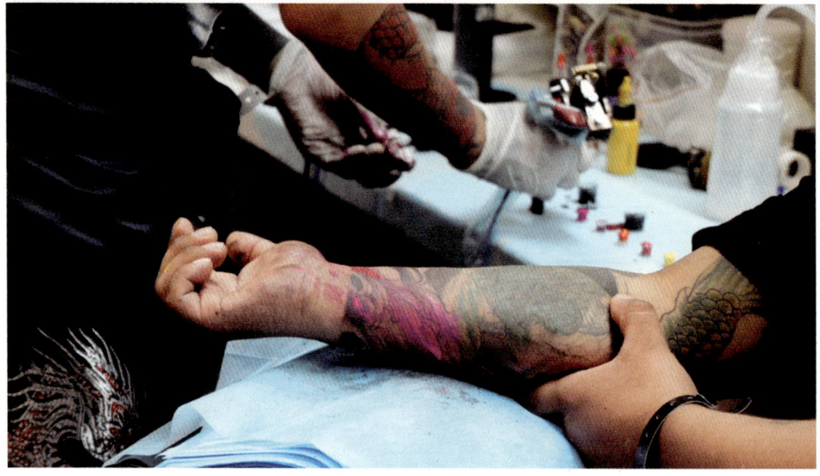

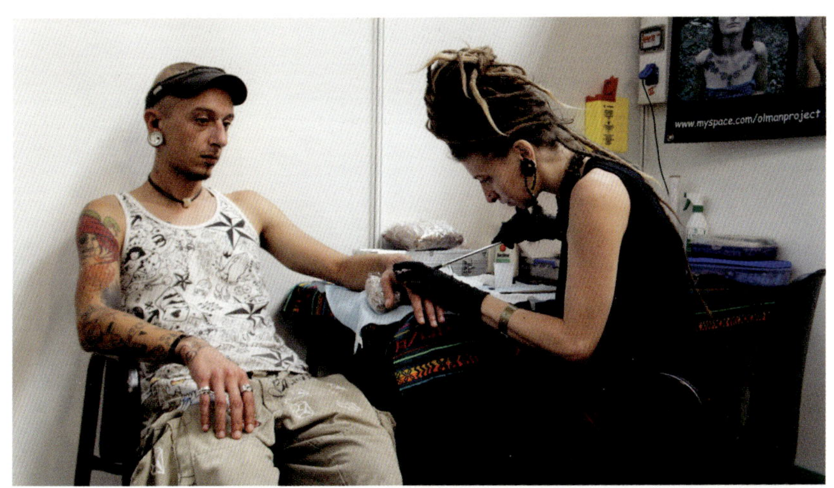
www.myspace.com/olmanproject

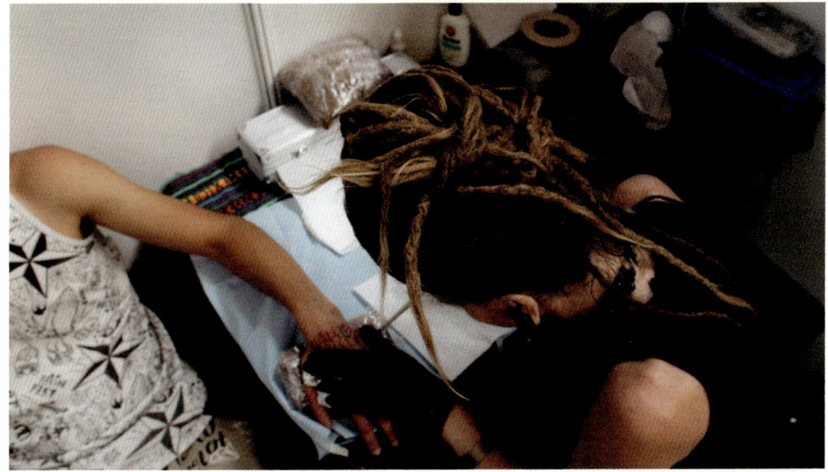

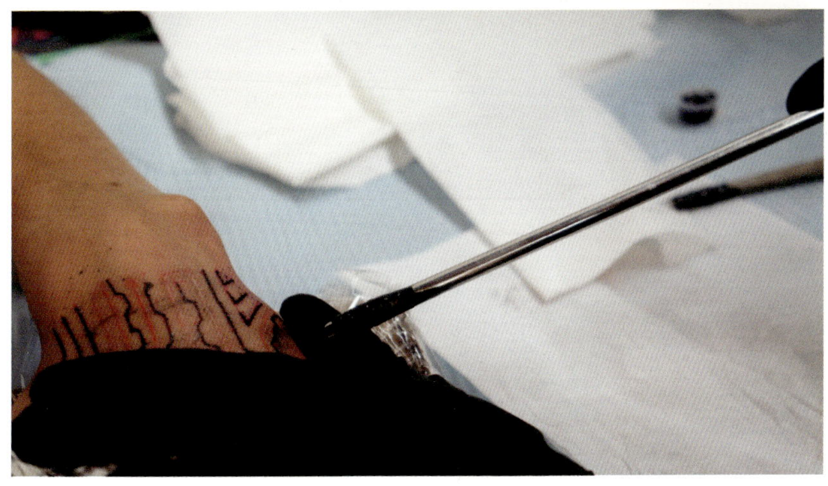

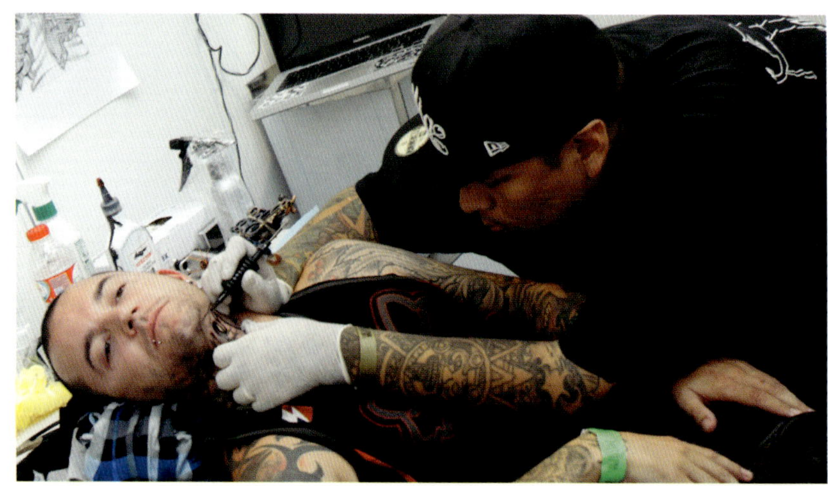
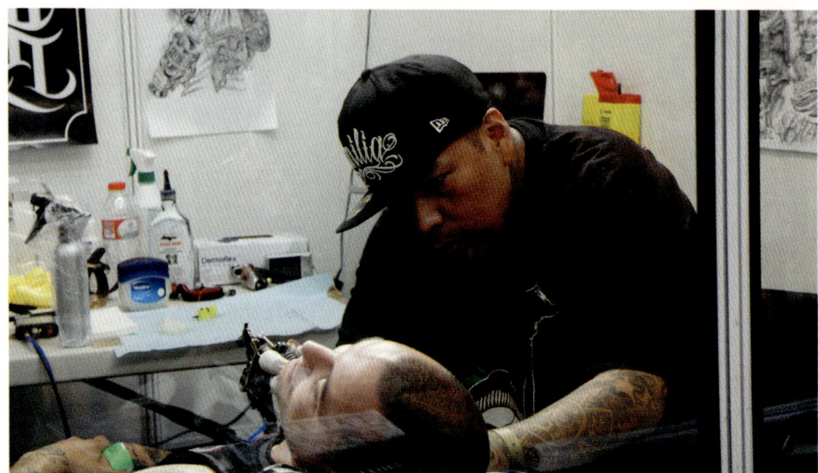
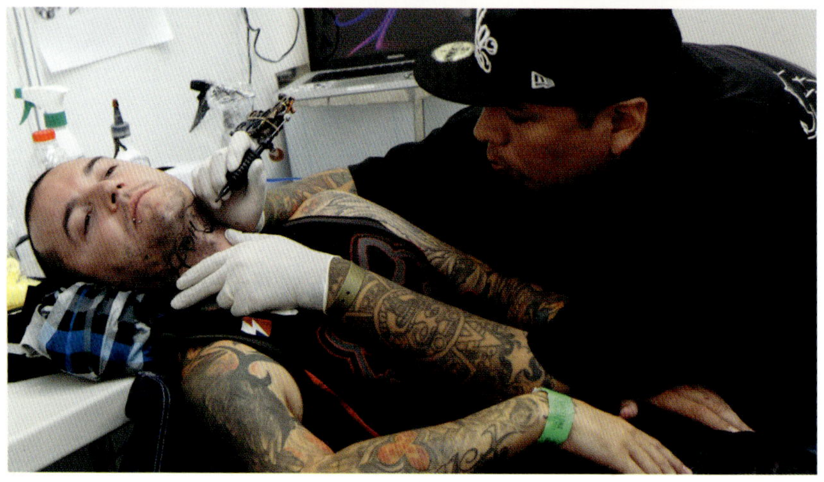

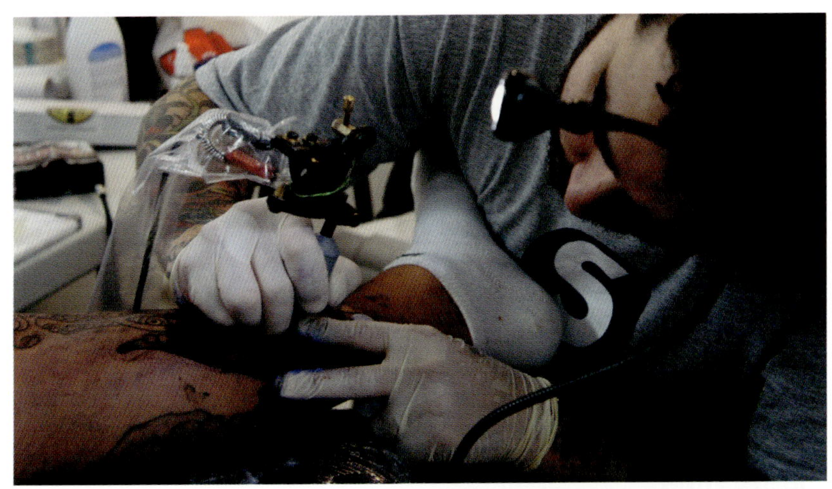

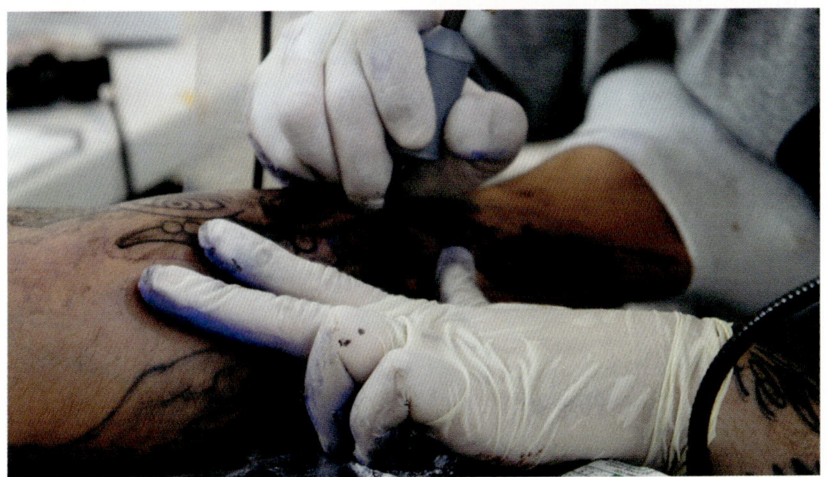

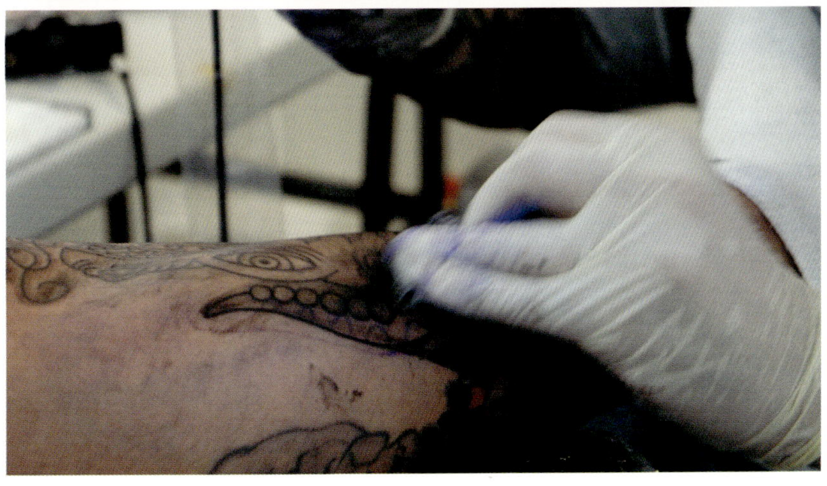

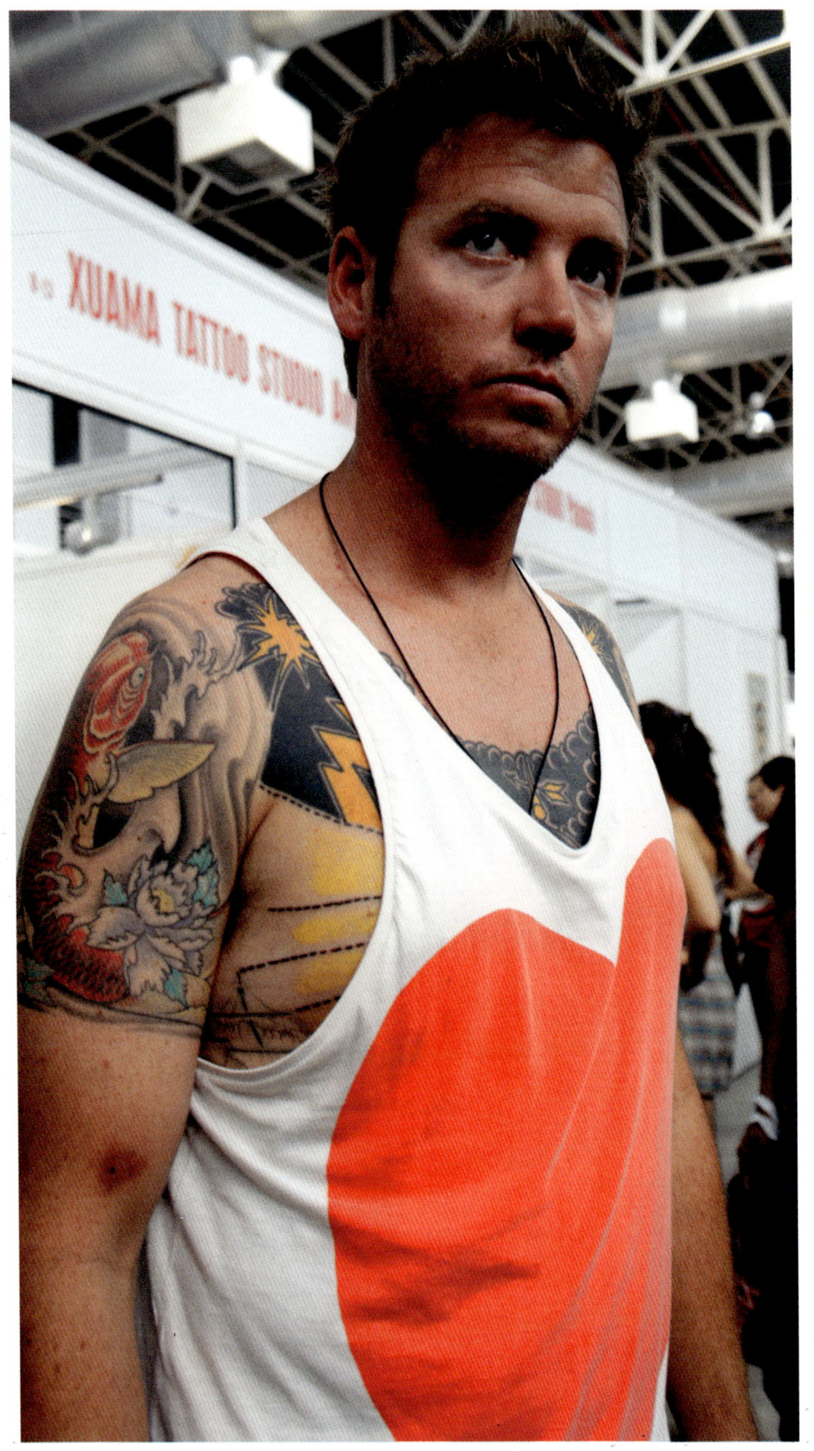
XUAMA TATTOO STUDIO

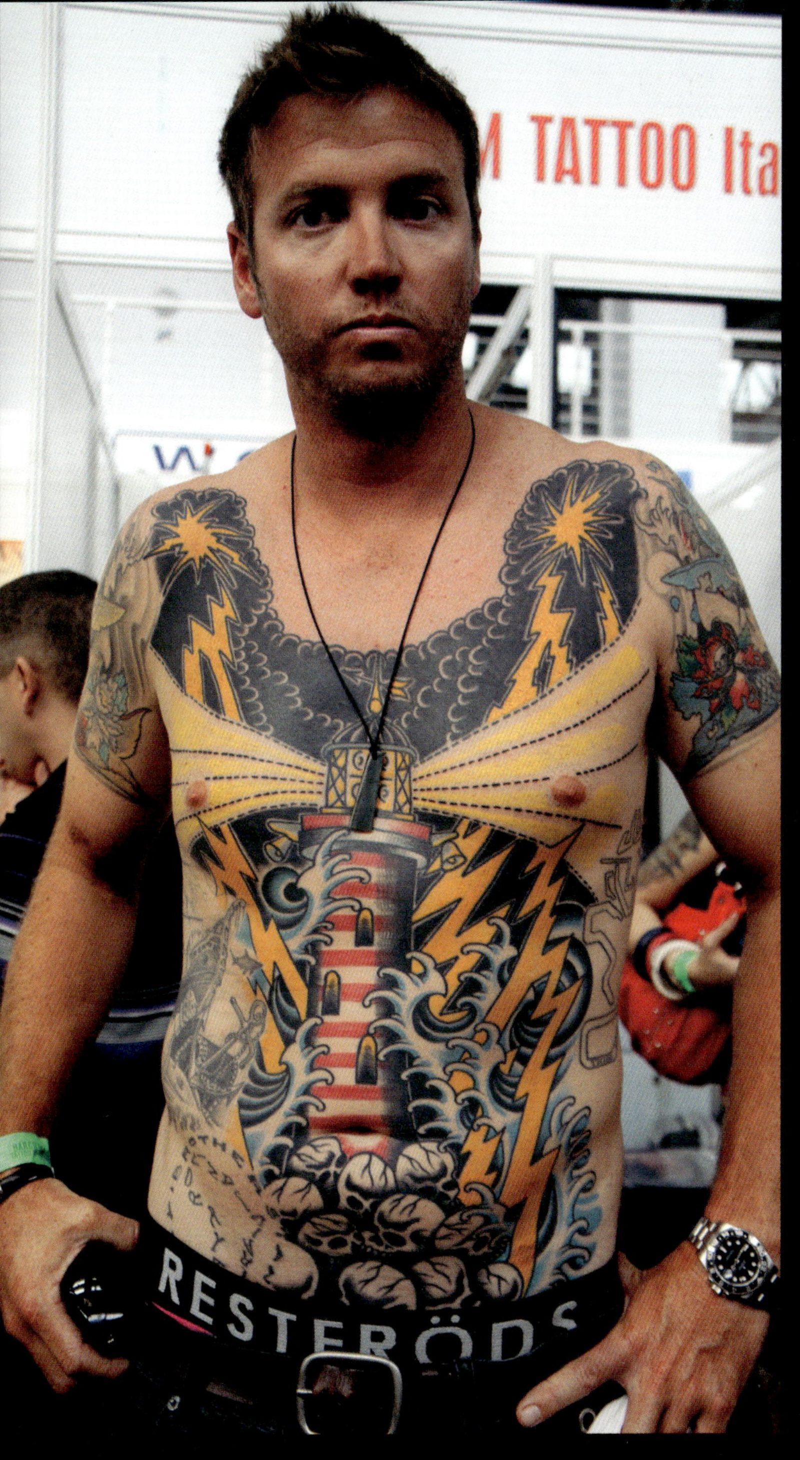
M TATTOO Ita
RESTERÖDS

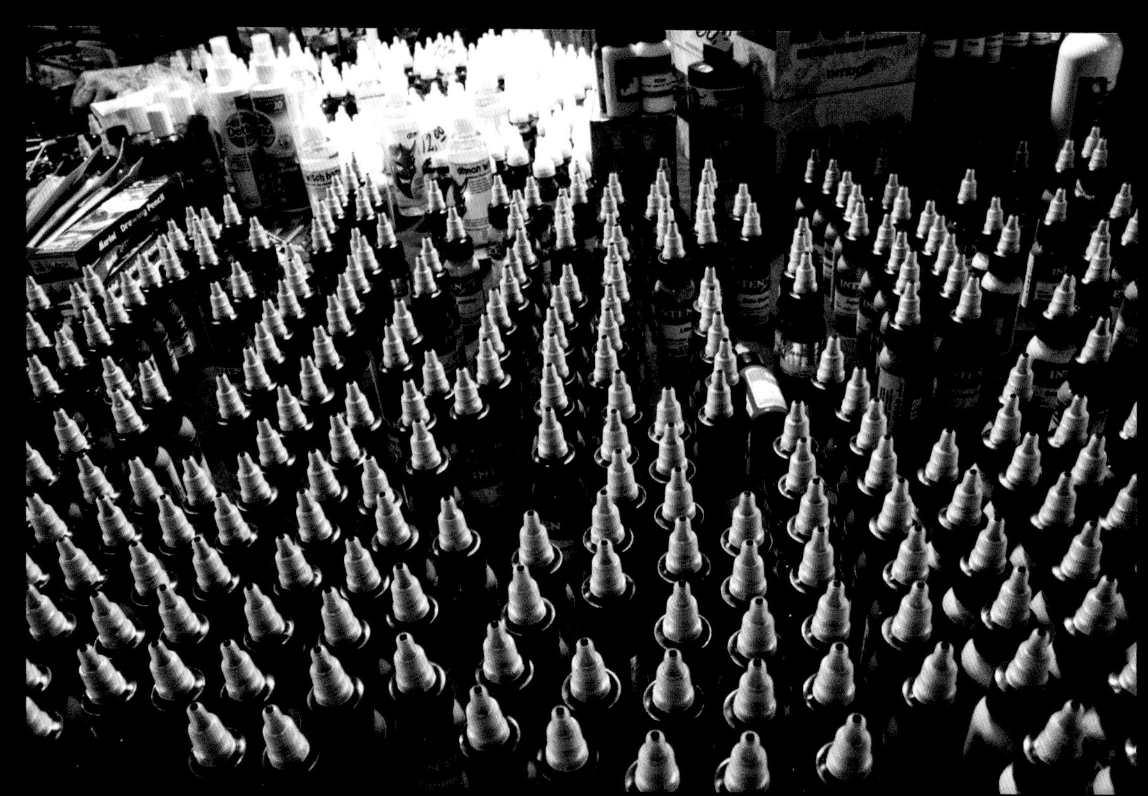

Ergo

www.wix.com/ergofashionphoto/one

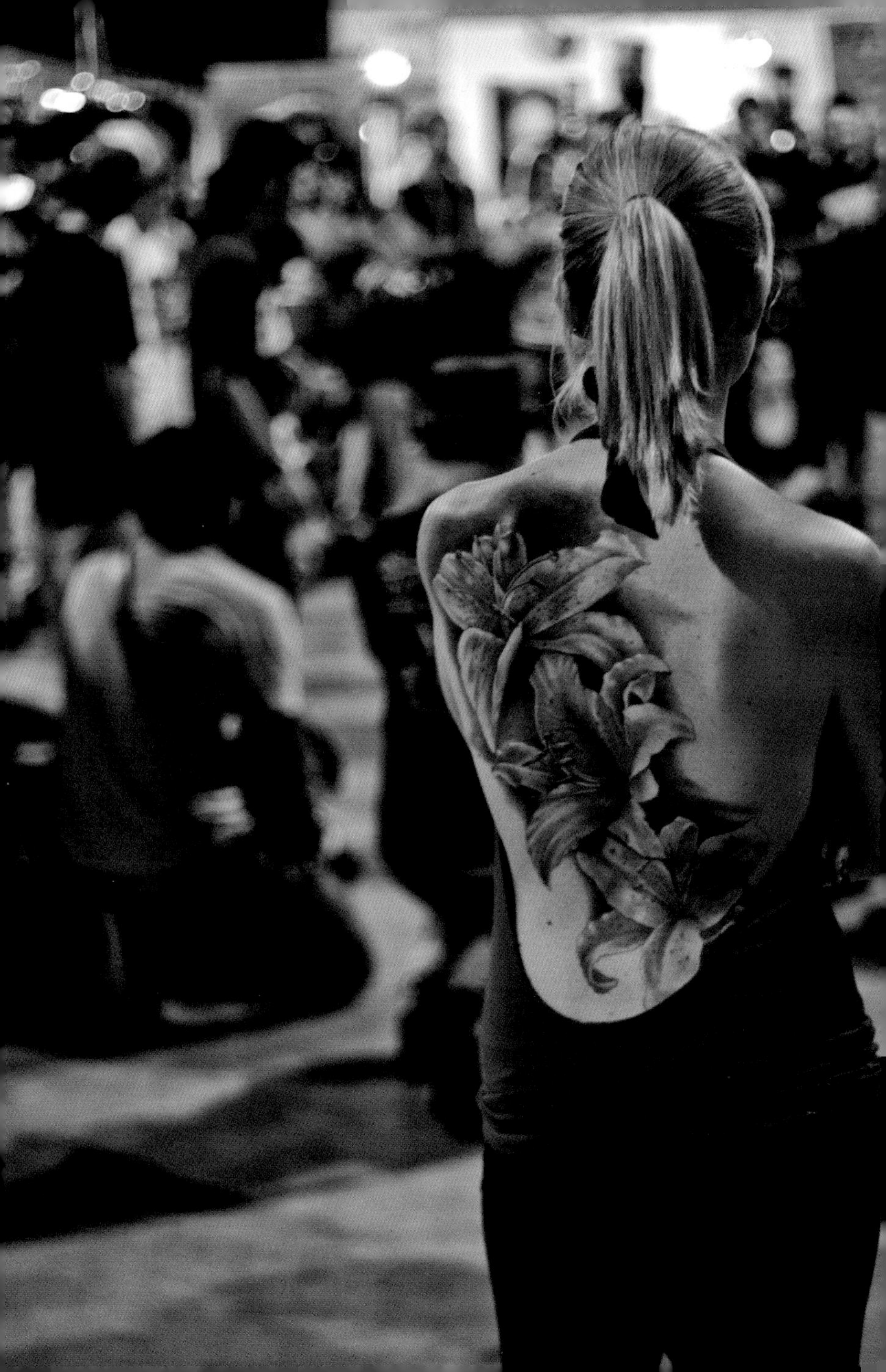

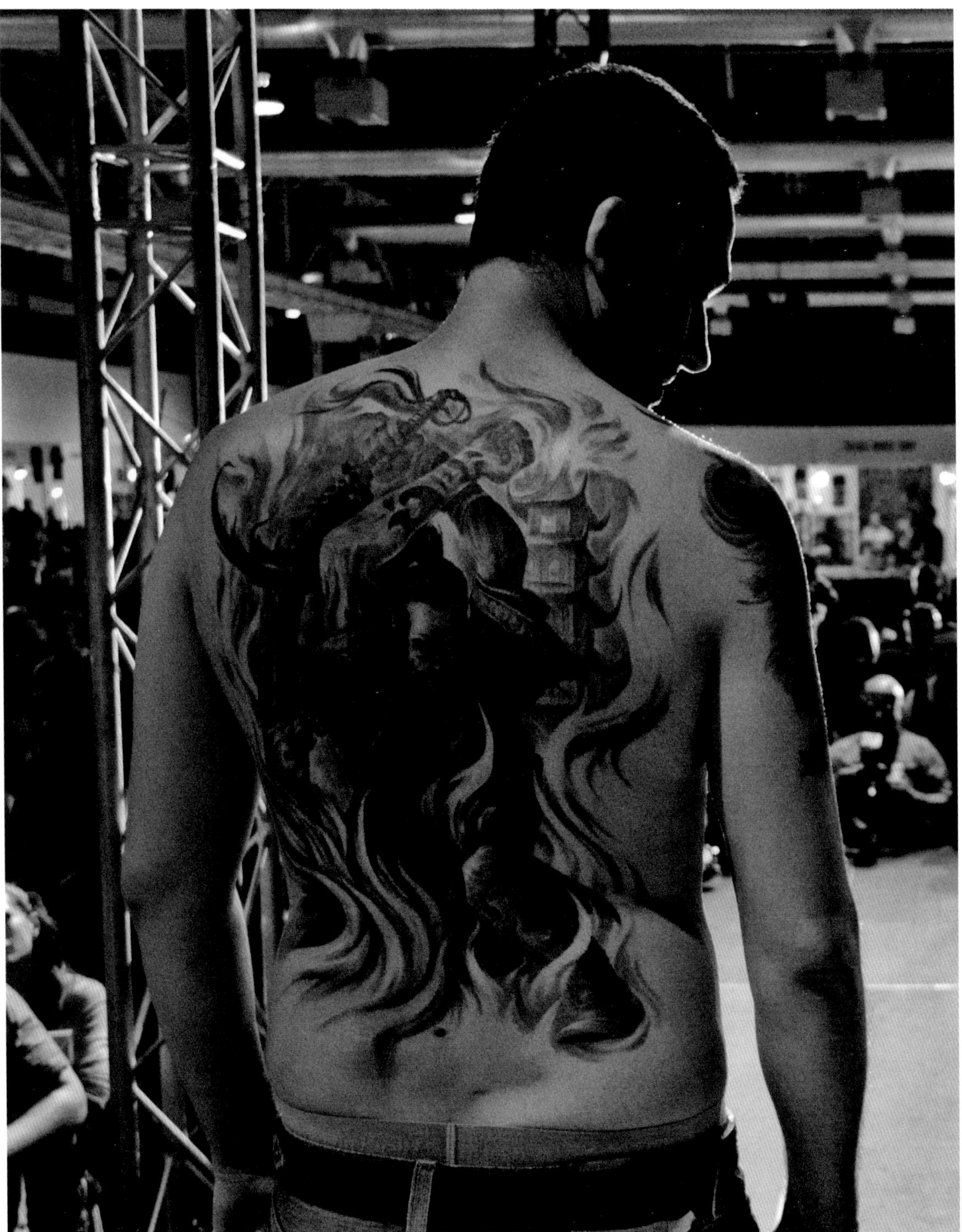

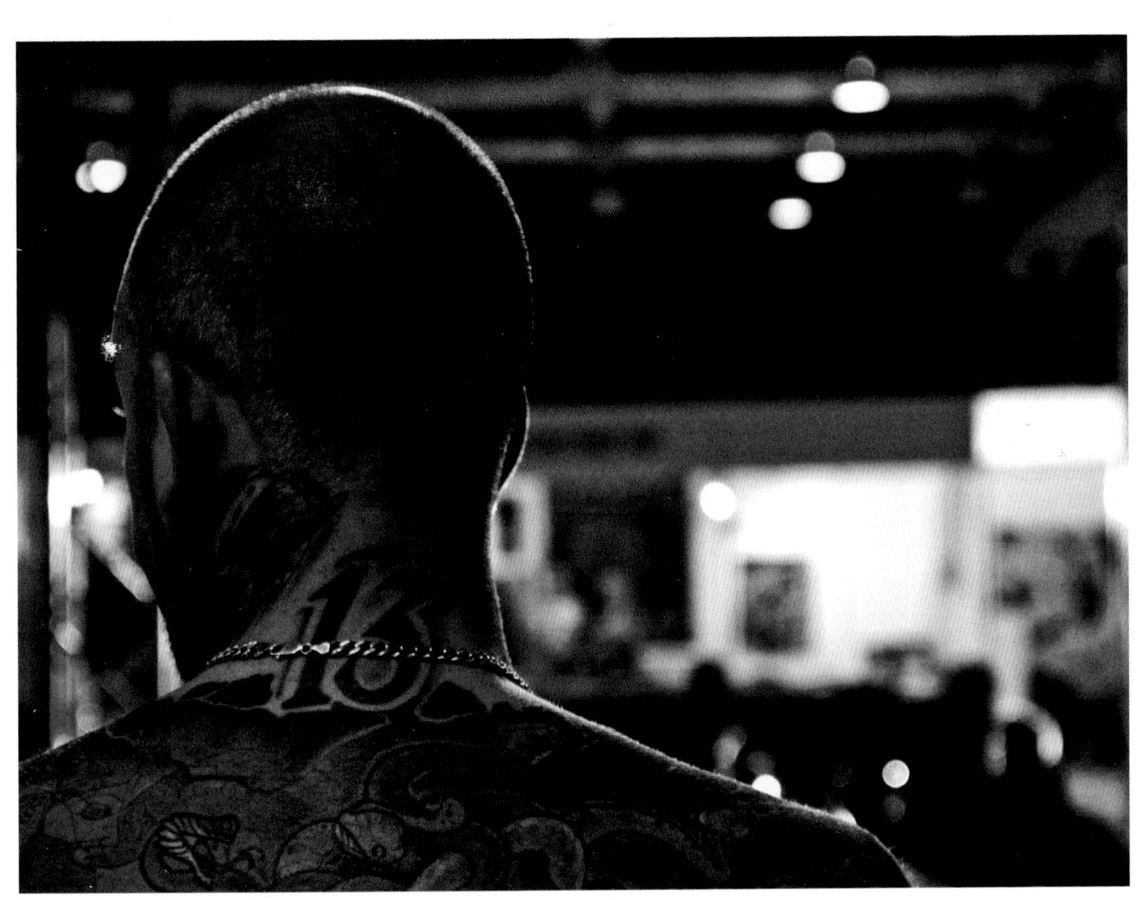

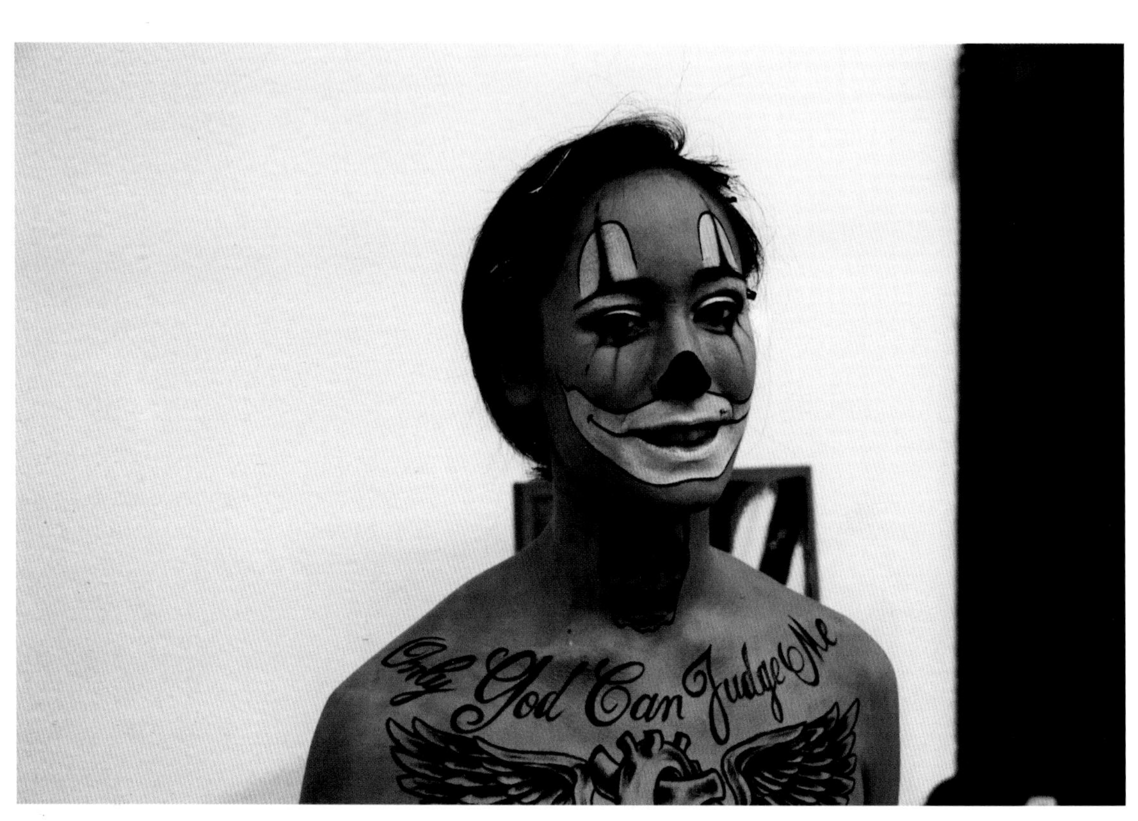
Only God Can Judge Me

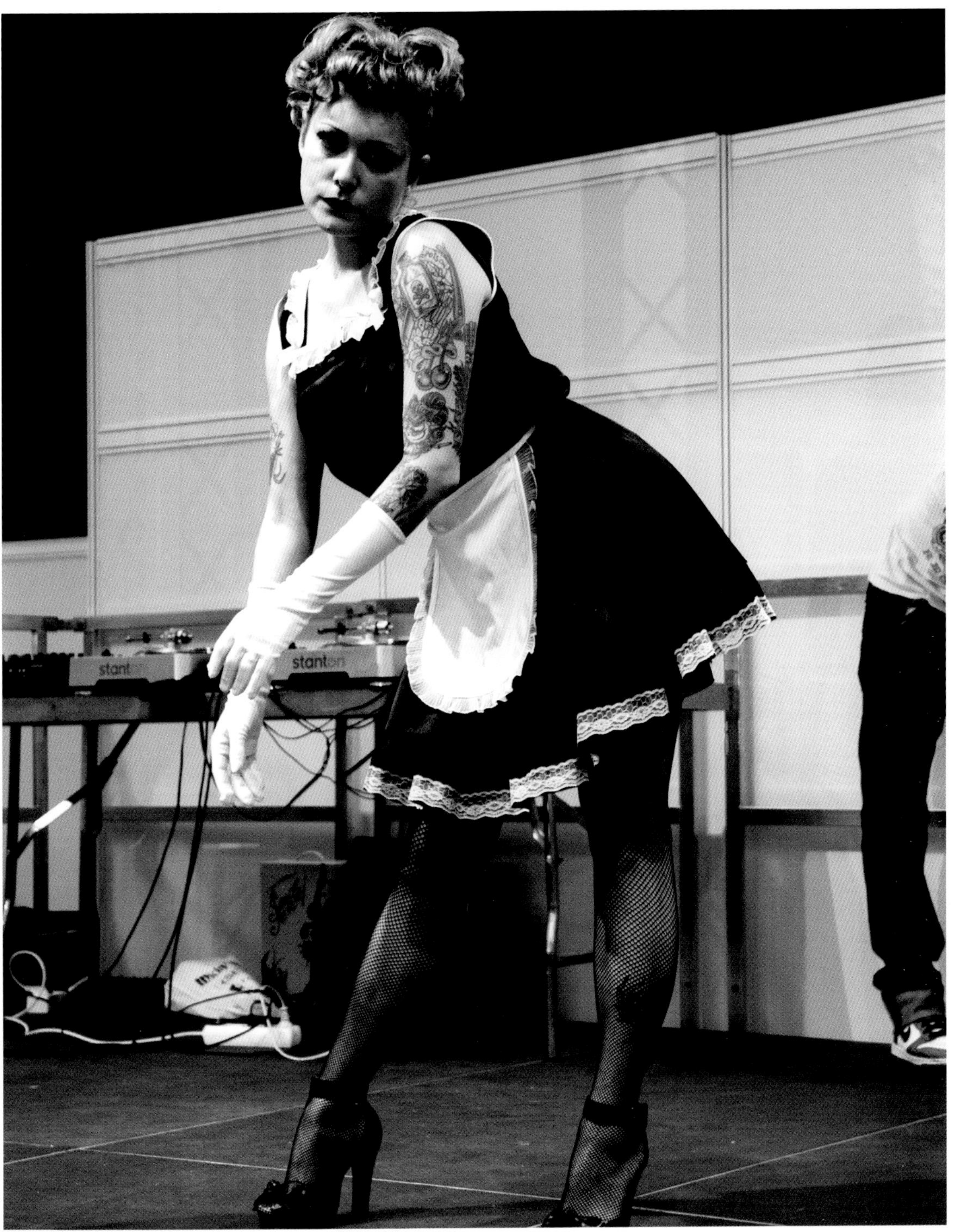
stanton

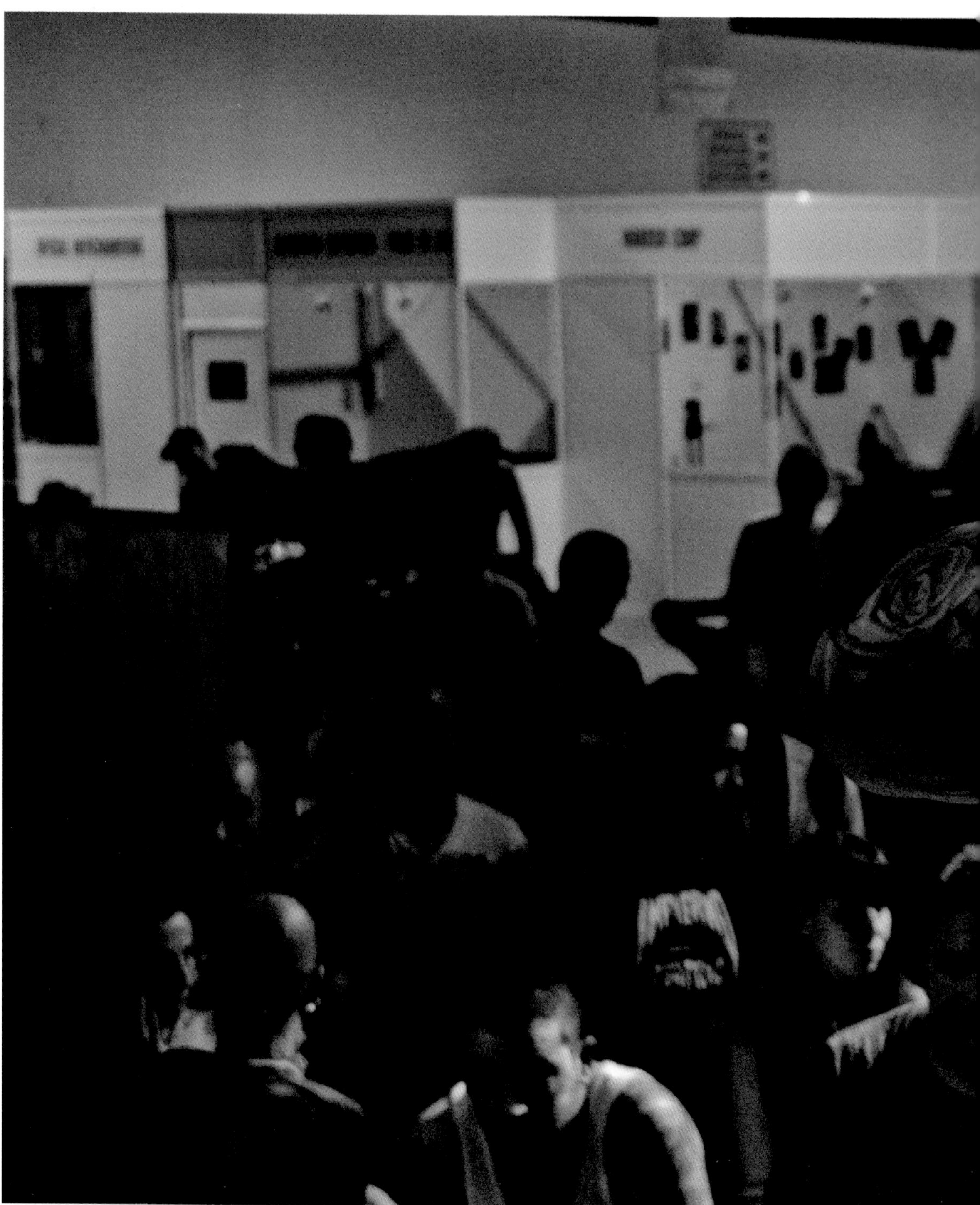

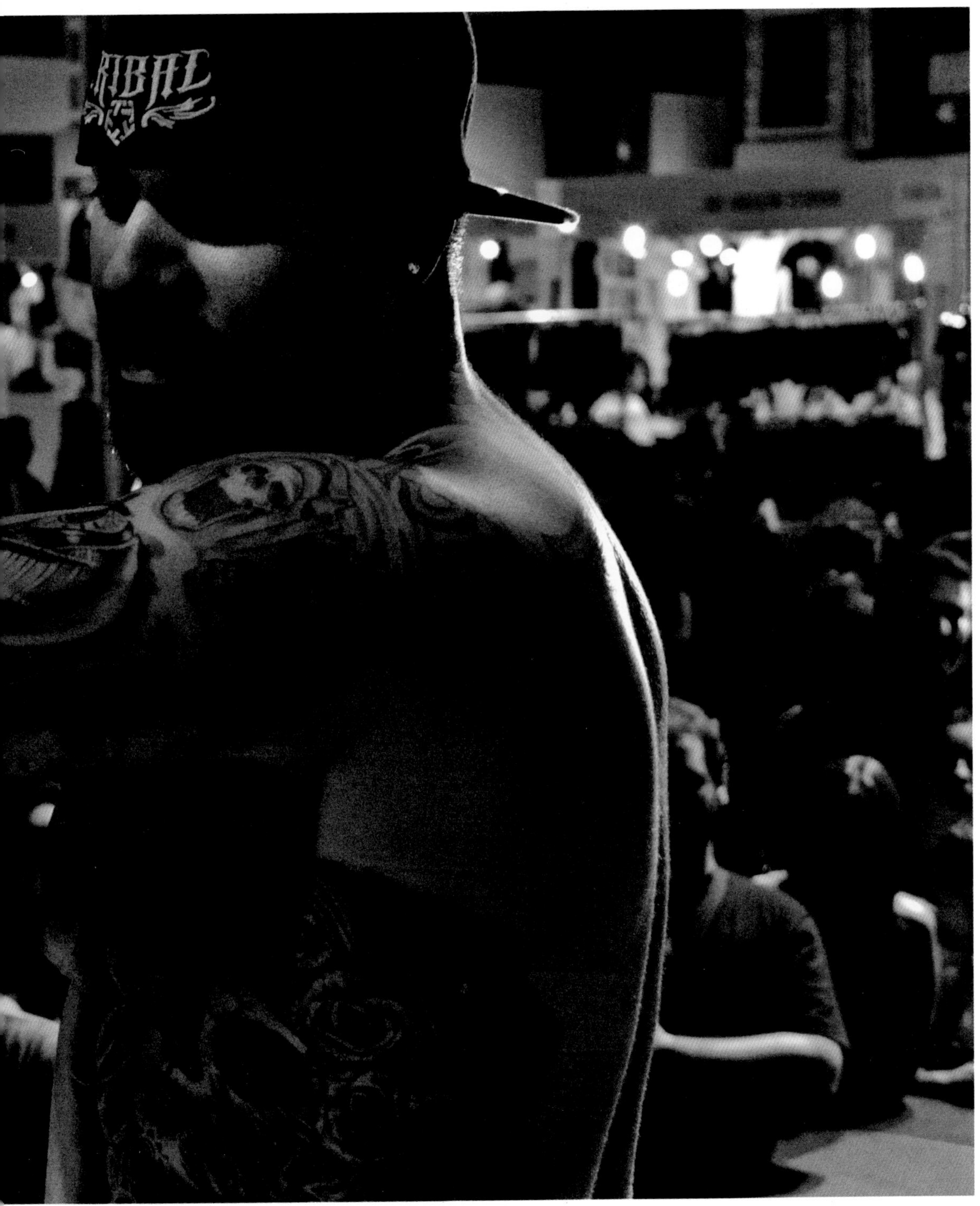

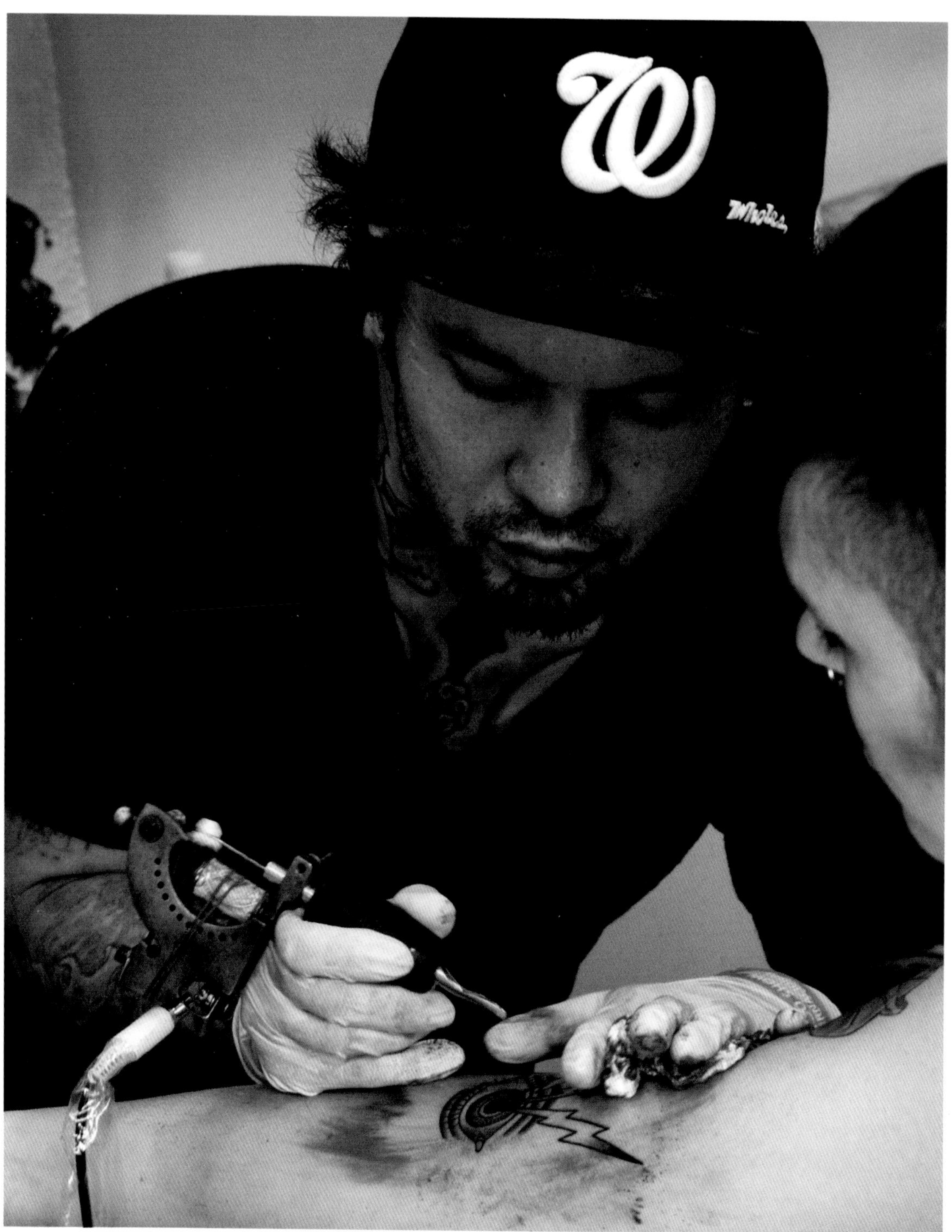
W

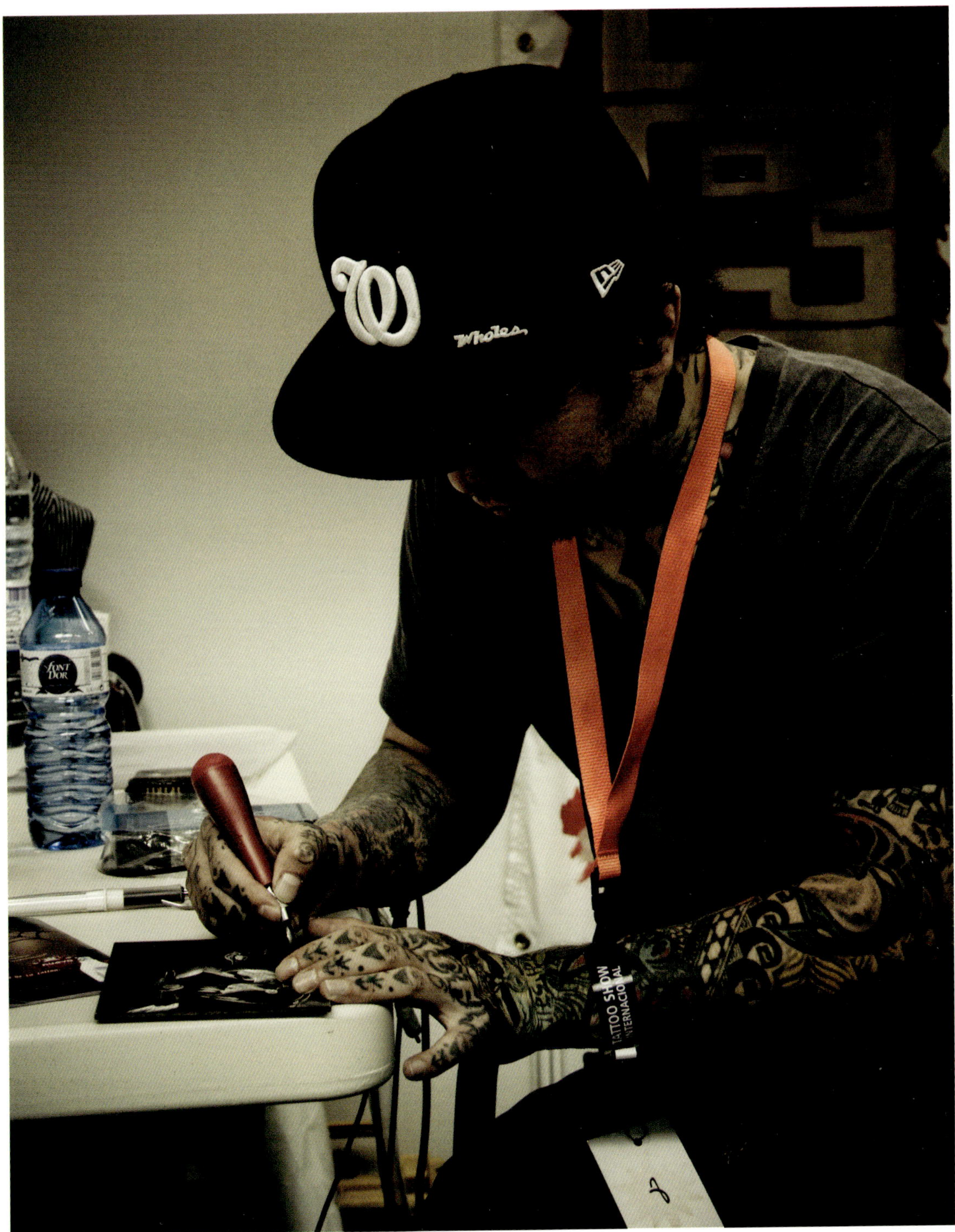
TATTOO SHOW

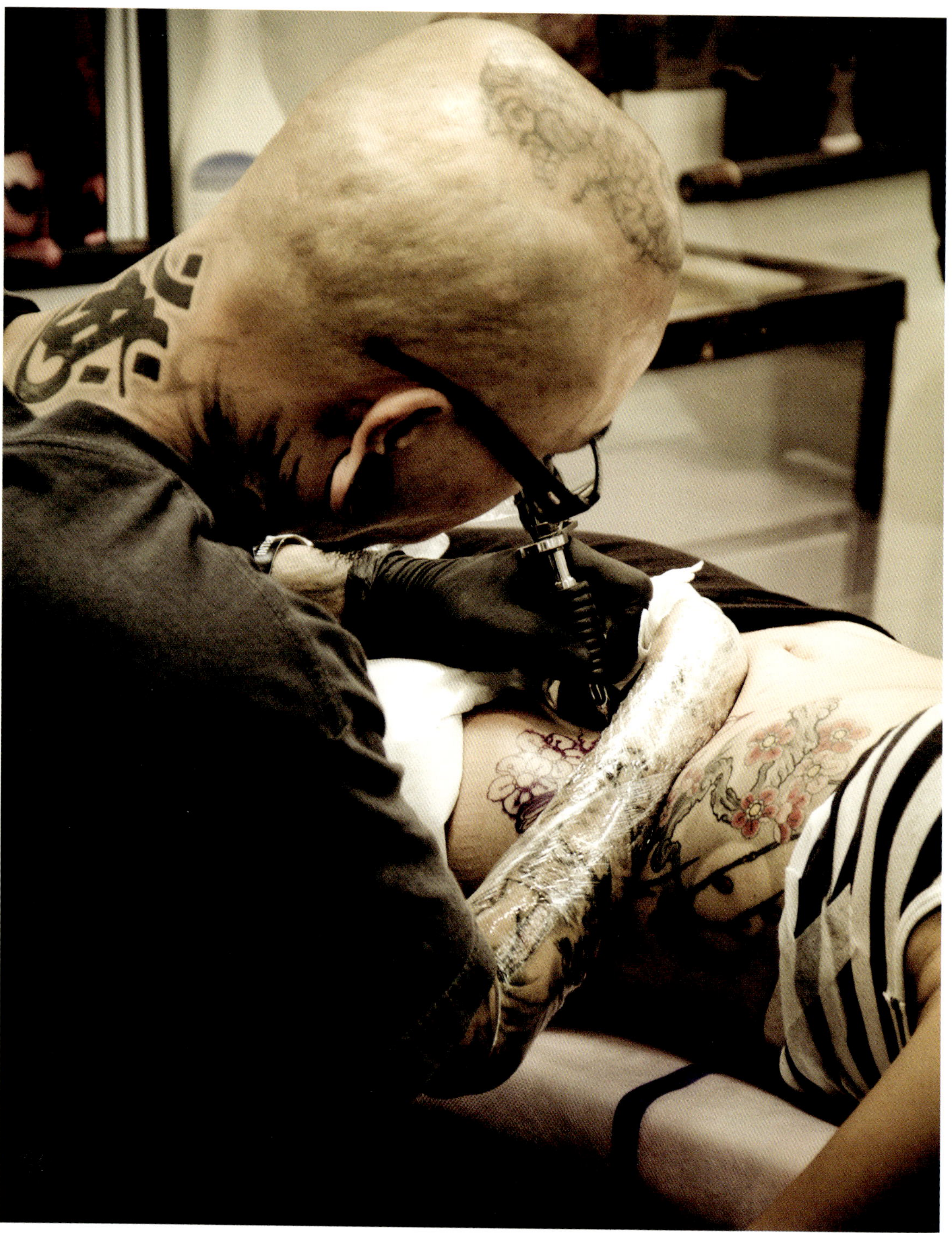

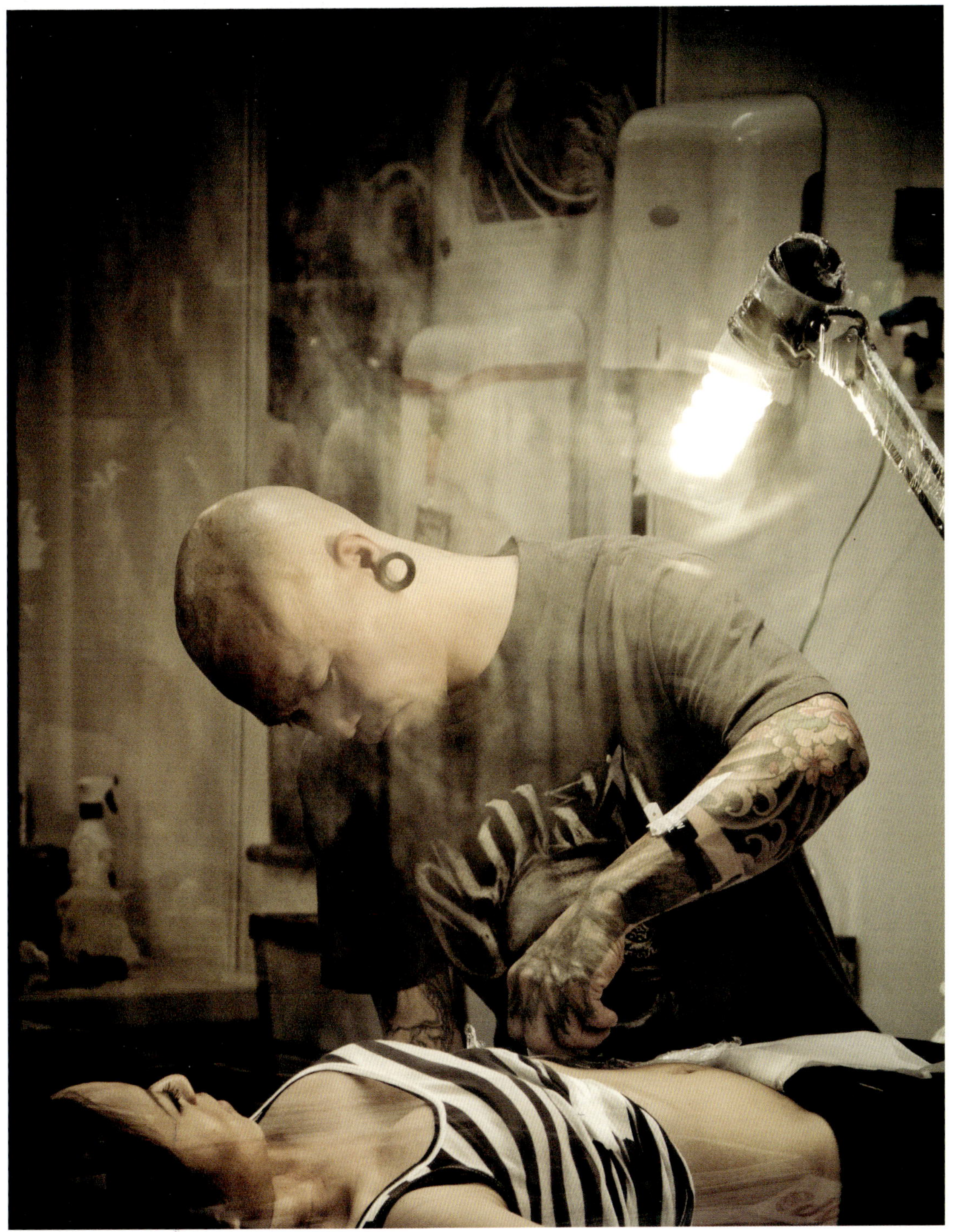

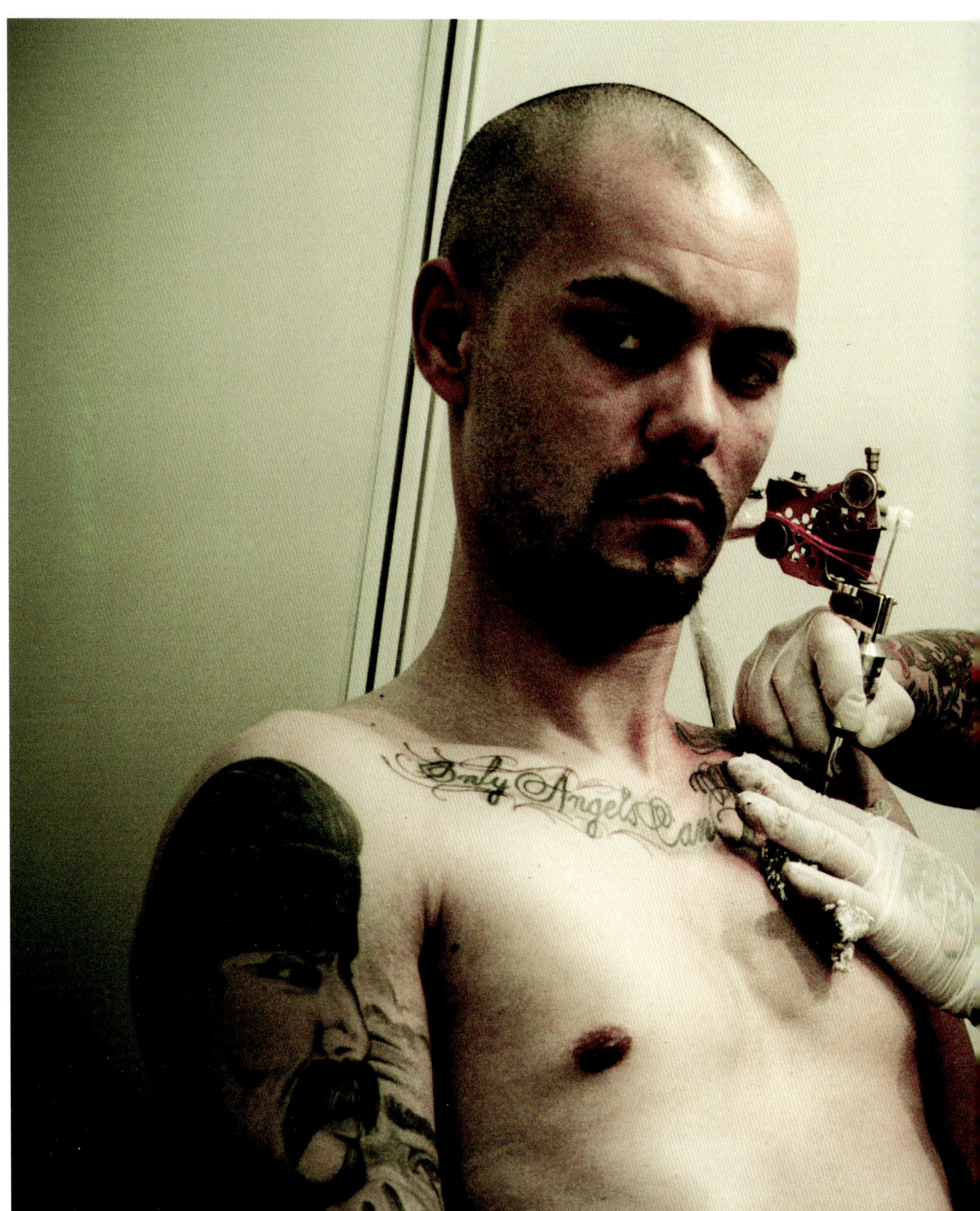
Only Angels Can

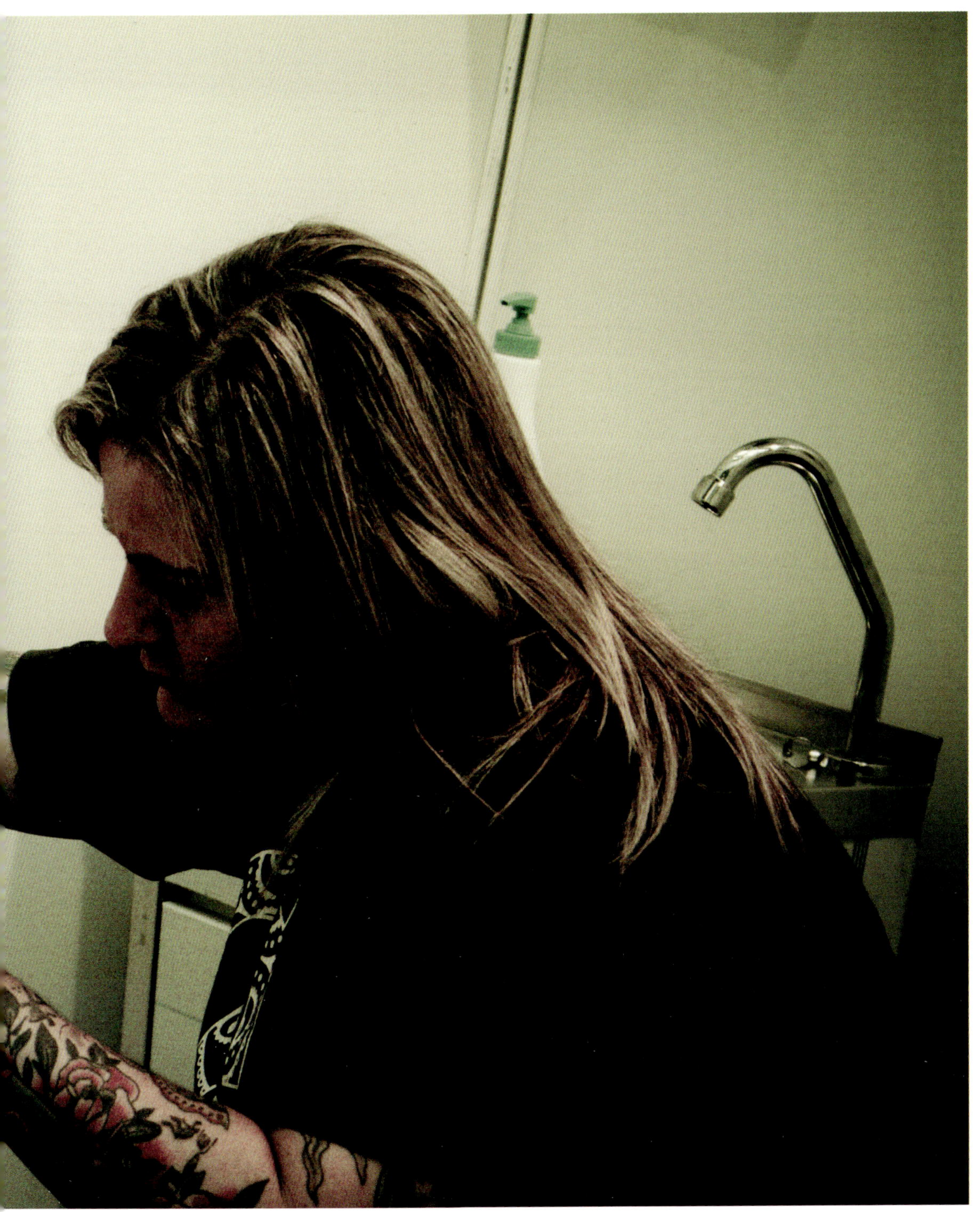

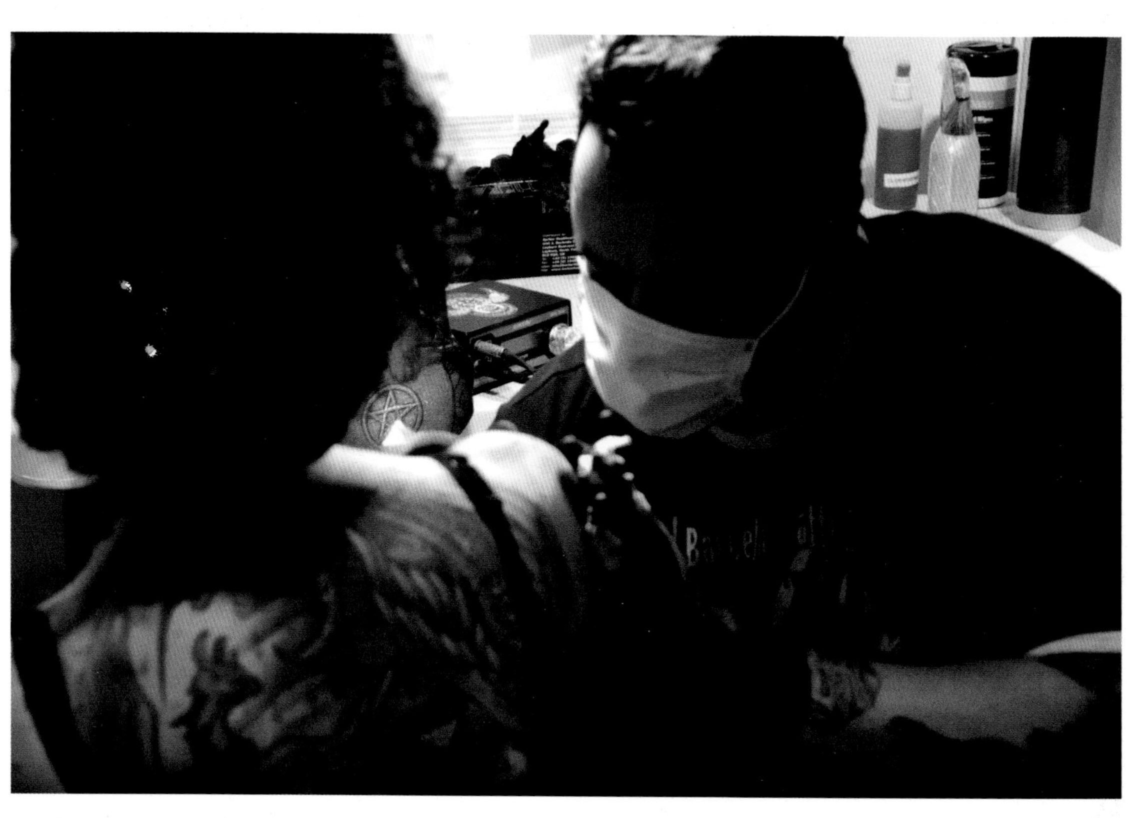

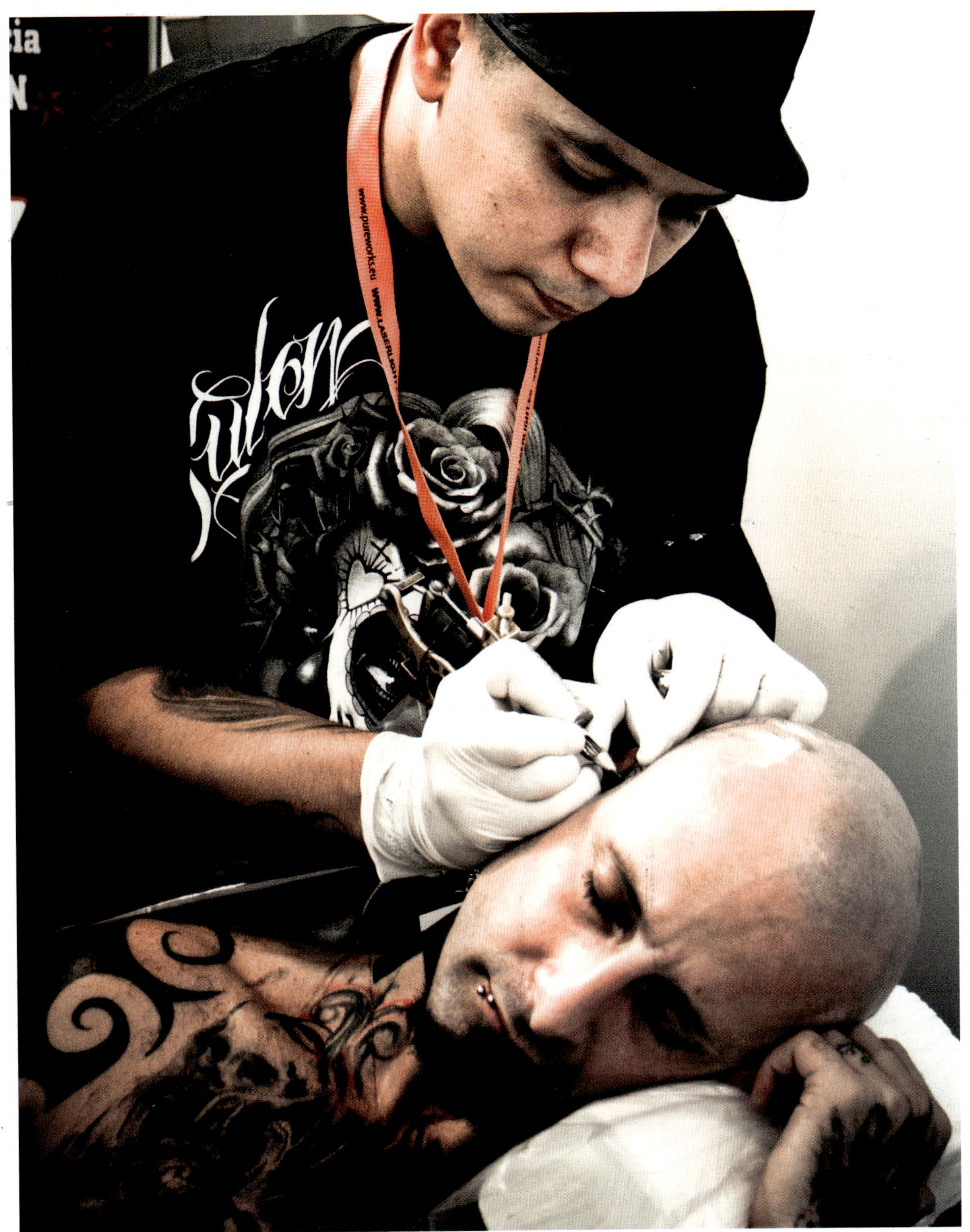

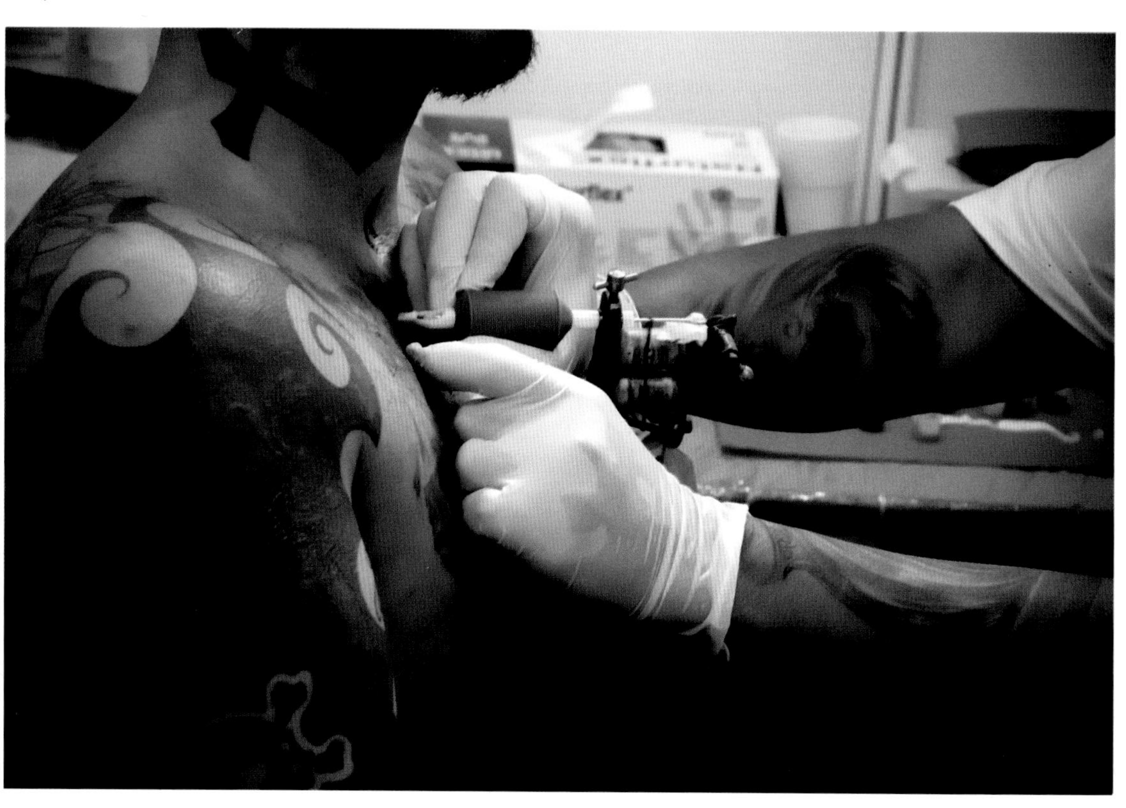

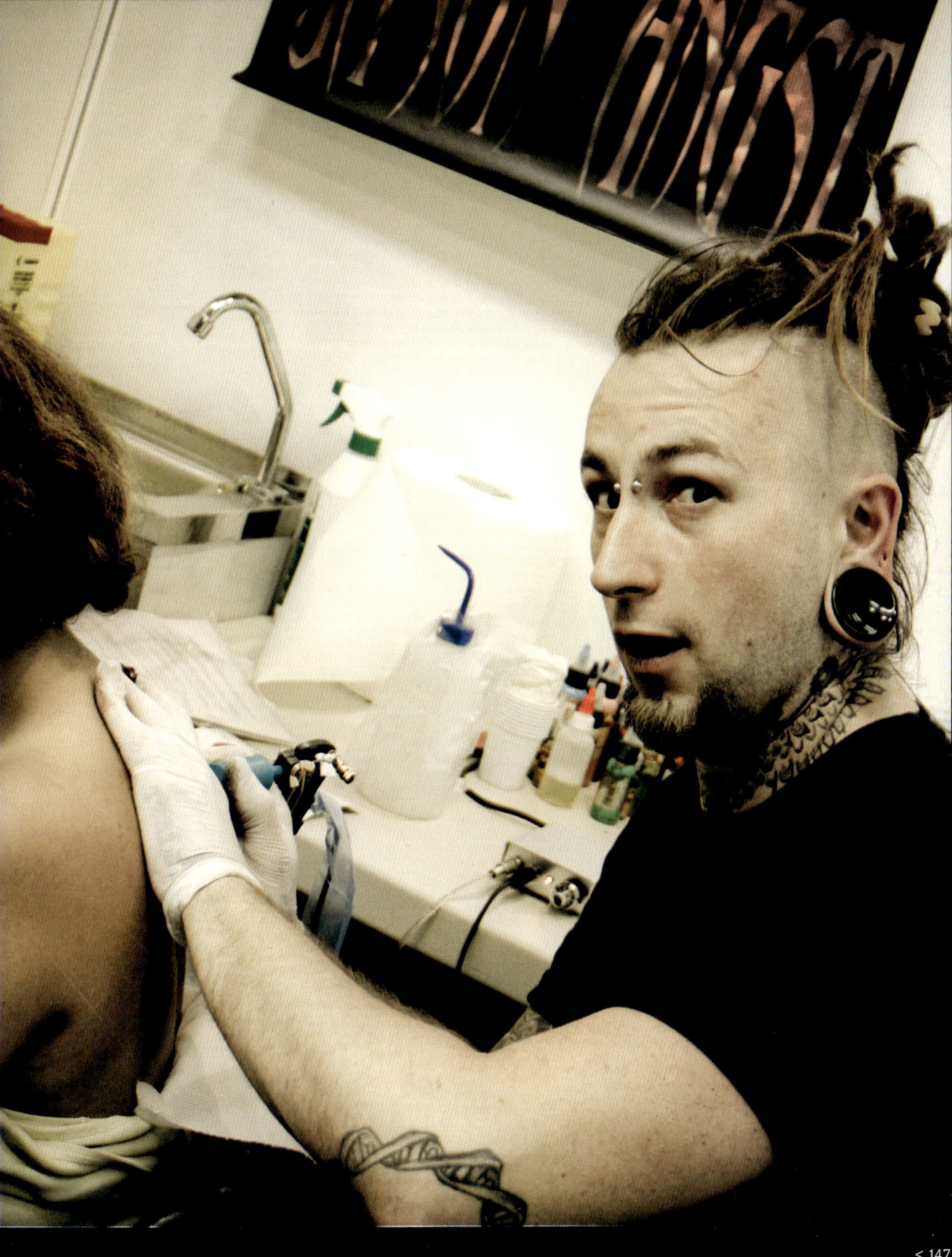

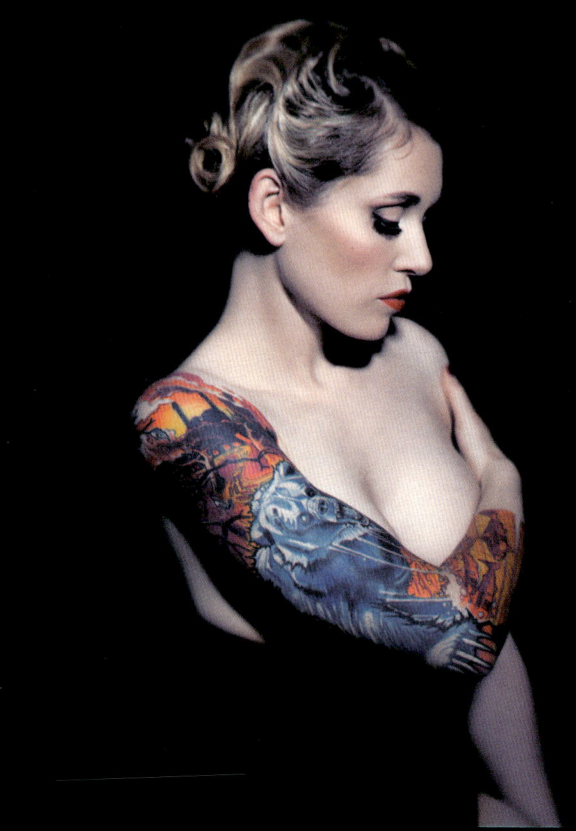

Melanie Jane

www.sugarcreative.ca

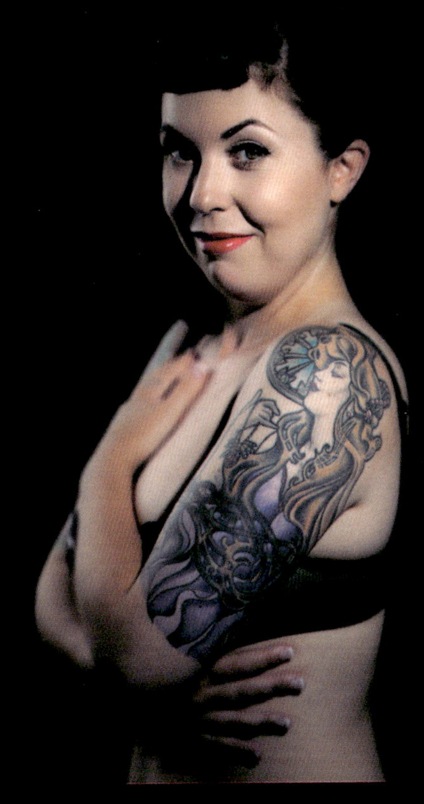

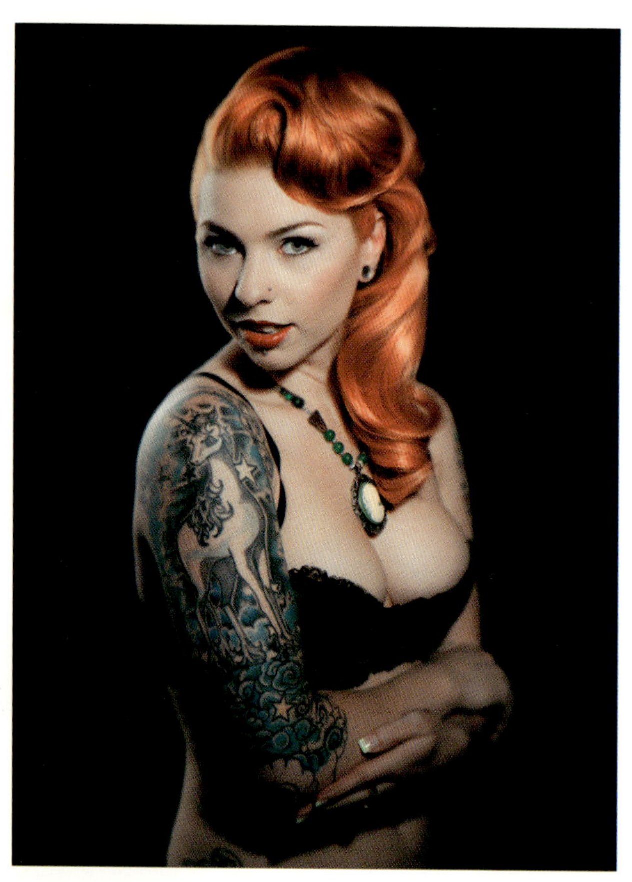

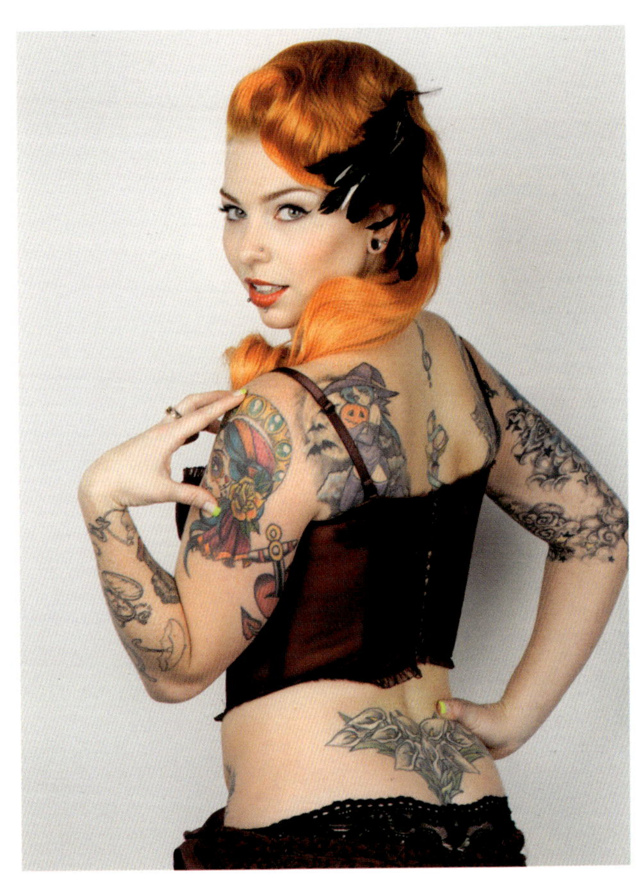

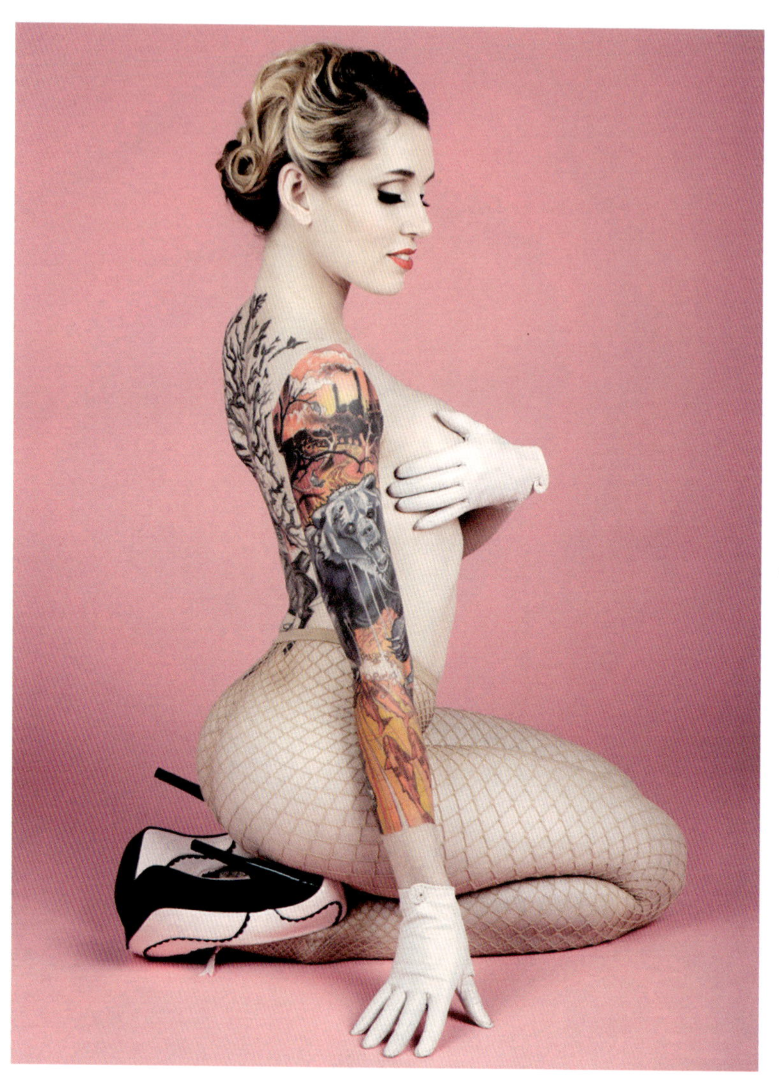

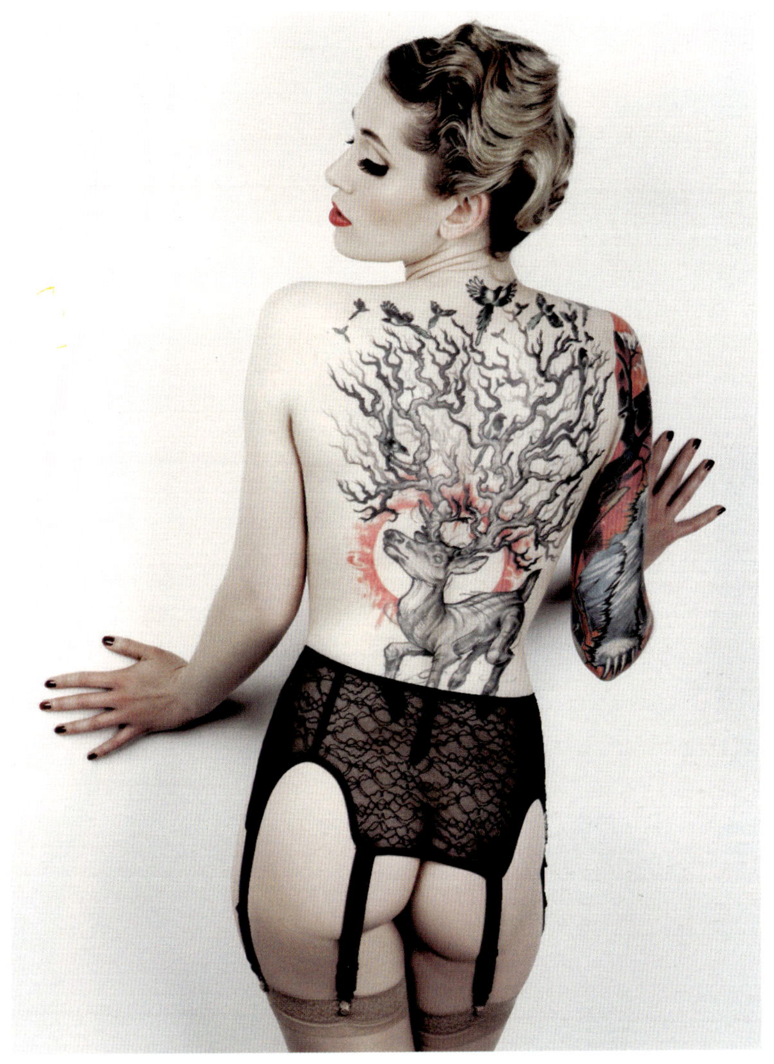

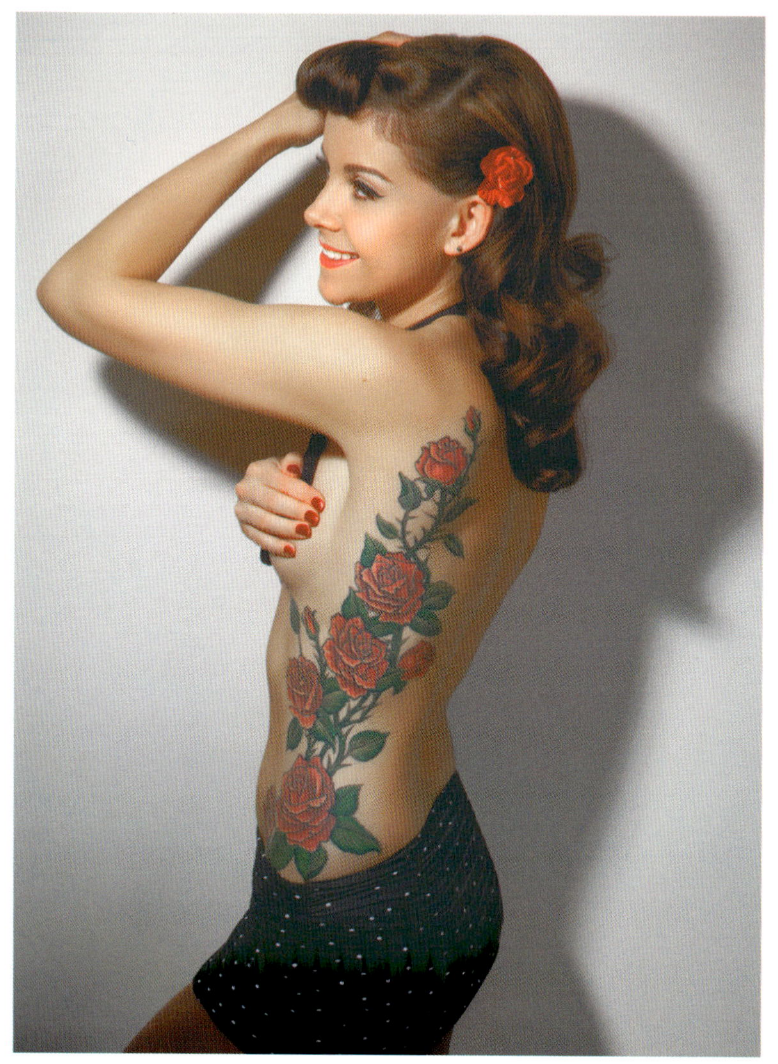

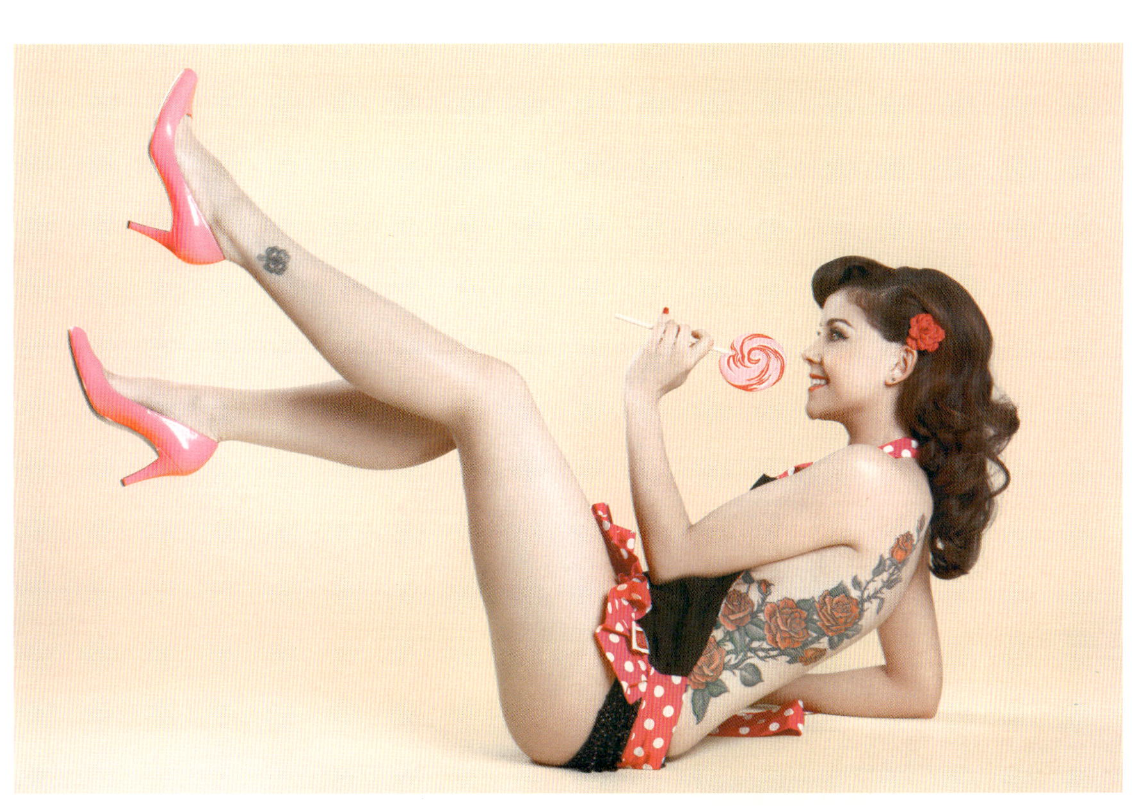

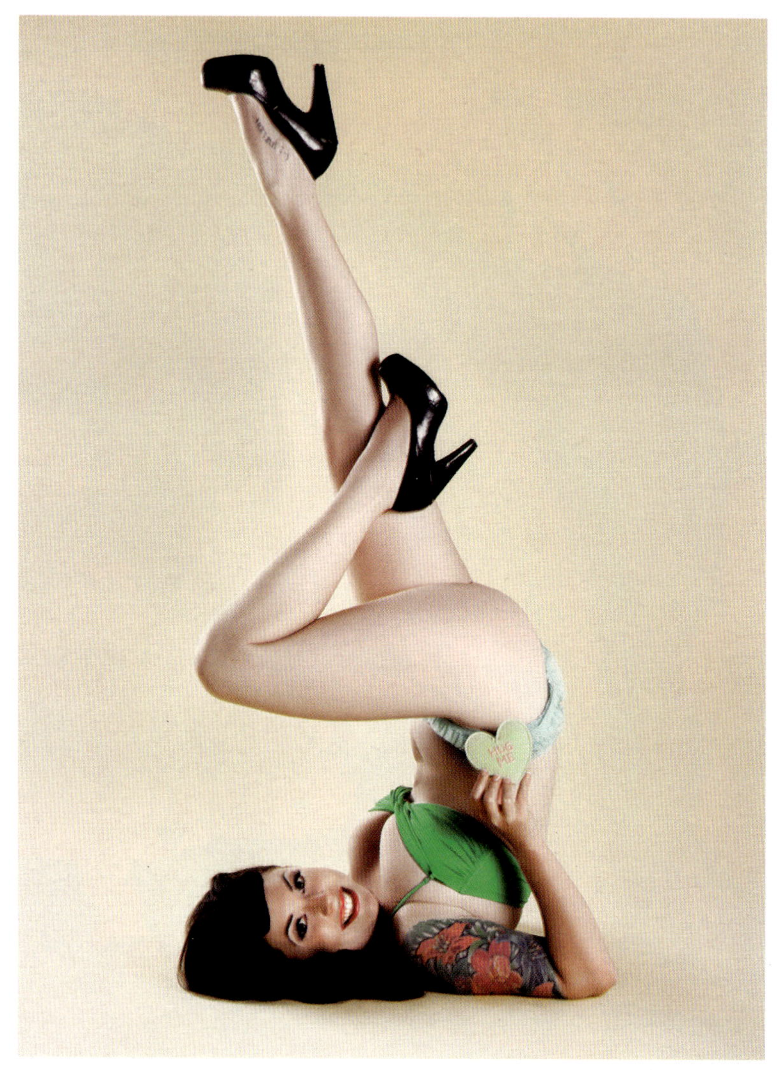
HUG
ME

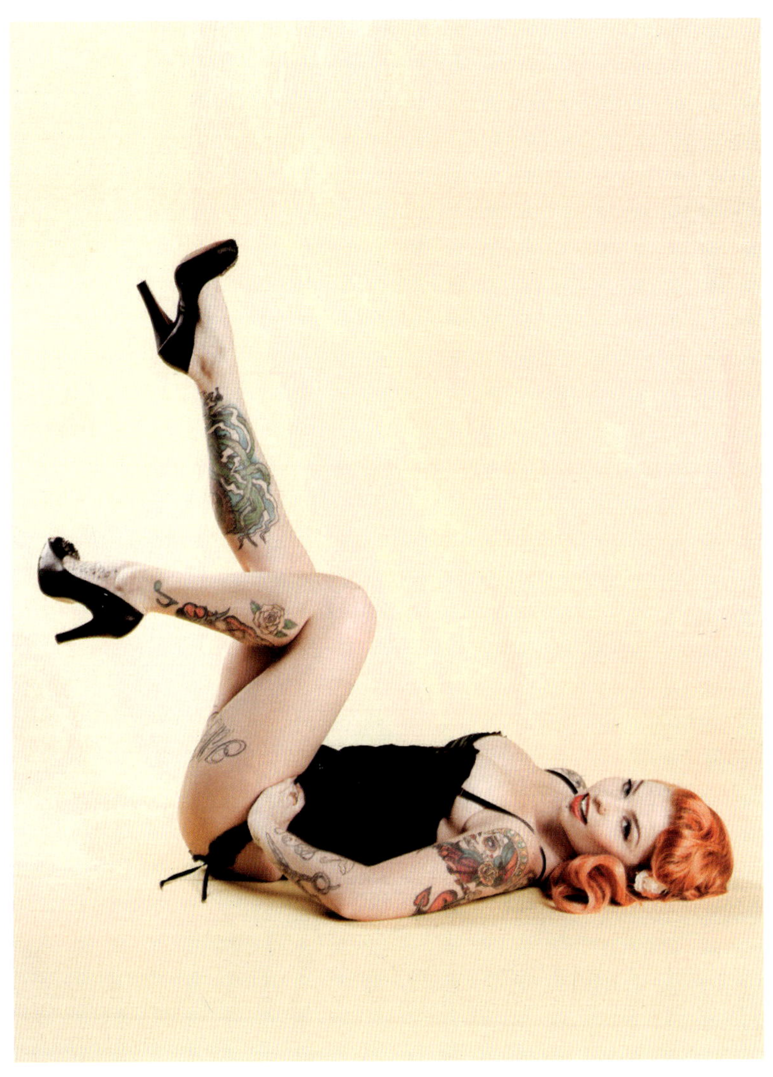

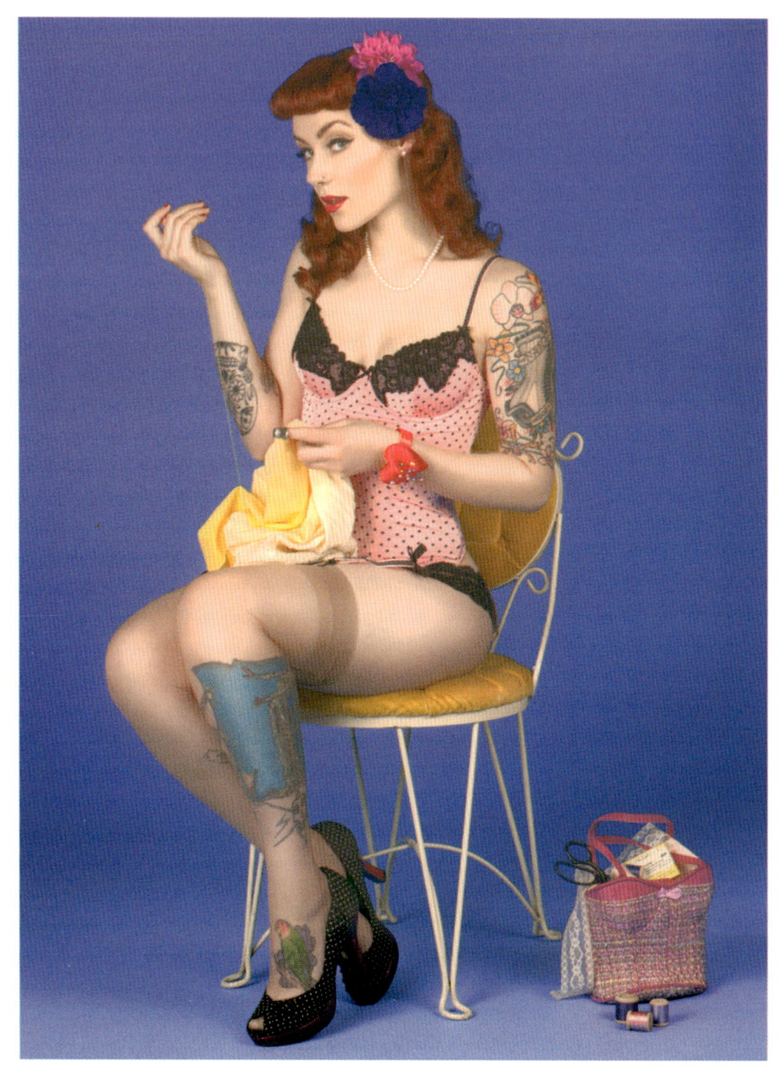

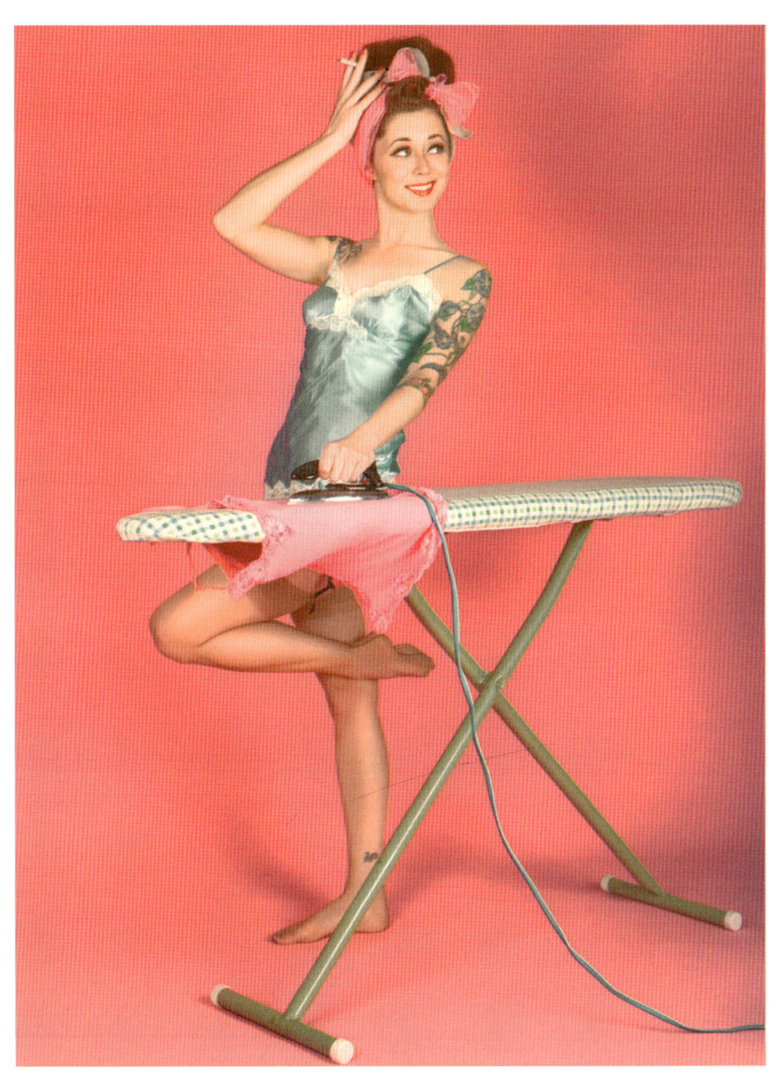

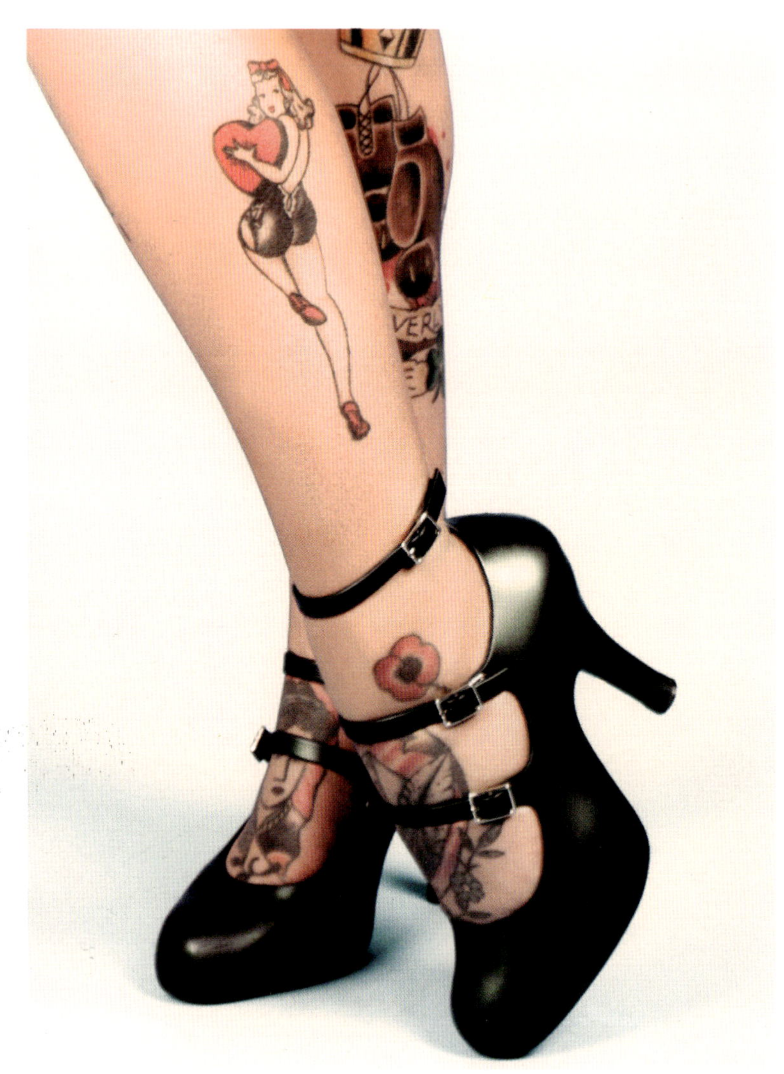

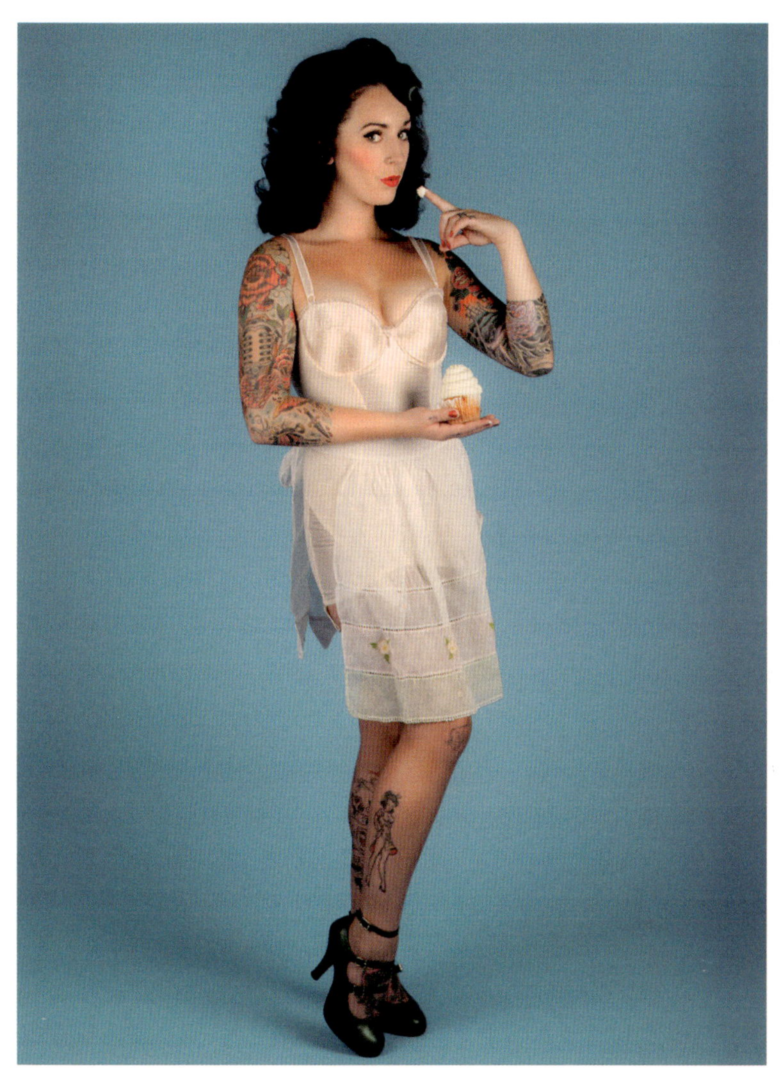

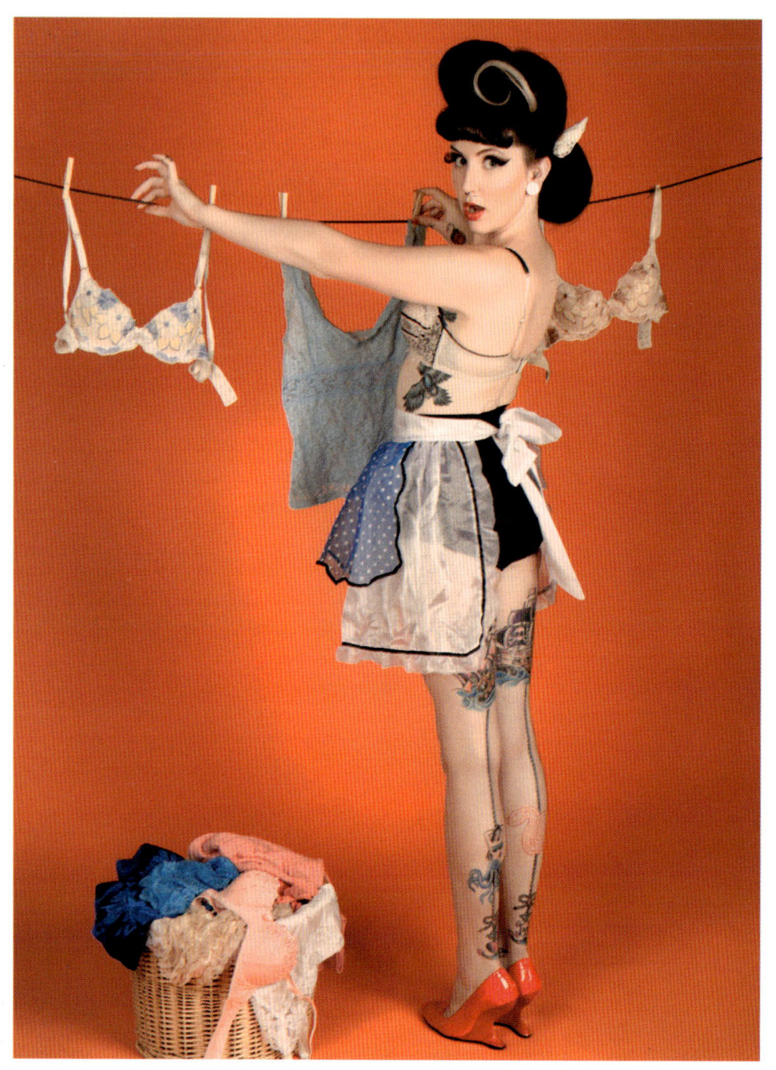

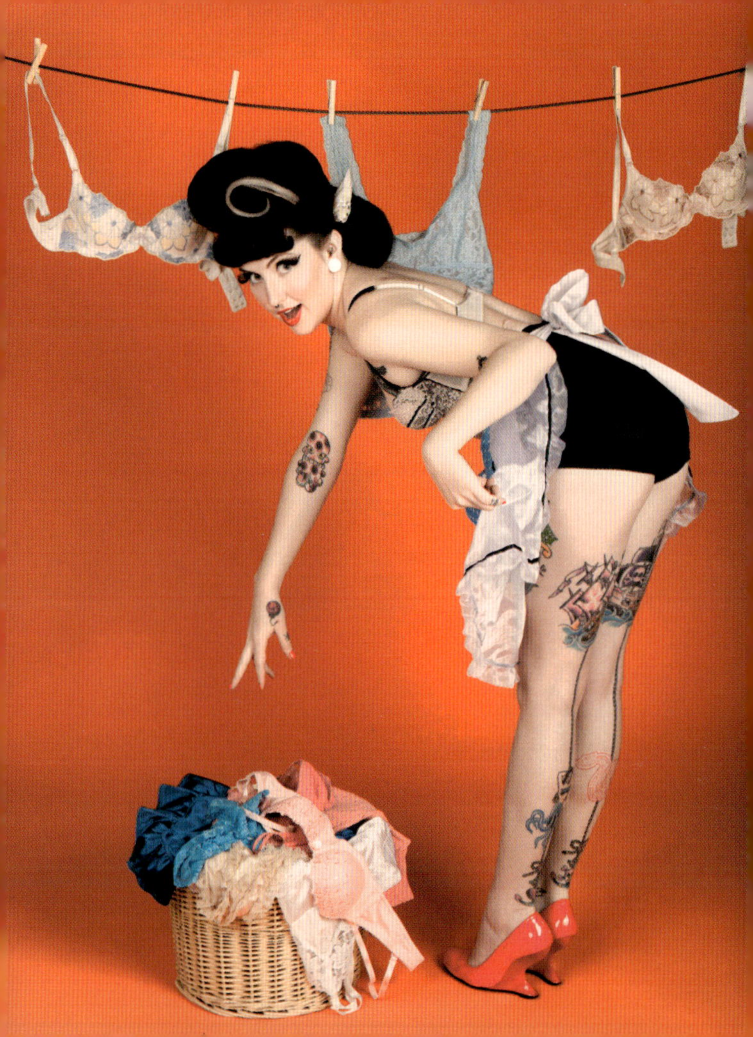

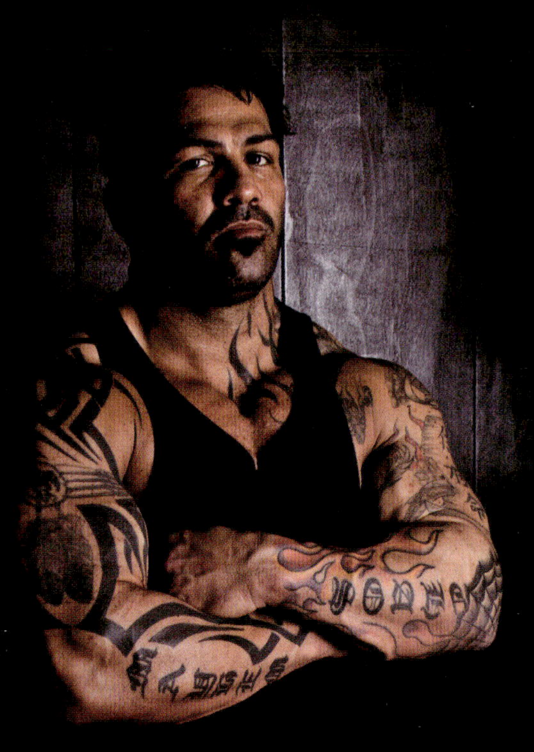

Mark V

www.markvclassics.com

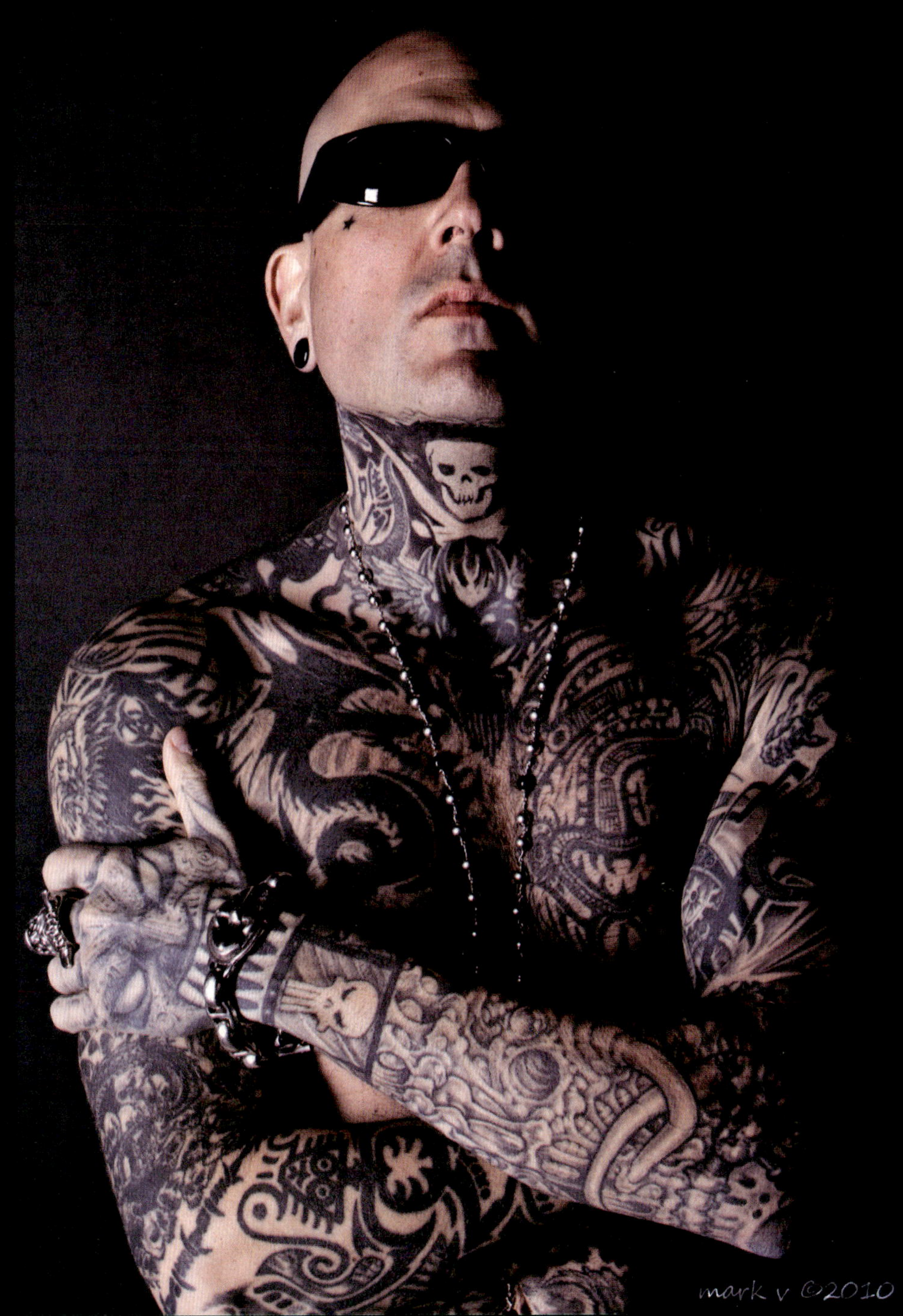
mark v ©2010

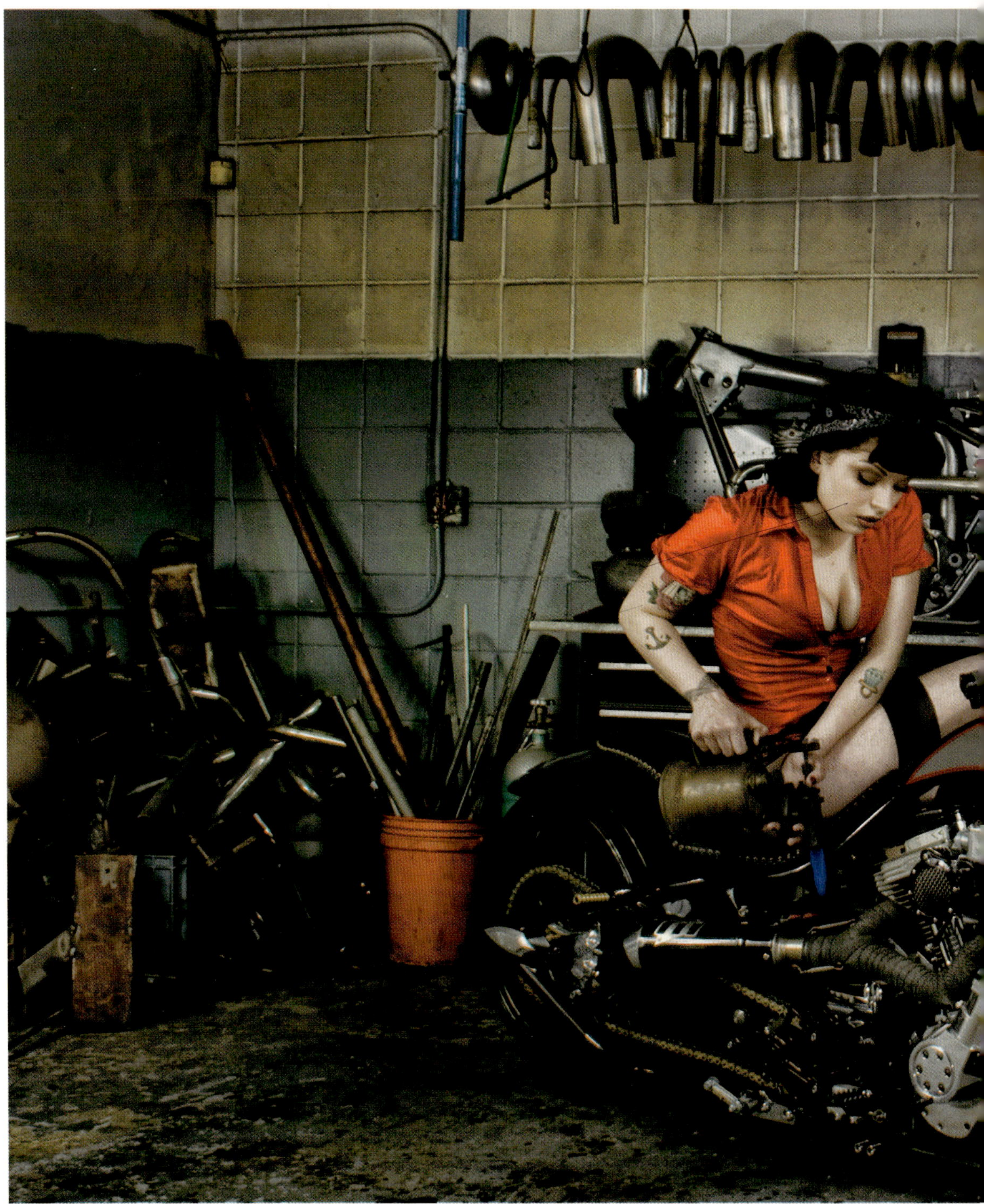

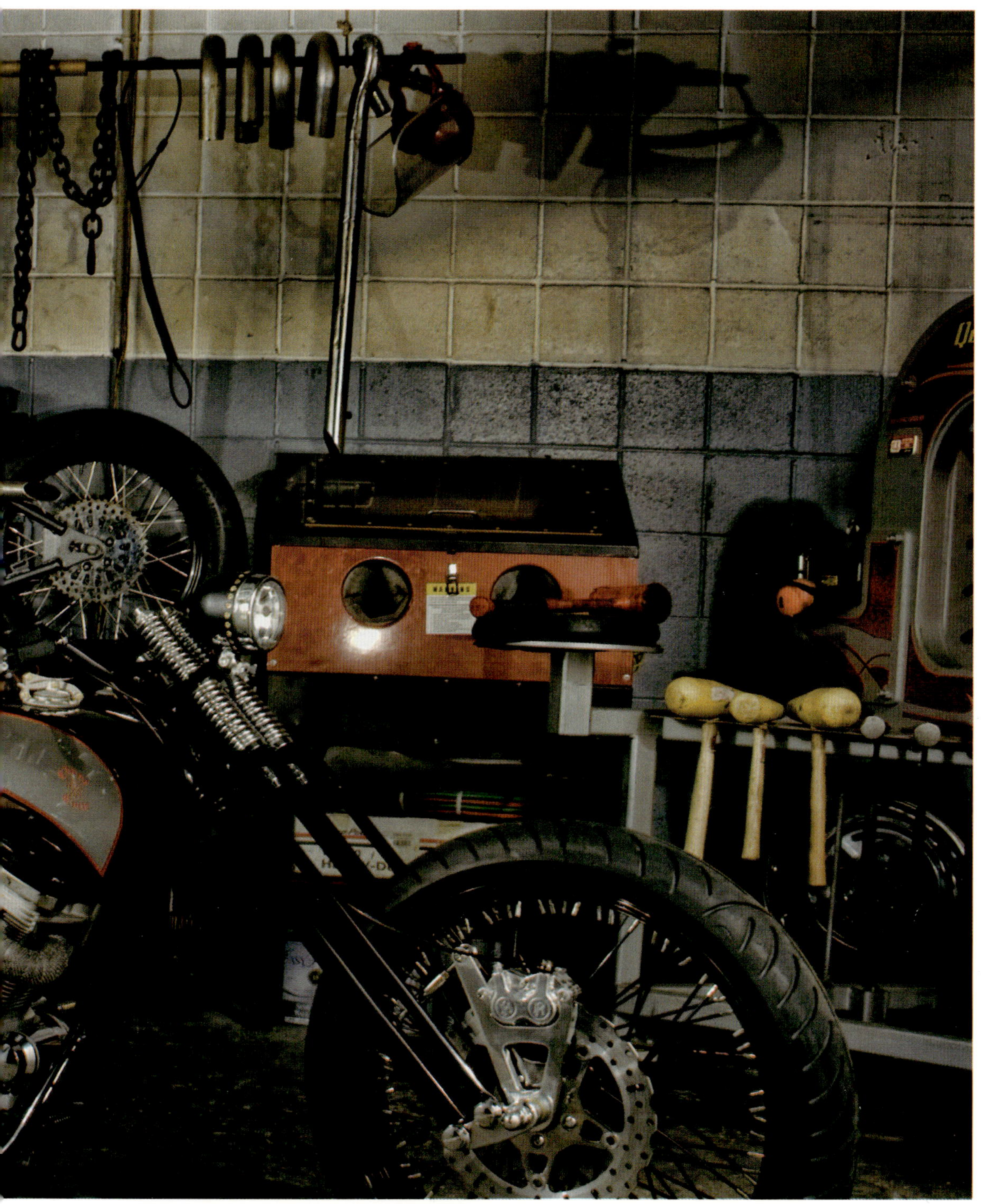

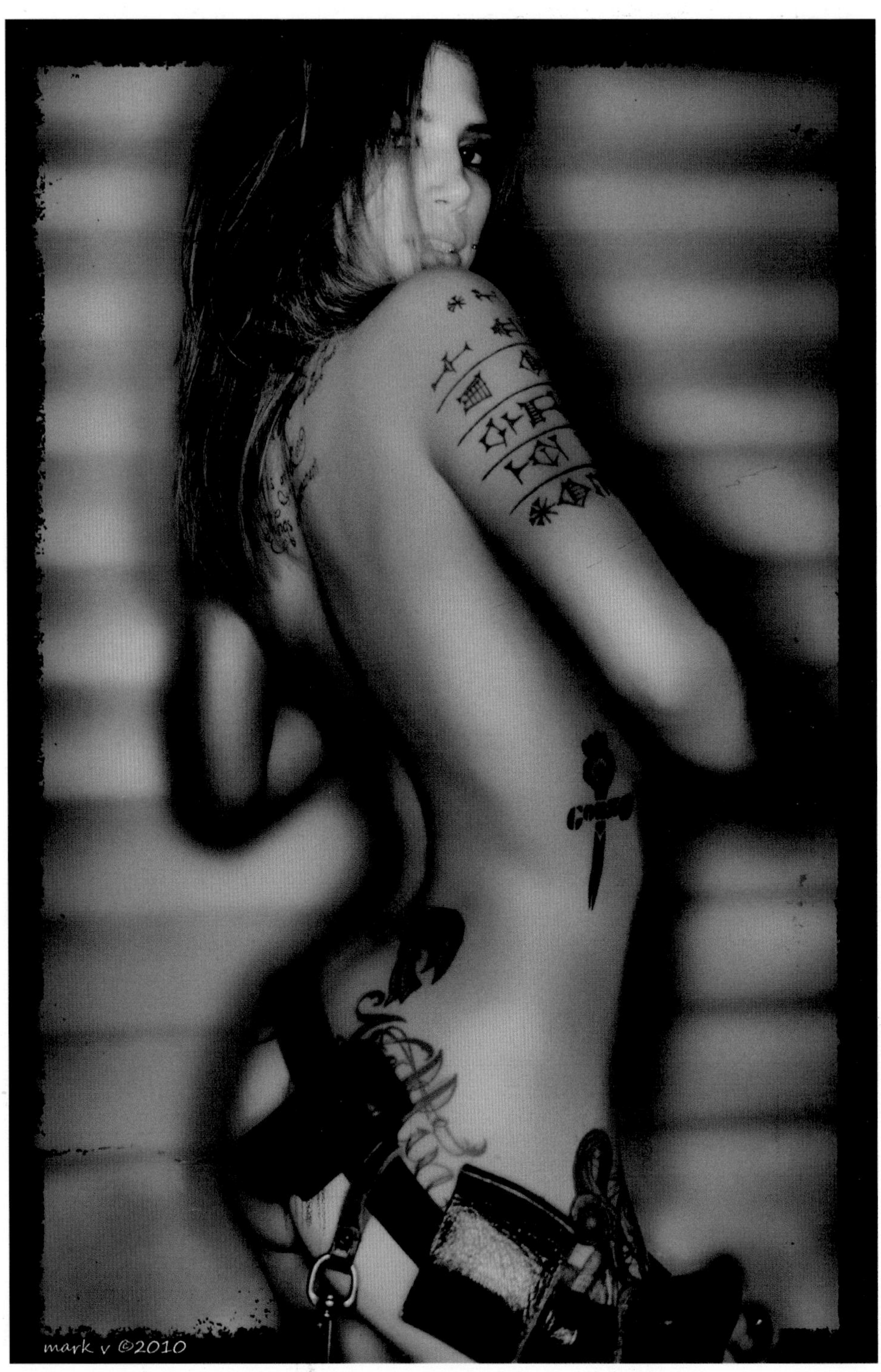
mark v ©2010

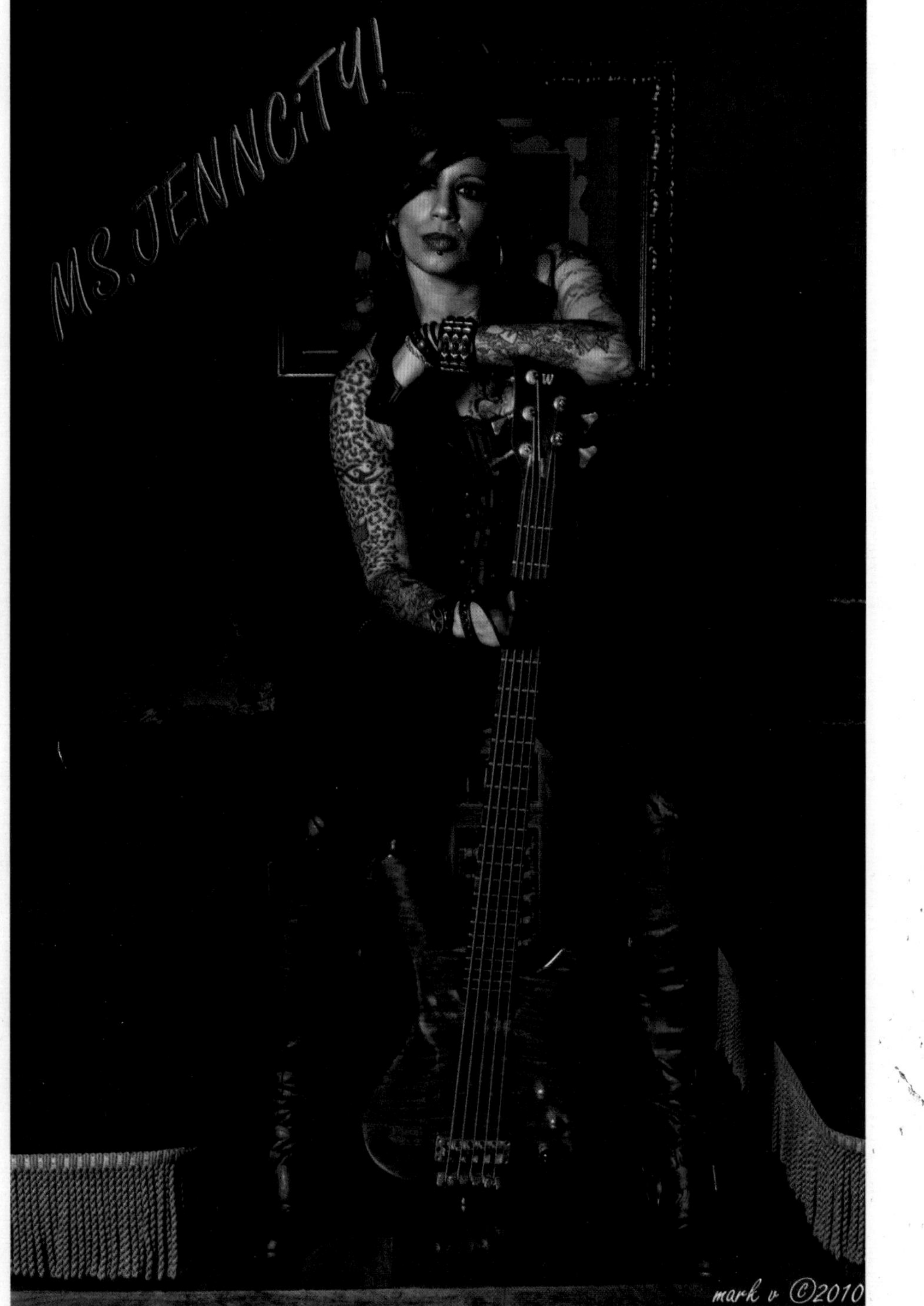
MS.JENNCiTY!
mark v ©2010

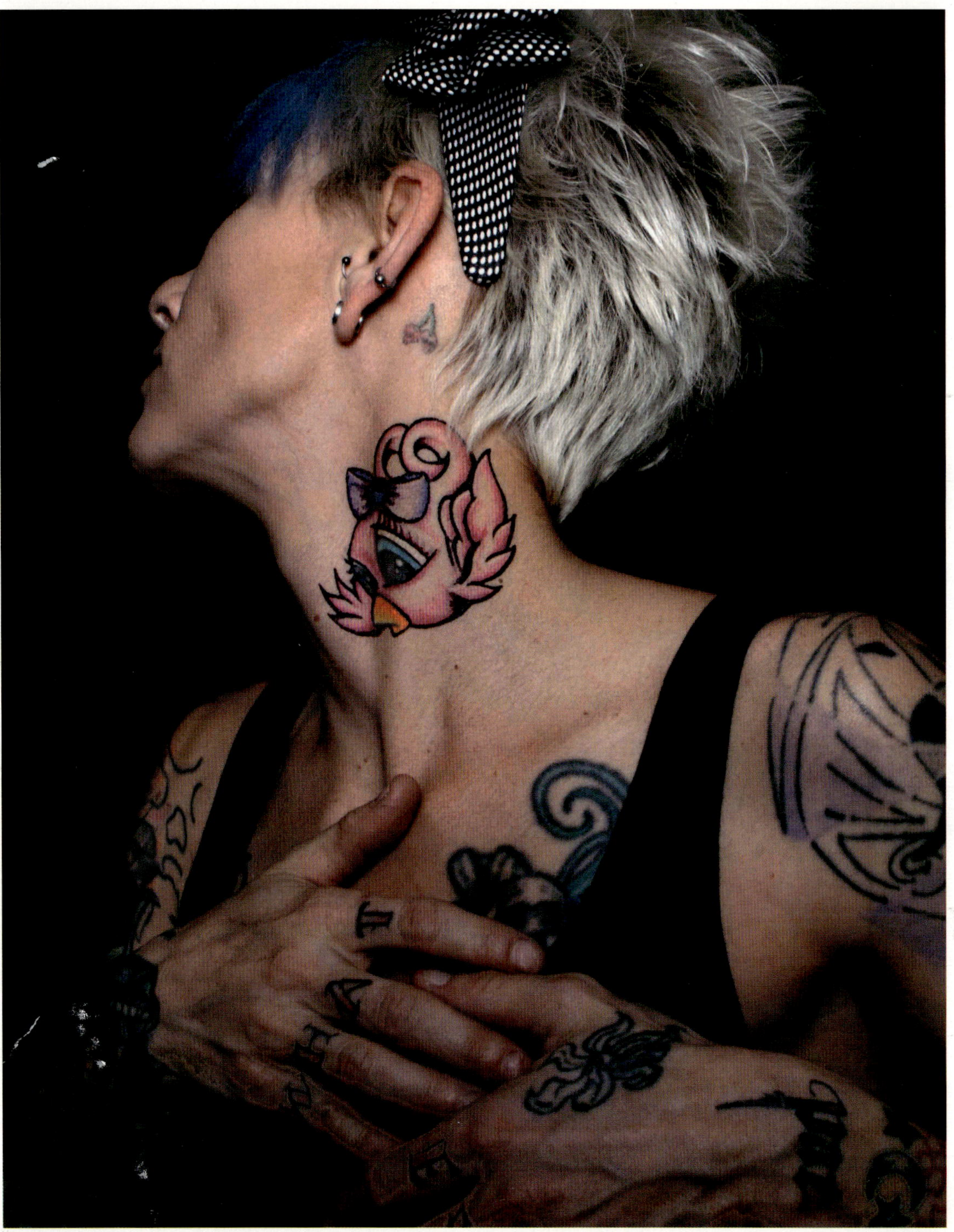

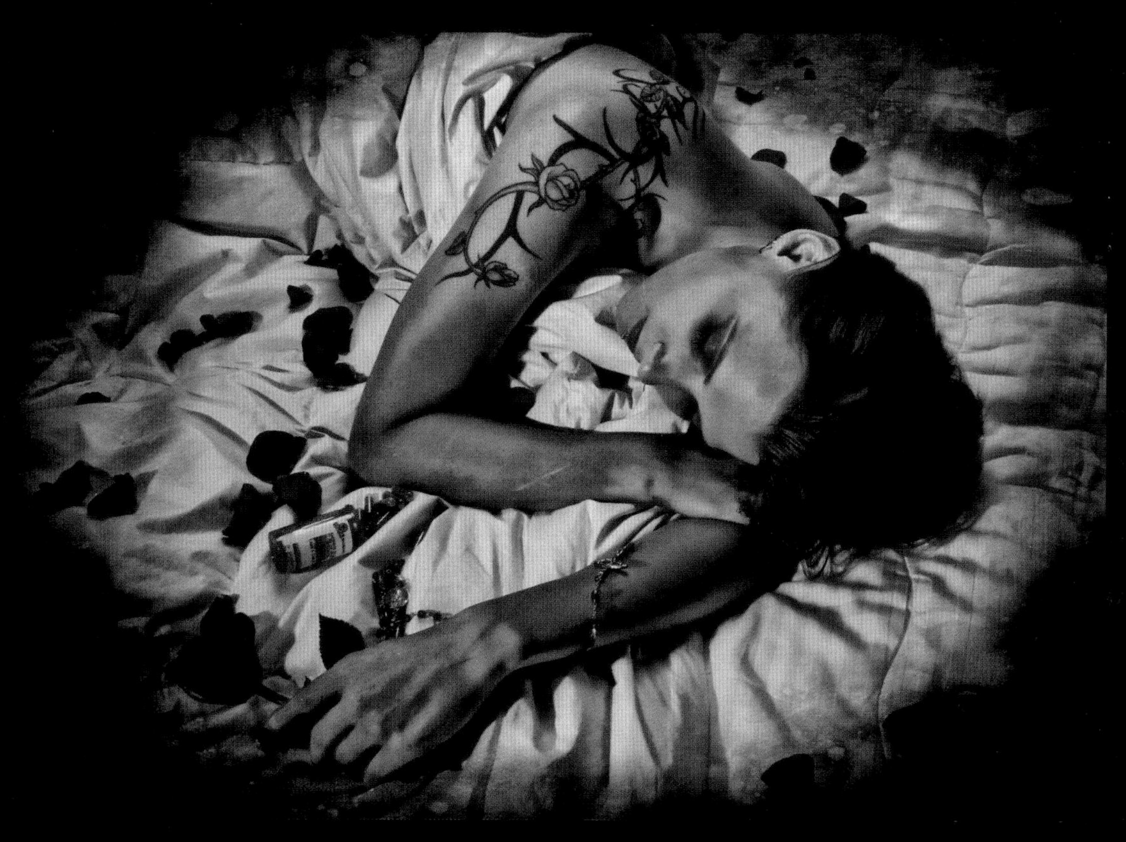

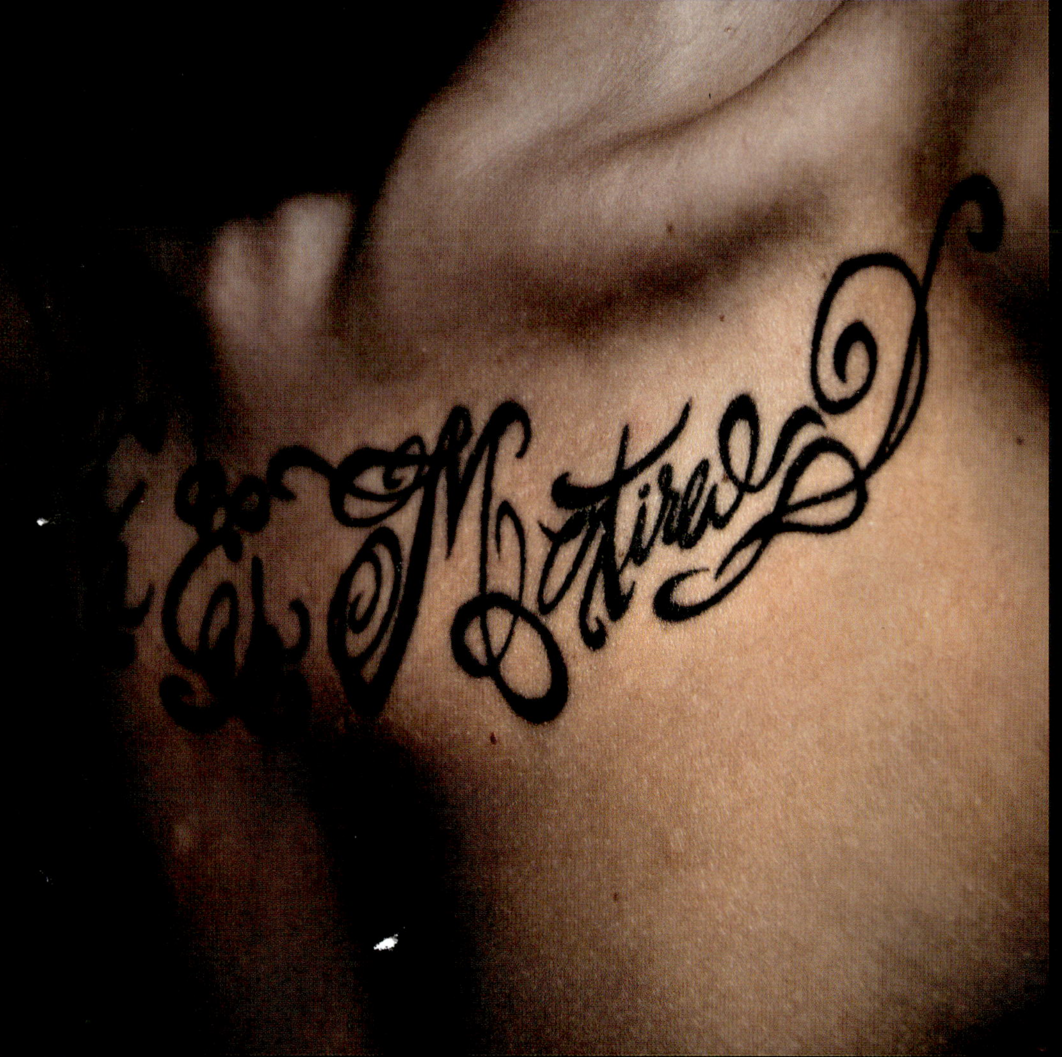

Yolanda G. Román

www.flickr.com/photos/bellakabiker/

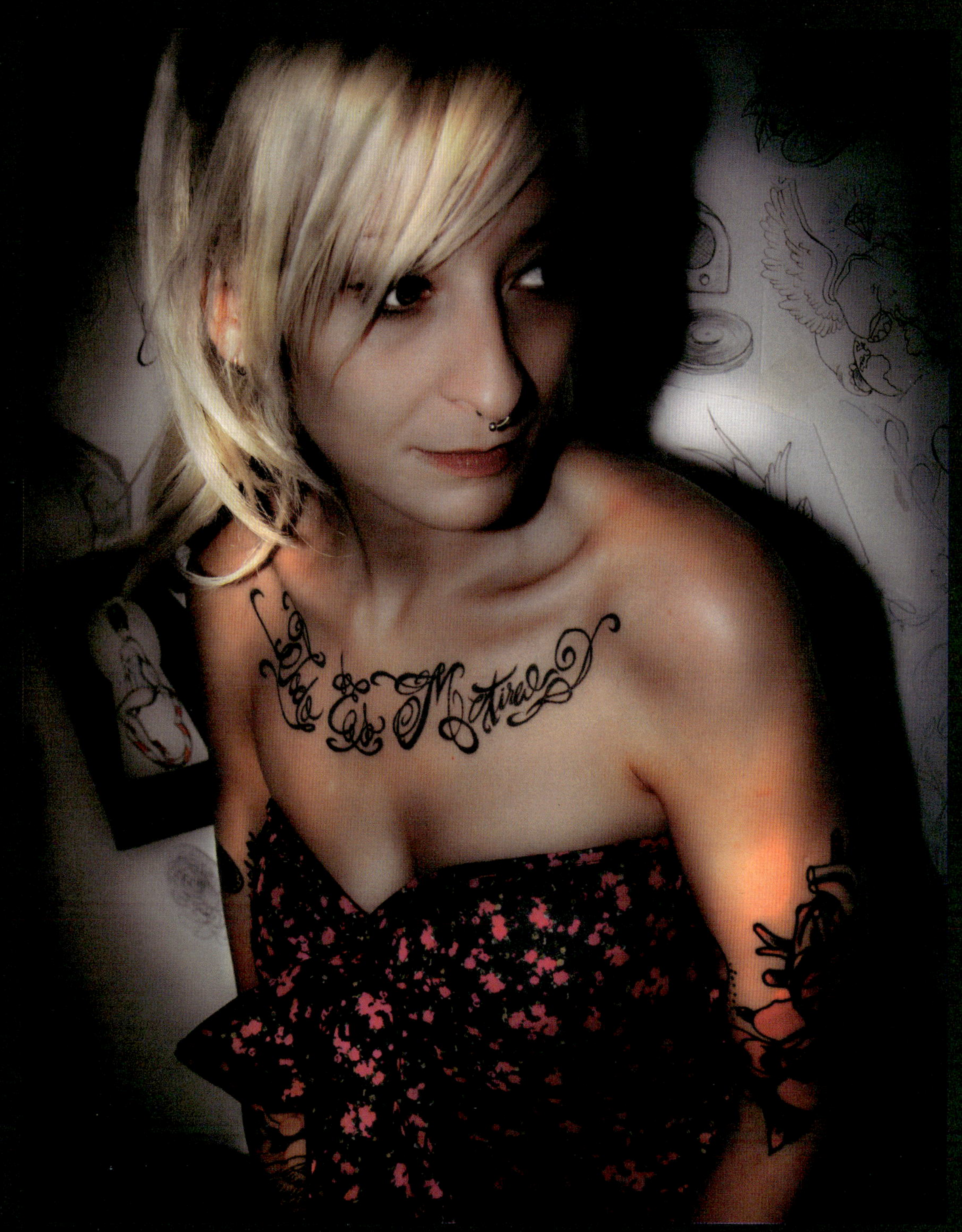
Todo Es Mentira

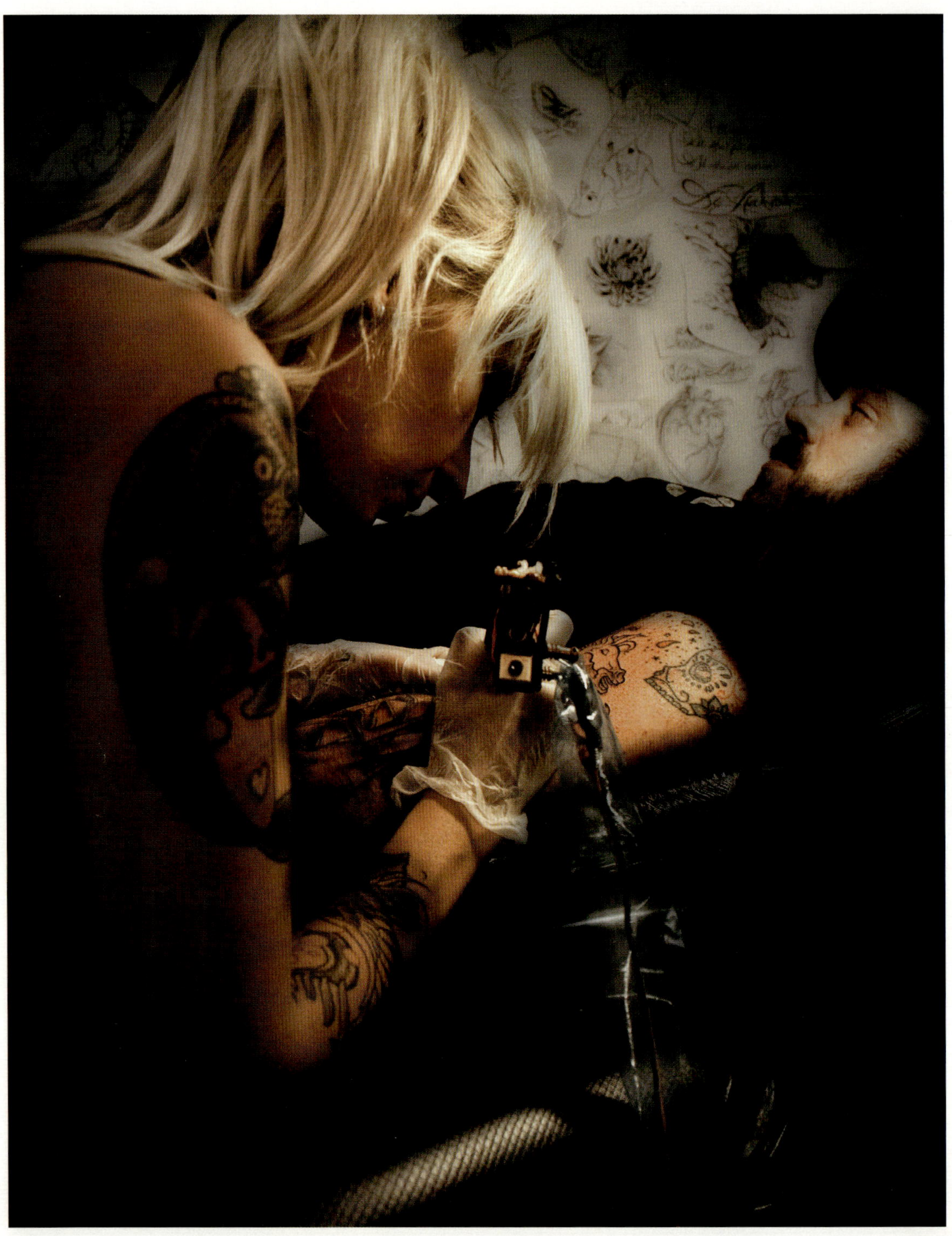

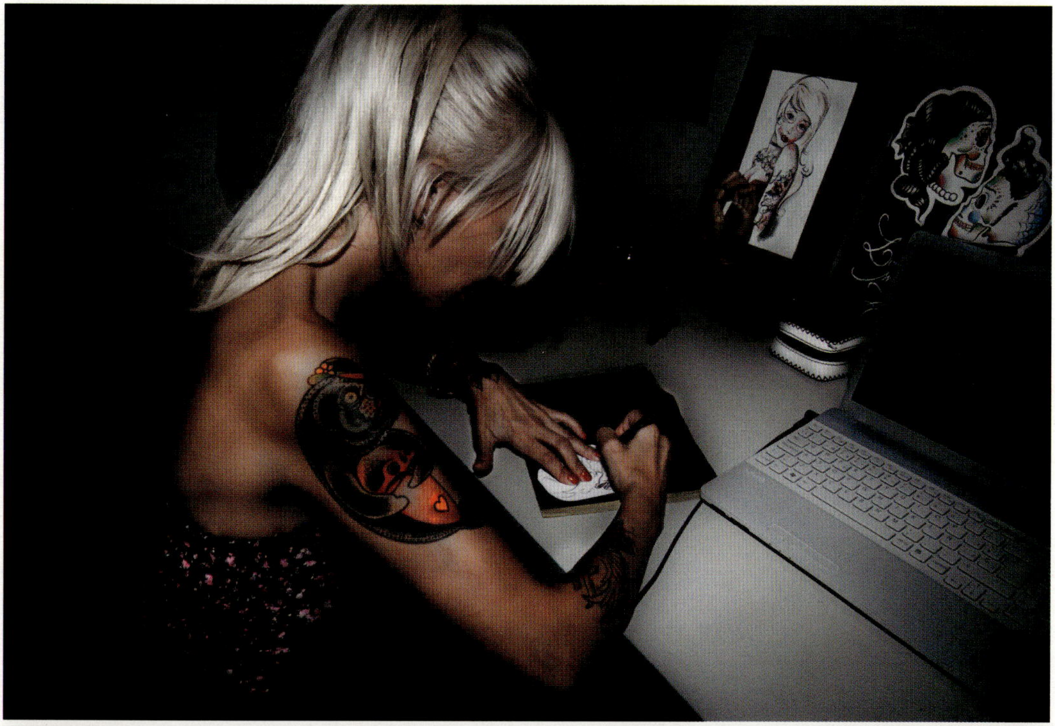

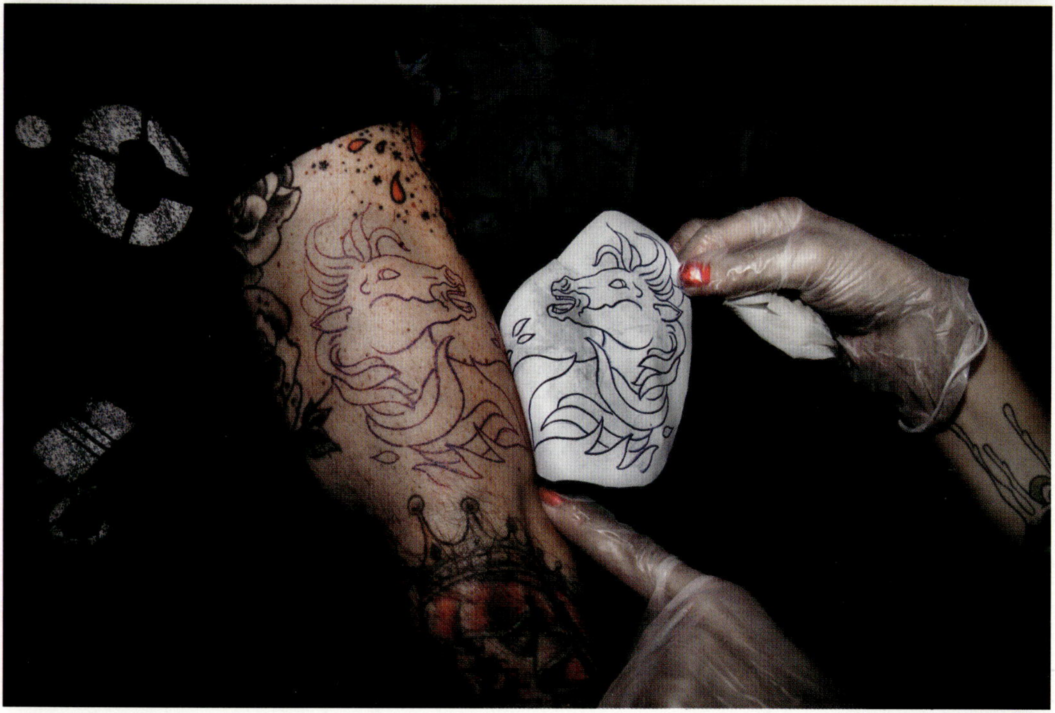

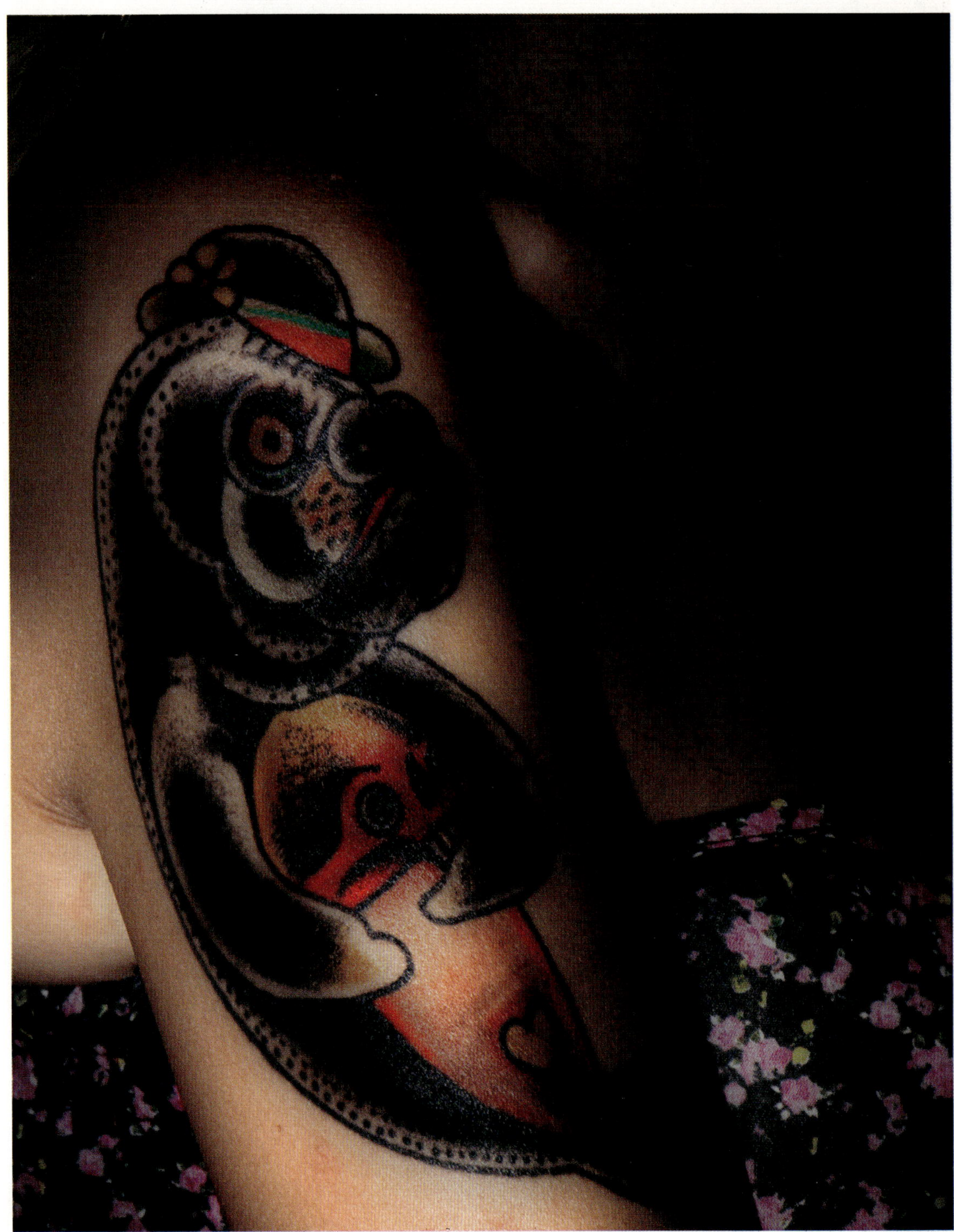

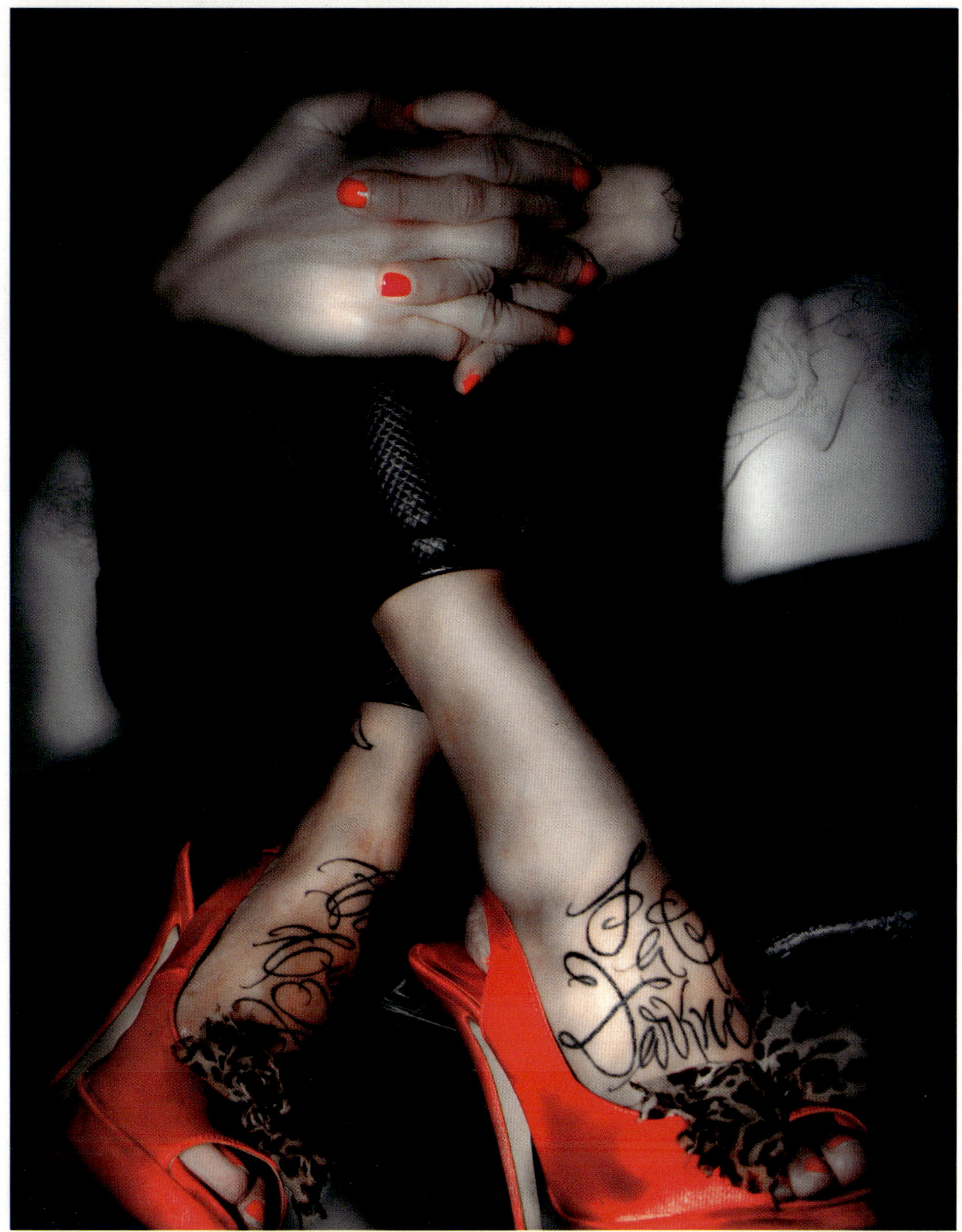

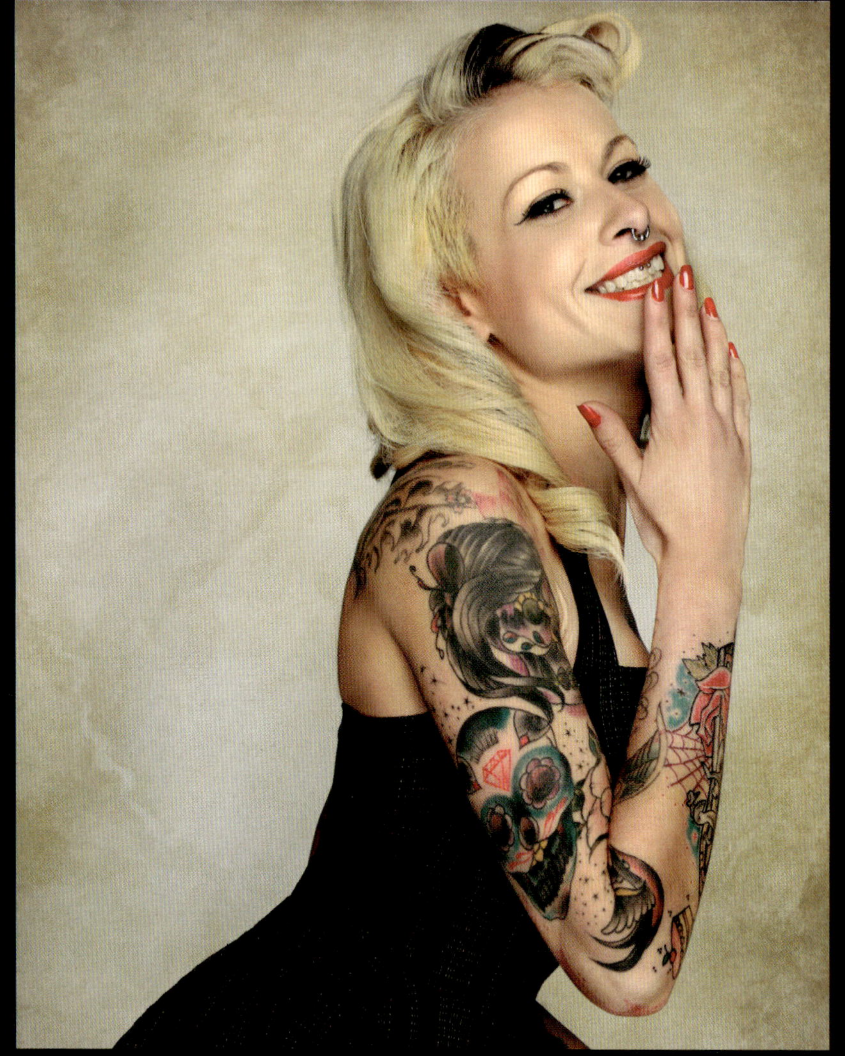

Marya García

www.maryagarcia.com

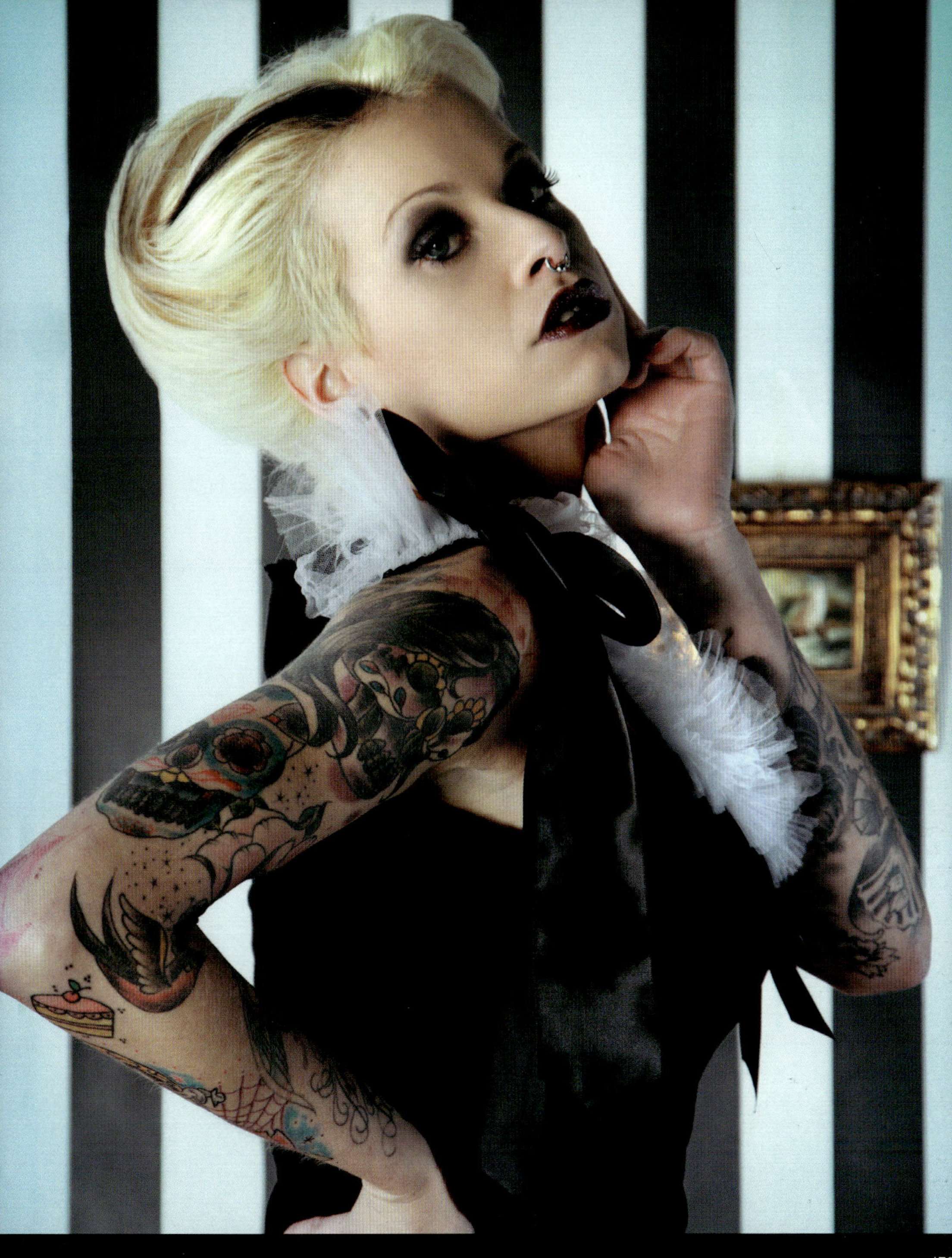

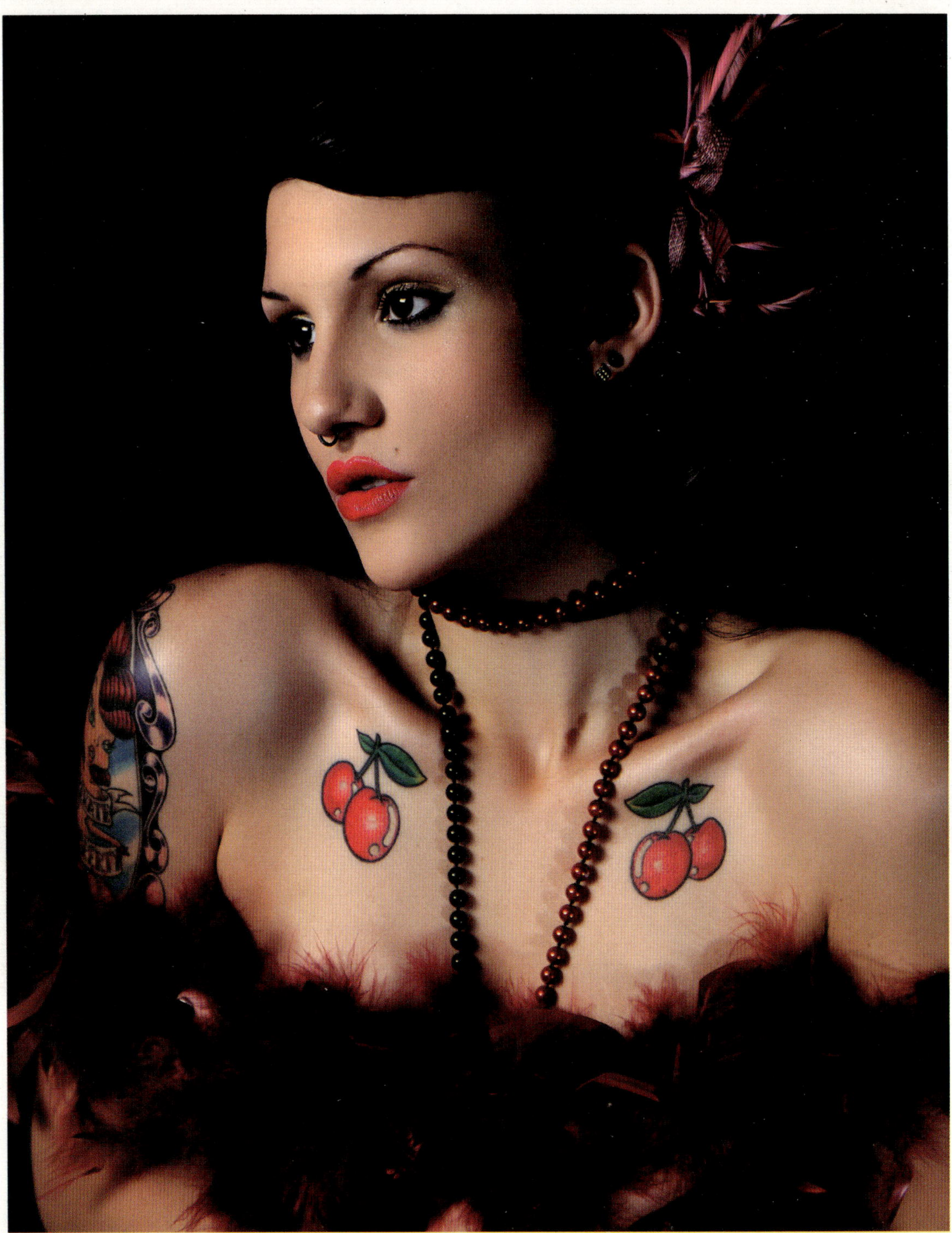

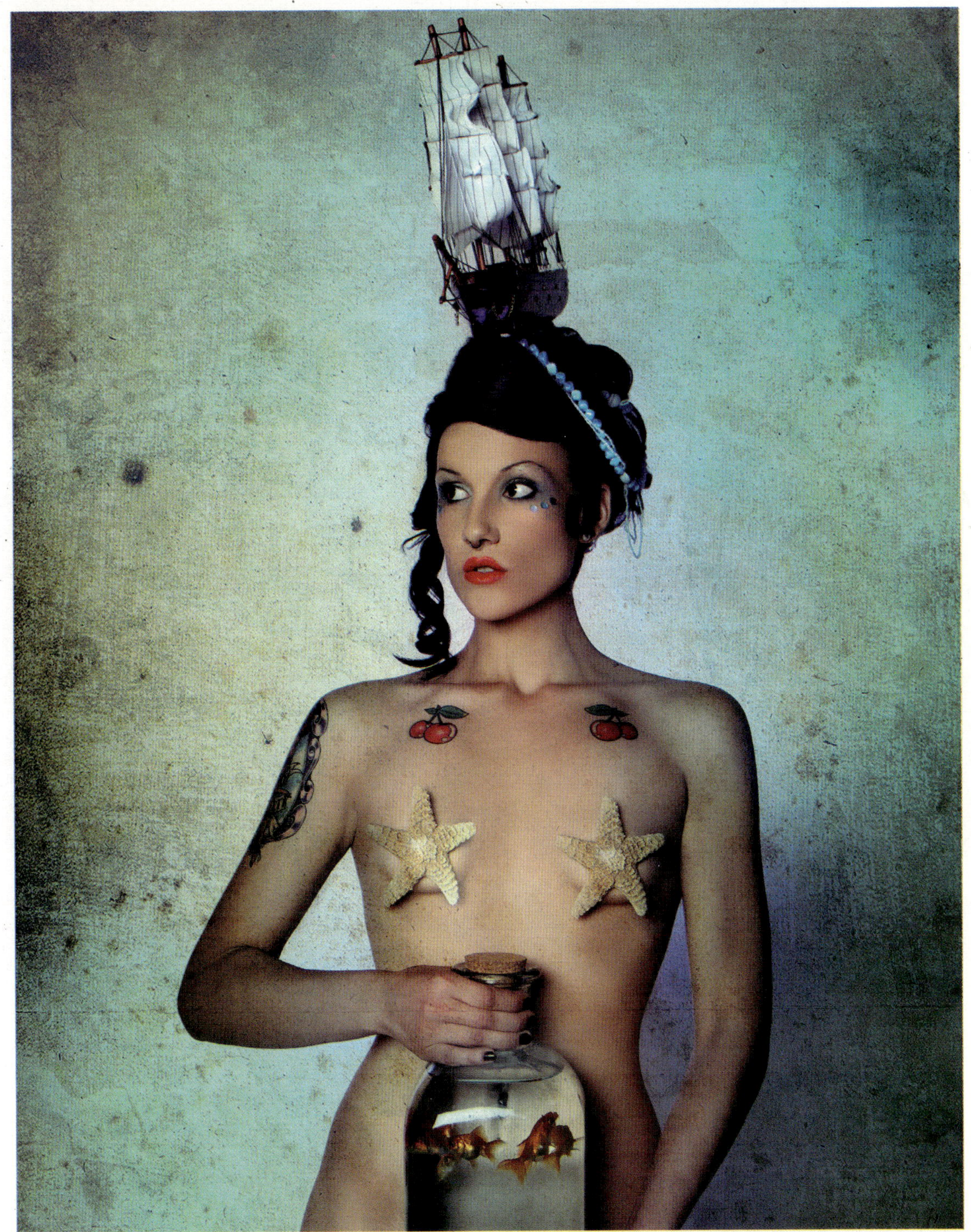

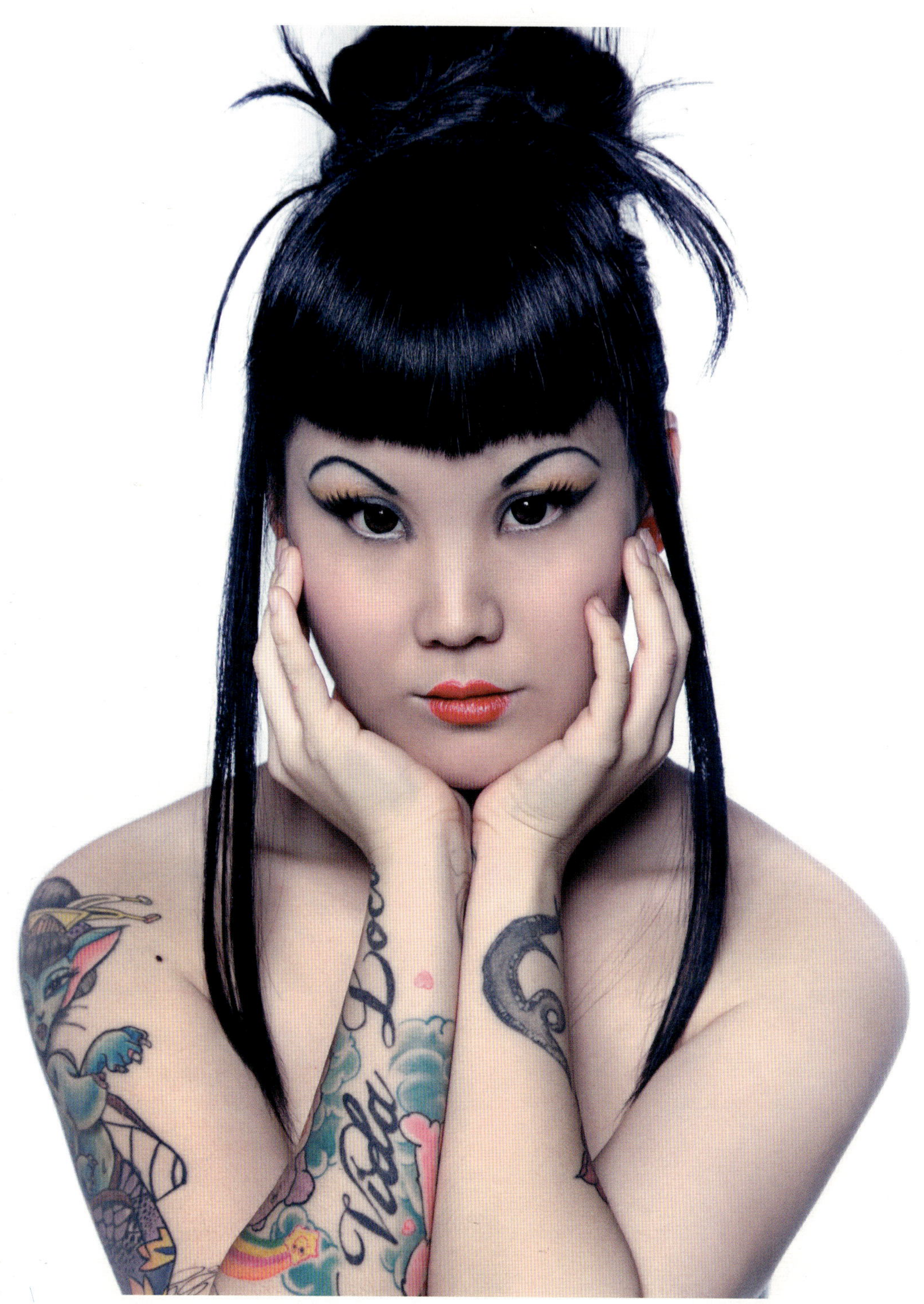
Vida

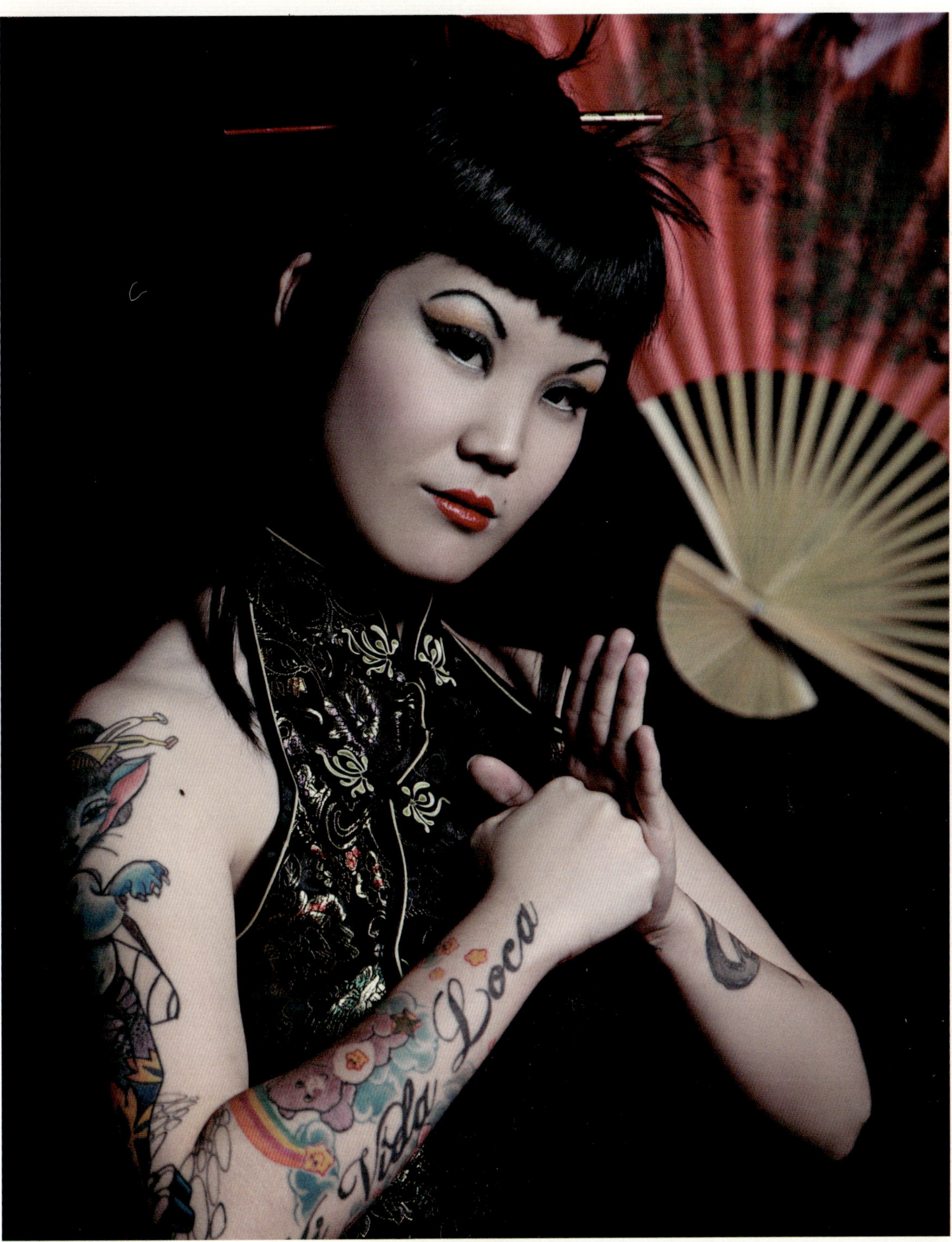
Vida Loca

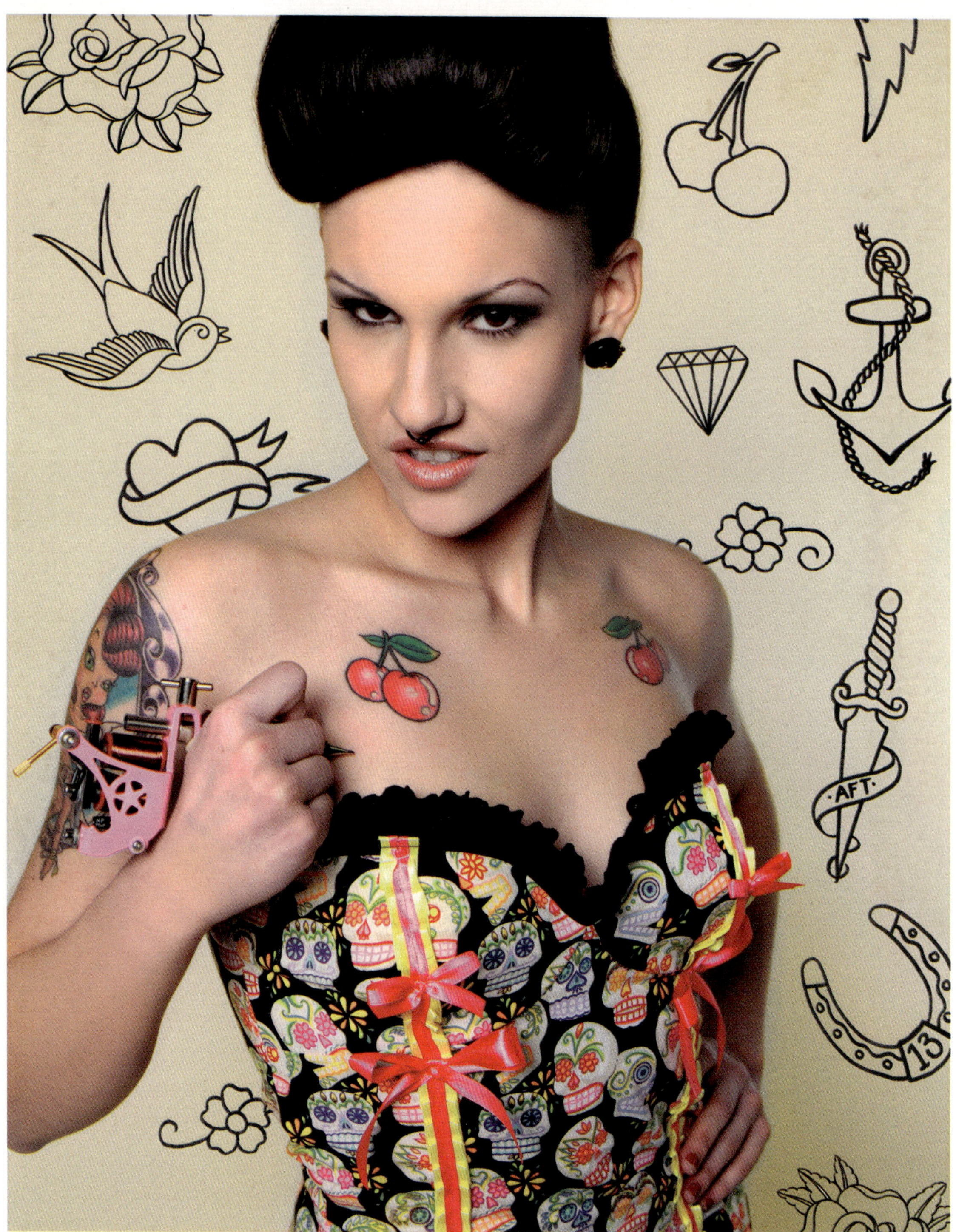
AFT
13

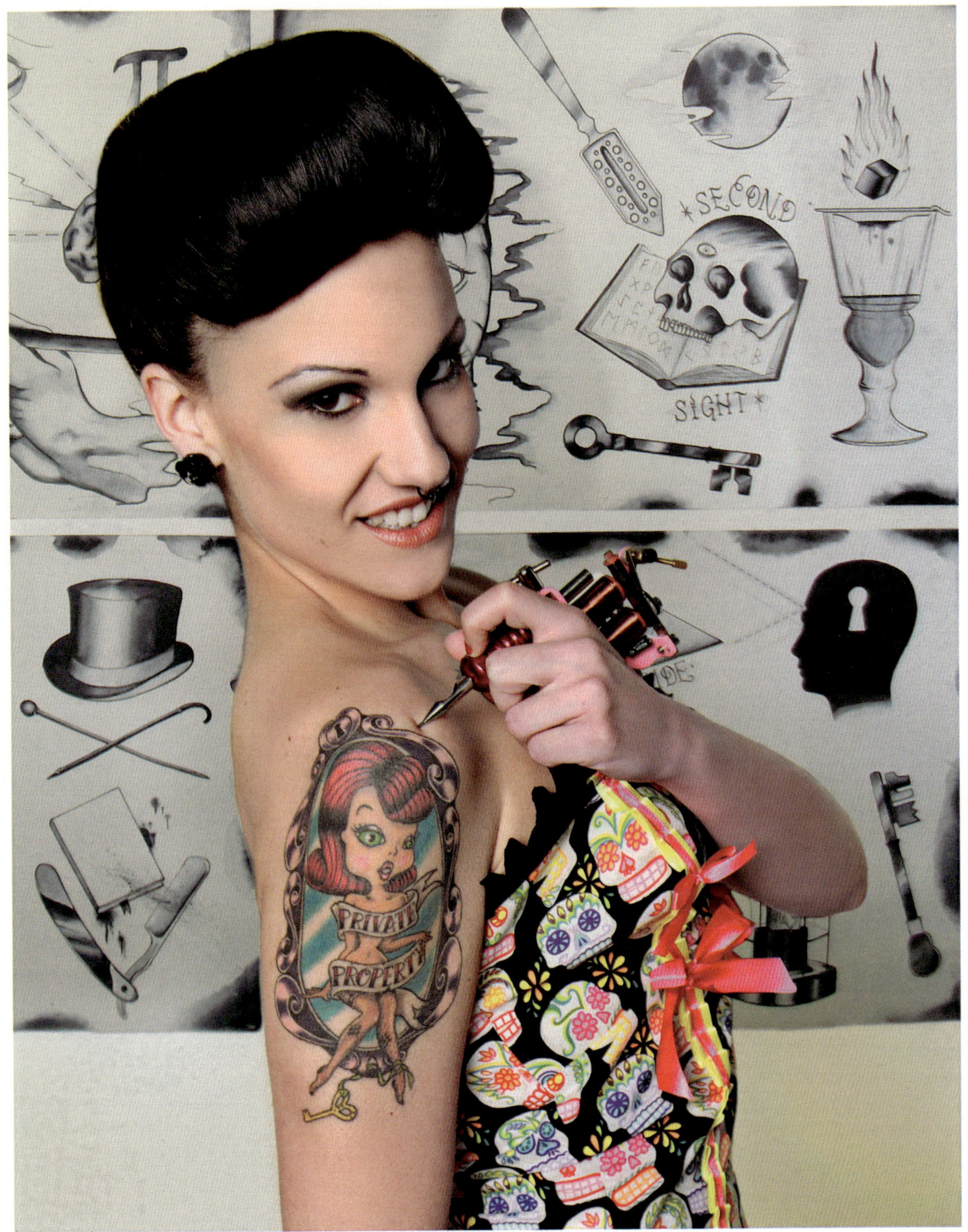
SECOND
SIGHT
PRIVATE
PROPERTY

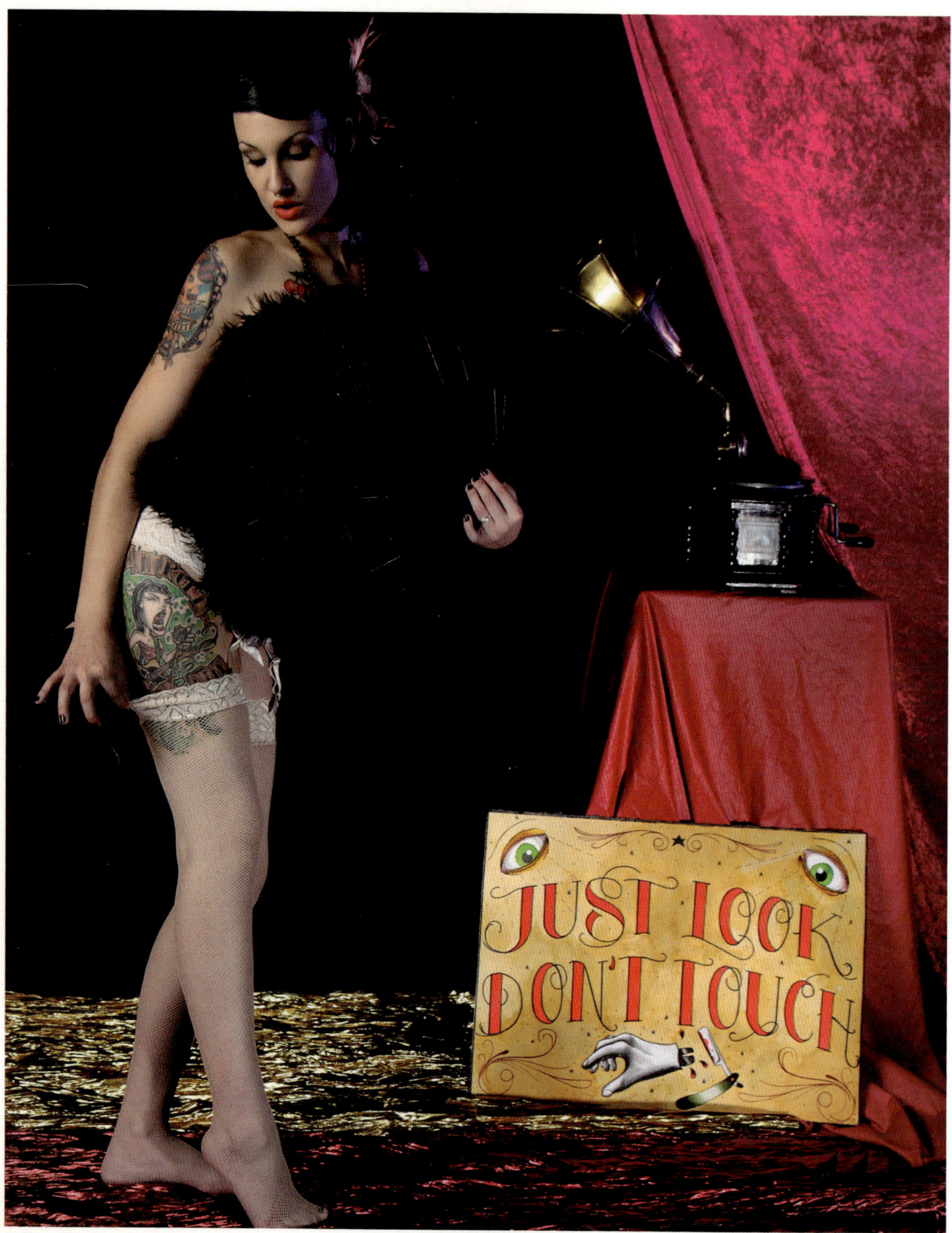
JUST LOOK
DON'T TOUCH

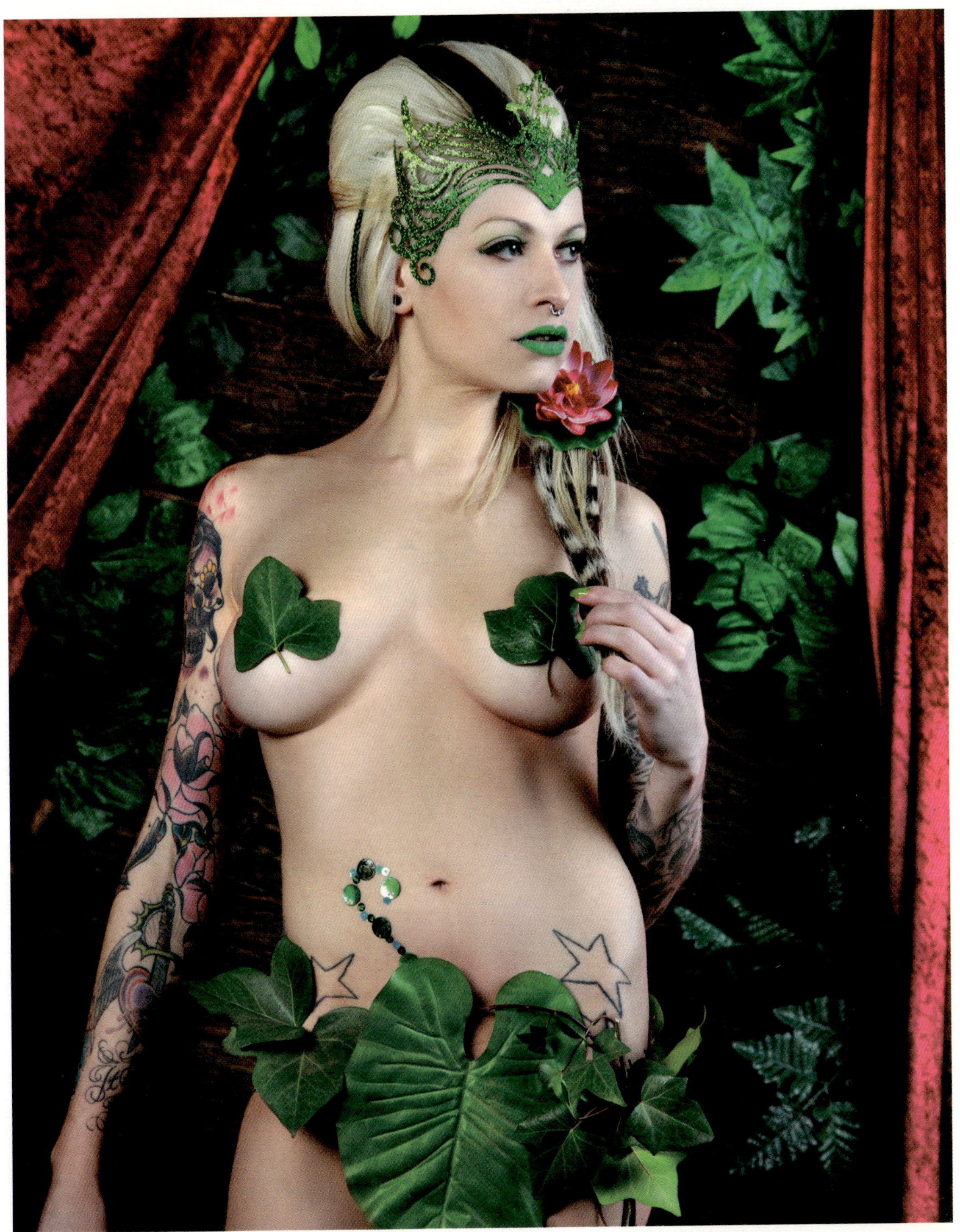

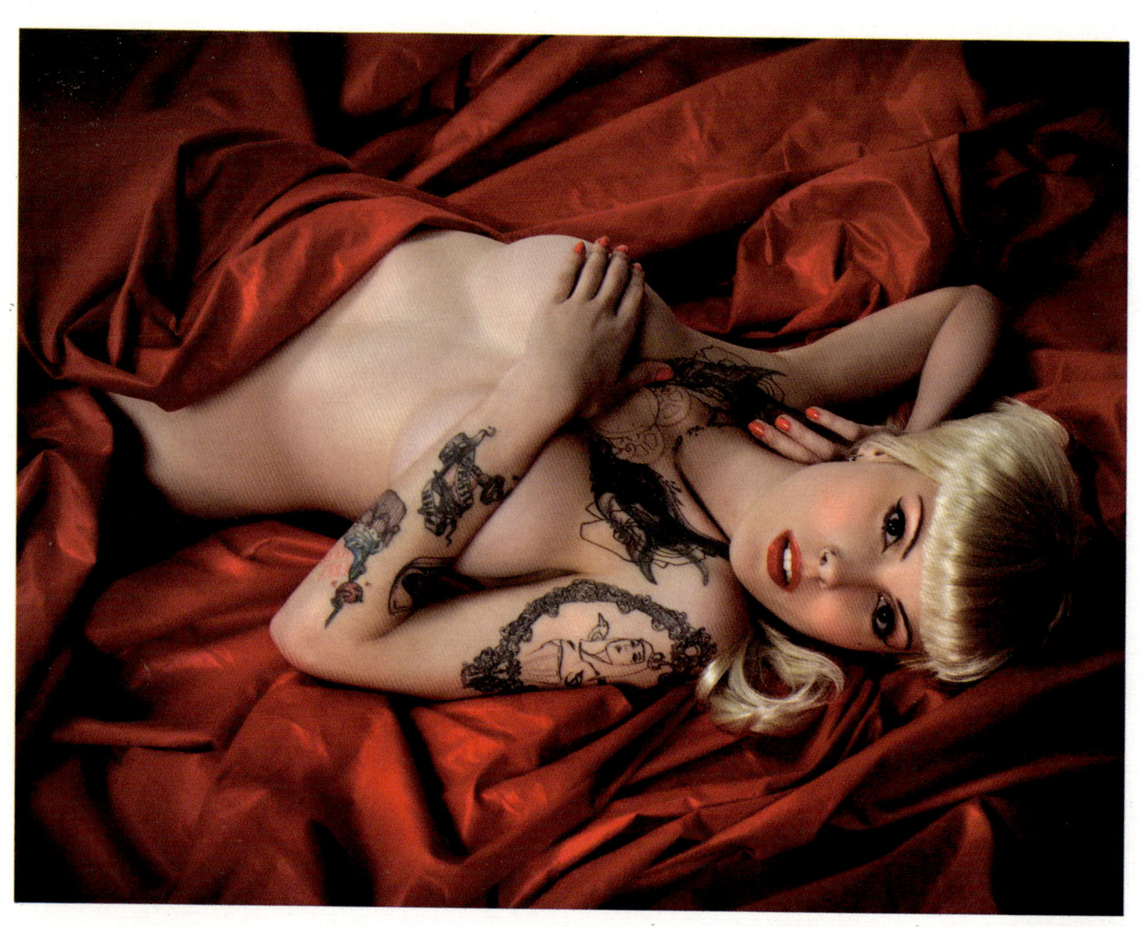

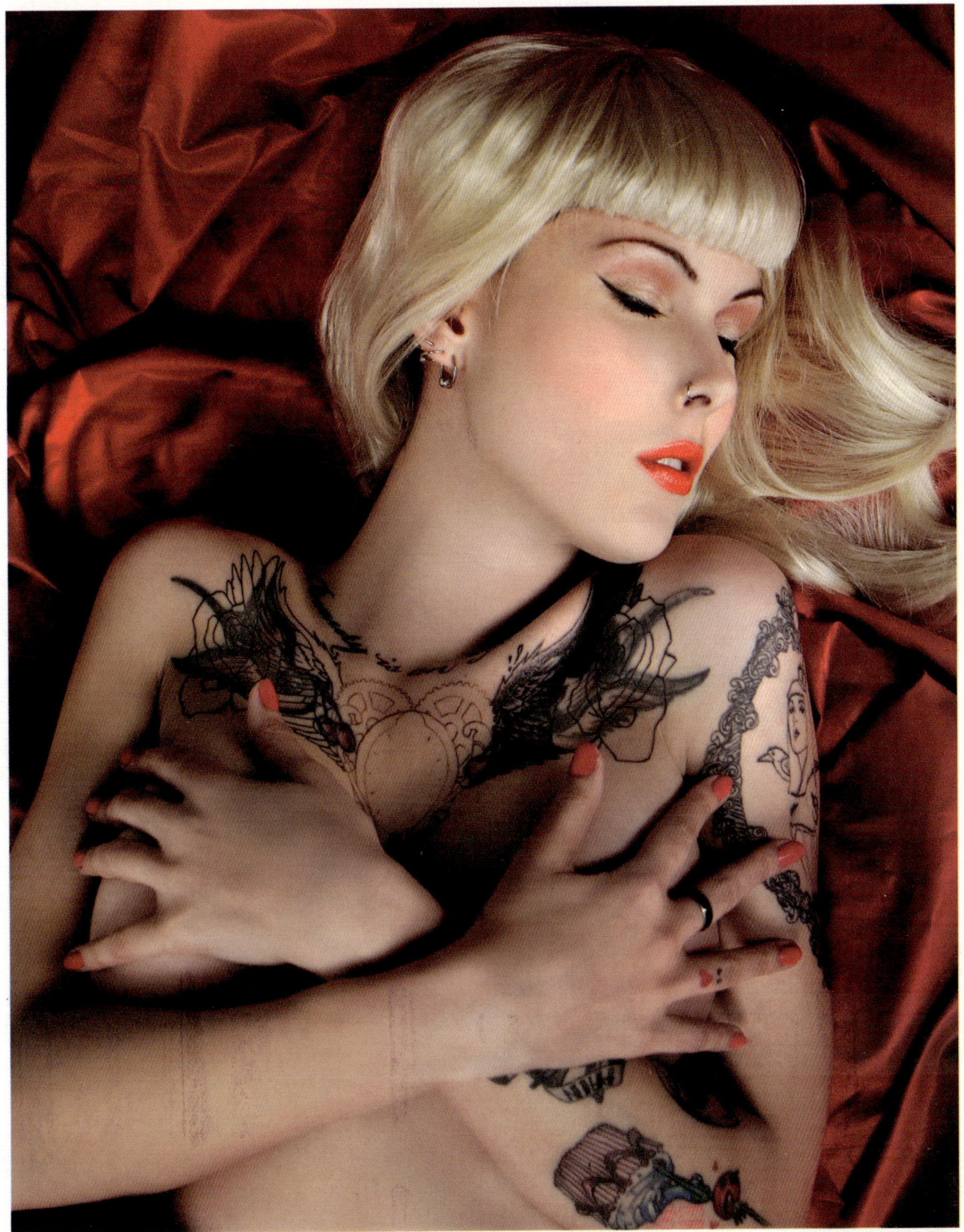

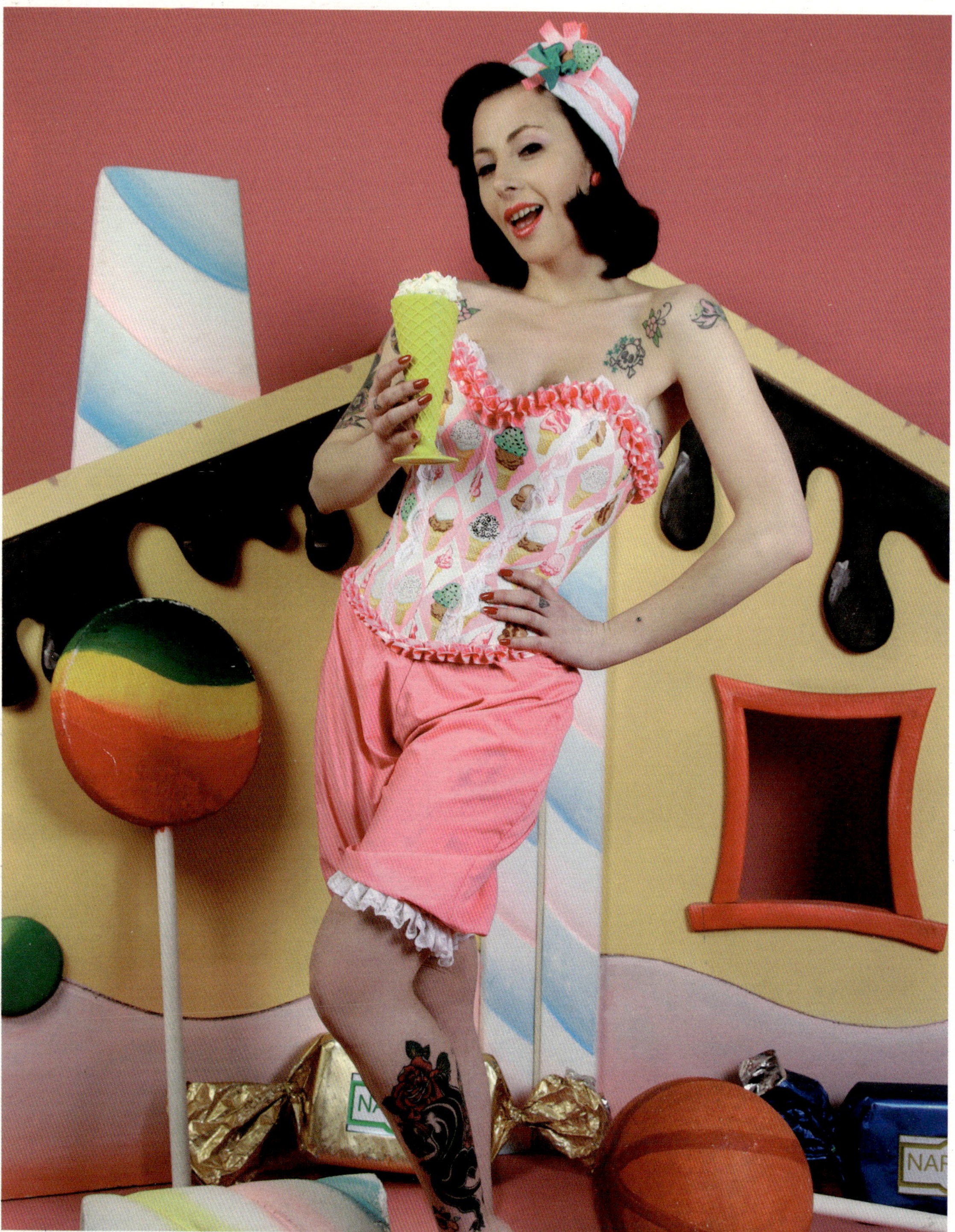

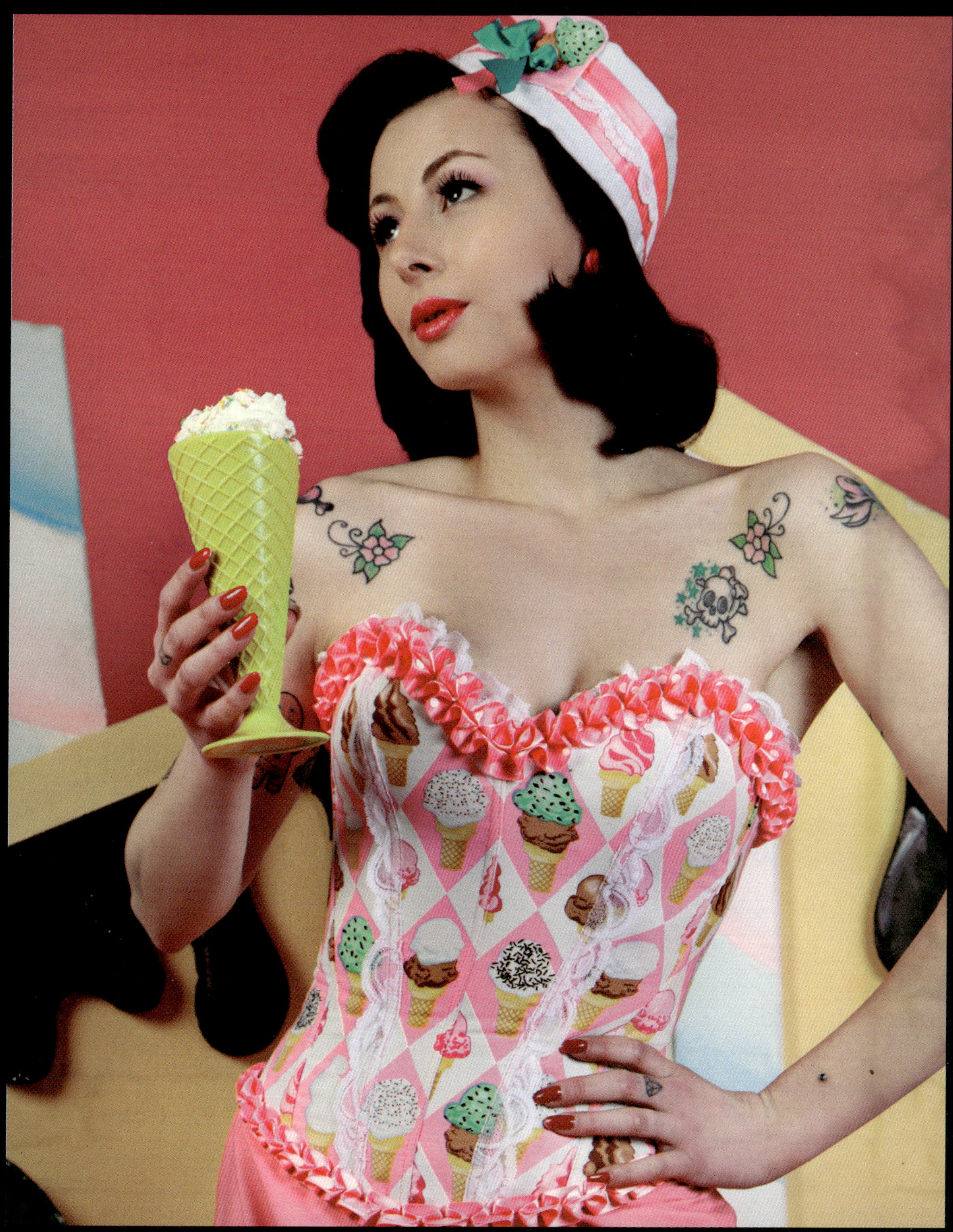